THE
RUPP
YEARS

THE RUPP YEARS

The University of Kentucky's Golden Era of Basketball

By TEV LAUDEMAN

ABOUT THE BOOK

There are only two reasons for writing a book: to entertain or to inform. It is difficult to write about Adolph Rupp and his University of Kentucky basketball teams without doing both. His career as a coach has been filled with drama—soaring triumphs, heartbreak, humor—a soap opera in which the plot has never dulled nor the parade of interesting characters ever diminished.

Laudeman

Rupp already had enjoyed some exciting moments as a coach, though the best were yet to come, when Tev Laudeman first started watching Kentucky basketball. As a youngster living in Lexington, Laudeman would often slip quietly into old Alumni Gymnasium where Rupp was conducting practice. The most fascinating times were on Mondays, when Rupp would gather his players around him at midcourt for a critique of their performances in the previous Saturday's game.

"Jimmy Goodman," Rupp would say (or the remark could be directed to Tub Thompson, Cab Curtis or Mickey Rouse), "you hit only two shots. That's not good enough. We have to hit 20 per cent to win."

That 20 per cent reveals how much basketball has changed. Thirty years later Rupp would have to say 40 or 45 per cent. One thing never changed: Rupp was a winner then, he was a winner throughout his long stay at Kentucky. This is the year-by-year account of his remarkable tenure. More, it is the story of the 700 or so players who came under his direction. It is important, the author believes, that it all be set down as a permanent record.

I am glad to see that a resumé of the 42 years of my teams has been put into print. Naturally, the story about many of these teams alone would make a complete book. As a history of basketball, Tev Laudeman's account is concise, accurate and interesting. I am sure that readers will enjoy this book tremendously and that it will serve as a history of many of the events that transpired during those adventurous years.

The journey through those years obviously was a labor of love for Tev. He stirs many memories and captures some great moments. The University of Kentucky and I are grateful.

ADOLPH RUPP

It is impossible to measure completely the impact Adolph Rupp has had on the game of basketball. We must leave that to history. His infinite knowledge of the game, his wisdom, his wit and his success rank him alongside the game's inventor, Dr. James A. Naismith, as one of the two greatest names in basketball annals. I am delighted that Tev Laudeman and The Courier-Journal and The Louisville Times have made available what must be considered a historical document: a mirror of the past 42 years of University of Kentucky basketball. It is a chronicle that is expertly pieced together in an entertaining and fascinating manner.

I am grateful for this work because I was fortunate enough to have played under Adolph Rupp. It was an exciting, rewarding experience which—as with so many others before me—provided my foundation for a professional career. I will remember Adolph Rupp as a warm, compassionate man, but also as a man who would not tolerate mediocrity. He was demanding, but he recognized and appreciated a total effort.

I commend the author and publisher for their foresight in producing this book. It is a service to the public and to the game of basketball, and a great tribute to Adolph Rupp.

DAN ISSEL

A freshman helps hire UK coach, then plays for him

Adolph Rupp, in his first year as Kentucky's coach.

If there had been anyone on the University of Kentucky athletic council with the gift of prophecy, he surely would have made high drama of a meeting the group held on a spring day in 1930.

Photographers, ringing phrases and maybe even champagne all around wouldn't have been overdoing it if the council had known exactly what it was about to accomplish.

All members of the council knew, though, that this wasn't a routine meeting. They were going to interview, and possibly hire, a new basketball coach.

And the council was in an uncomfortable position. Many fans thought it had erred in not matching or bettering the offer Miami University (Ohio) had made in luring coach Johnny Mauer from UK. After all, Mauer had taken over after a season in which UK had won only three games and produced three straight winners. His last team had won 16 of 19 games, and he had recruited brilliantly for the future.

One member of the athletic council represented the student body. He was only a freshman, and it was unusual for a first-year man to be on the council. But this youth was not an ordinary freshman. He had been a high school All-American in both football and basketball at Ash-

land, Ky., and was a star in baseball and track. He was the greatest athlete UK had ever landed.

The interview came off well. The freshman didn't just sit back and listen to his elders. He took an active part in the session.

When the meeting was over and the coach had departed, the members of the athletic council agreed they were impressed with the coach's manner and his refreshing approach to basketball. They reached the decision quickly: UK would hire the man.

That's how freshman Ellis Johnson helped hire his own coach, Adolph Frederick Rupp. Johnson went on to become a three-year starter and an All-American as a senior. Rupp would win more games than any other coach in college basketball history. It was truly a momentous day for the UK athletic council.

The announcement was made formally on May 21, 1930, that UK had signed the 29-year-old Rupp to a two-year contract as head basketball coach, freshman football coach and assistant to Bernie Shively with the track team.

Born in Halstead, Kan., on Sept. 2, 1901, Rupp had been a senior guard on Dr. Forrest (Phog) Allen's undefeated University of Kansas team in 1923. Rupp's

Freeport, Ill., high school teams had won more than 80 per cent of their games over a four-year period.

Ellis Johnson got a chance to talk more basketball with Rupp when they ran into one another on the campus. Johnson was delighted when Rupp told him of plans to install the fast break, a sharp contrast to the slow, meticulous offense run by Mauer.

Later Rupp sent for Carey Spicer, captain-elect of the basketball team. Spicer was curious but mildly apprehensive. An all-round athlete, Spicer was starting quarterback on the football team and a member of the tennis squad, although he admitted he played tennis "just to get out of spring football practice."

As a sophomore Spicer had been named an All-American in basketball under Mauer, only two years after winning All-State honors at Lexington High School. Now, after two seasons with Mauer, Spicer was going to play his senior year under a strange coach. Is there any wonder he was troubled?

As he shook hands with Rupp, Spicer saw a man nearly equal his own 6 feet, 1 inch height, already a bit on the portly side, dark hair combed neatly in place. But the impact of the coach's personality was greater than his visual impression.

Rupp told Spicer that set patterns would be retained, but when possible UK would run, with more chance for individual initiative on the part of the players.

Rupp questioned Spicer carefully about the returning players. Spicer painted an encouraging picture. Paul McBrayer, the All-American guard, and Lawrence (Big) McGinnis were gone, but among those back were 6-4 George Yates and clever Louis (Little) McGinnis, along with such promising players from the freshman squad as 6-4 Forest (Aggie) Sale and rugged Ellis Johnson.

Both Spicer and Rupp were pleased with their first meeting. The coach now was certain he had the personnel to make the fast break work, and he liked Spicer's eager acceptance of the forthcoming changes. Spicer felt his misgivings vanish under the spell of Rupp's sales talk.

Six players were missing when Rupp called the first practice of the 1930-31 season. Spicer, Johnson, Yates, Jake Bronston, Darrell Darby and Bud Cavana still were with the football squad. Spicer was adding luster to an already bright football career by scoring 75 points in his senior season, highest total in the state and the Southern Conference. Practice tempo picked up after the footballers reported.

On Dec. 18, UK opened its schedule at home against nearby Georgetown College. On the first play of the game, Aggie Sale tipped the ball to Spicer, who threw it to Johnson under the basket. Johnson laid it in to become the first player to score for Rupp at UK.

Carey Spicer of Lexington made All-American for UK in 1931.

UK won the game 67-19 as Sale, the lanky sophomore from Lawrenceburg, scored 19 points, and Louis McGinnis of Lexington hit 17. Other starters were Spicer, Johnson and Bill Trott of Evansville, Ind.

Lancaster Scores 10

Yates, the tall pivotman from Elizabethtown, came off the bench to get 10 points. Other UK players in action were Bronston, Vernon Congleton, Walter Crump, Allan (Doc) Lavin, George Skinner, Cecil Bell, Charles Worthington, Bill Kleiser, Ercel Little and Cavana. Before the season was over Bronston, from Lexington, and Worthington, from Louisville, would be starting.

Georgetown had little to offer in offensive punch except a husky guard, Harry Lancaster, better known for his halfbacking on the football team. He scored 10 points and played well on defense. Eighteen years later he would become Rupp's first full-time assistant.

By the middle of February, UK had won 10 straight. The toughest game was at Vanderbilt, where Spicer scored 27 points. The score was tied 18-18 at halftime. Rupp, who always wore a brown suit with brown socks and tie to the game for good luck, asked Jake Bronston, "What were you thinking out there?"

Bronston, who was having a miserable night, replied, "Coach, I was just wondering if you had on those brown socks." Kentucky won 42-37.

A 36-32 victory at Tennessee was costly as Ellis Johnson suffered a sprained ankle and was ordered to the sidelines for at least two weeks.

If Rupp wasn't already 100 per cent superstitious, he had reason to be after he took his 10-game winning streak to Georgia. UK was upset on Friday, Feb. 13, 25-16. Chief Georgia weapons were a defense that smothered Carey Spicer (he got one point) and a forward named Bill Strickland, who hit three straight goals late in the game.

Making the loss embarrassing for Rupp, Georgia was coached that night by football coach Harry Mehre, filling in for Herman Stegeman, who was out of town.

Still stunned by its first defeat, UK bowed to Clemson 29-26, then closed the trip by defeating coach Roy Mundorff's Georgia Tech team 35-16. UK finished the season with a 12-2 record by returning home to beat Vanderbilt 43-23, a week before the Southern Conference tournament in Atlanta.

About 300 fans were at the railroad station to see UK off for Atlanta. Ellis Johnson was there but only to say goodby. Because of his ankle injury, Johnson had to yield his place on the tournament squad to Ercel Little.

Long Shot Beats UK

Rupp's starting team for the tourney was the same as it was for the last few games of the regular season: Carey Spicer and Louis McGinnis, forwards; George Yates, center, and Jake Bronston and Charles Worthington, guards.

UK beat North Carolina and Duke in the first two games, McGinnis getting 18 points against Duke. Carey Spicer put on a spectacular show as Florida was crushed 56-35, scoring 11 points in one two-minute stretch on his way to a 22-point total.

The championship game between UK and Maryland was one of the most exciting played in the South all season. With less than a minute to play, McGinnis hit from near the sideline to give UK a 27-25 edge, but Maryland came right back to tie the score on a layup by guard Bozzy Berger. Then, as the final seconds ticked off, Berger swished through a long shot to give Maryland the title 29-27.

Back home, Rupp called spring practice for April 21. In the meantime, the coach wore painful blisters on his feet refereeing district high school tourney games. Louisville Manual won the state crown, and the play of a guard for the champs, Russell (Duke) Ellington, caught Rupp's eye. Next fall Ellington would enroll at UK.

Rupp's success in his first year at UK would be overshadowed by conference and national championships of later seasons. Yet it is doubtful if any of the years to follow were more important to his career.

He took over strange personnel, introduced a new style of play and had the difficult task of following another successful coach.

So well did he blend his players and system of play that Carey Spicer, Louis McGinnis, George Yates and Jake Bronston were named to the All-Southern squad, and Spicer was selected to an All-American team for the second time in three years. Under Rupp, Yates was able to fully develop an unorthodox backhand flip shot, which Mauer had discouraged.

"Rupp didn't care how you shot as long as you put the ball in the basket," Yates recalled years later. The tall center doubts that Aggie Sale would have been nearly as good under Mauer.

"Aggie would shoot off balance, falling down, or sitting on the floor if he had to," explained Yates. "Mauer wouldn't have permitted that."

All in all, you'd have to say that freshman on the athletic council helped hire the right man.

Ellis Johnson of Ashland was first to score for the new coach.

Basketball a slice of cake for Aggie

Aggie Sale liked cake almost as much as he enjoyed playing basketball and at least once there was a conflict between the two.

It happened while he was averaging 15 or 16 points a game for Kavanaugh High School in Lawrenceburg. On the day Kavanaugh was to play nearby rival Versailles, Aggie broke training—he ate a big piece of angel food cake.

Coach Rice Mountjoy decided to suspend his leading scorer and rebounder, then changed his mind when the other members of the team asked that Aggie be allowed to play. Mountjoy must have been tempted to pass out cake before every game after that because the 6-foot-4 Sale scored 14 points as Kavanaugh won 18-14.

Aggie Sale got his early basketball experience shooting at an outdoor goal on his father's farm. There were times when Aggie's father wanted to chuck the goal off the premises. It wasn't unusual for him to send his lanky son out to do some farm chores, only to find him an hour later firing away at the basketball hoop. And—perhaps this was the redeeming feature—even then dropping the ball through consistently.

Aggie was an immediate success as a high school player with the simple formula, he admitted, of "doing most of the shooting." He improved each season and by the end of his senior year was head and shoulders above most of the state's centers. Not only a good shooter, he was fast and agile and an excellent rebounder. One of his favorite plays was to outjump the opposing center, tip the ball to himself, and dribble in to score.

Had Aggie played high school basketball 20 years later, he would have been swamped with college offers. But in the days before organized, competitive recruiting his reputation was confined largely to his home state. Even so, Ohio State University beckoned to him.

He chose UK because "it was close to home."

This gangling youngster was to go high—to the very zenith before he finished at UK. He would twice be voted All-America, would captain the Wildcats as a senior, be voted Player of the Year for the entire nation and would lead UK to its first national championship.

So lightly would he wear his honors that three decades later when the Louisville Courier-Journal and Times ran an item referring to him as UK's first Player of the Year, it came as news to him. He had forgotten it.

One thing he never forgot in the years he was flying high as a player—he went to UK to get an education. He was a serious student and when he was graduated, Dr. Thomas Clark, head of the UK History Department, said of Aggie, "He had the best attitude of any athlete I ever taught."

Aggie Sale was as proud of that as anything he ever did on the basketball court.

Only 19 as a sophomore at UK, Aggie (he got the nickname because he was studying agriculture) was further away from his physical peak than most of his classmates, and he was handicapped his first varsity season with minor injuries. Yet his flashes of brilliance convinced

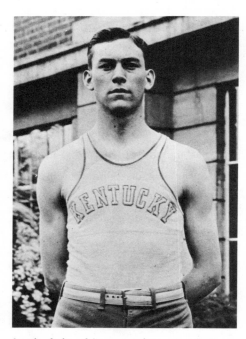

Aggie Sale of Lawrenceburg was twice a UK All-American.

UK coach Adolph Rupp that Sale was a great player of the future.

Rupp Is Optimistic

With the return of Sale and other experienced players, Rupp predicted as practice started for the 1931-32 season that UK would be strong again.

Rupp and most UK fans had a fairly clear idea of how the starting five would shape up even before the first practice. Ellis Johnson and Charlie Worthington, experienced guards of the previous season, were back. Sale and Darrel Darby were heirs apparent to the forward positions vacated by Carey Spicer and Louis McGinnis.

George Yates was due back to play center but came out of the UK-Tennessee football game with an injured shoulder and couldn't report for practice. After a few weeks, a 6-foot-6 sophomore from Walton, John (Frenchy) DeMoisey, won the job. Yates, the captain-elect, never was able to join the squad and yielded his captaincy to Ellis Johnson.

While the Wildcats were tuning up for their opening game with Georgetown, Madisonville Democrat Ruby Laffoon was being swept into office as governor of Kentucky by a 71,523 majority over Louisville's William B. Harrison. Laffoon's lieutenant governor was A. B. (Happy) Chandler of Versailles, later to be governor and senator, commissioner of baseball and one of Rupp's staunchest boosters.

With Sale, Darby, DeMoisey, Johnson and Worthington starting, UK breezed by Georgetown 66-24. Carey Spicer, in his first season as Georgetown coach, tried to employ the fast break style he had learned under Rupp. Spicer didn't have the horses to stay with UK although his No. 1 guard, Harry Lancaster, scored nine points.

UK's national prestige soared with a 36-34 triumph over Carnegie Tech. DeMoisey hit for 15 points and Sale for 13 against Tech, which had Louis Jagnow, a high school All-American from Jackson, Mich. Jagnow scored 12 points despite some all-out defensive work by Johnson.

Carnegie Tech coach Ralph Hogan had no excuses. "My team is considered strong," he said in Lexington after the loss. "At least it's as good as anything around Pittsburgh, and Kentucky beat

1931-32 UK team. Front, from left: Cecil Bell, Ercel Little, Gordon George, Harvey Mattingly, Evan Settle, Bill Kleiser. Middle: Berkley Davis, Crittenden Blair, Darrell Darby, Ellis Johnson, Howard Kreuter, Charles Worthington. Back: Assistant coach Len Miller, Jim Hughes, John DeMoisey, Aggie Sale, George Skinner, Adolph Rupp.

us." Tech went on to win 17 games, a school record for one season that still stands.

Sale and DeMoisey continued their double-figure scoring as UK whipped Berea and Marshall. Bill Kleiser, Howard (Dutch) Kreuter, Cecil Bell, Ercel Little and Crittenden Blair were reserves used by Rupp as he tried to develop depth.

As 1931 came to an end, Rupp was jolted by the news that DeMoisey was ineligible because of a deficiency in sociology. Rupp filled in for the big man by shifting Sale to the pivot and moving Kreuter in at forward. Sale scored 17 points as UK downed Clemson, and UK was ready to take its 5-0 record on the road.

After Rupp promised that UK would "deal a whole lot of misery some place," Clemson fell again, then Sewanee, with Darby and Sale doing the hot shooting. Next stop—Tennessee.

Sale's teammates were fond of heckling him about his defensive play. His usual joking answer was, "Oh, I'm too busy scoring to worry about defense."

He gave a more eloquent rebuttal against Tennessee. He blocked five shots near the end of the game to enable UK to win 29-28. Rupp called it Aggie's "greatest game."

For Aggie Sale, the trip had one embarrassing moment. Late one night after the players were in their Pullman berths, someone tossed water into his bunk. Aggie leaped into the aisle after the vanishing culprit just as Rupp strolled into the car. The coach told Aggie to "get back to bed," and Sale didn't try to explain.

With a 9-0 mark, Rupp got the news that DeMoisey was eligible again. Reserve center Berkley Davis also became eligible.

Ellis Keeps a Promise

Washington and Lee was routed 48-28 as Sale got 20 points, but DeMoisey almost had to sit out the game. The night before he and Ellis Johnson got in from a movie 20 minutes late and Rupp was waiting for them. He gave them both a tongue lashing with Johnson catching the brunt of it. Rupp wound up by telling DeMoisey, "We don't need you against Vanderbilt (an important game coming up)."

"If you leave us alone," pleaded Johnson, "we'll get 30 points between us against Vandy." They did, too, Frenchy pouring in 29 points in 29 minutes, and Johnson getting one as UK won 61-37.

Duke, Alabama and Tennessee fell to hike UK's record to 14-0. Only a return match with Vandy stood in the way of a perfect season. But DeMoisey and Sale were ill with the flu, although they played and UK lost 32-31.

Still below par physically, UK went to the Southern Conference tournament in Atlanta. Tulane was beaten 50-30, but UK faded late in the game to bow to strong North Carolina 43-42. Although Carolina put two men on him, Sale scored 20 points.

Rupp was obviously disenchanted with the tournament. He told Lexington reporter Brownie Leach that if the Wildcats were unbeaten next season, they would pass up the tournament because "we would have everything to lose and nothing to gain."

Sale and Johnson were named All-Conference and Sale picked to an All-American team. Sale finished the season as high scorer with 235 points in 17 games, Darrell Darby was second with 145, DeMoisey third with 142 in 12 games and Ellis Johnson was fourth with 66.

The annual state high school tournament was won by Hazard, which defeated Louisville Male 15-13 for the title. Male had the consolation of landing the only unanimous choice on the all-tourney team. He was 6-foot, 200-pound Jim Goforth, who would attend UK.

DeMoisey reaches stardom, UK named nation's best

John (Frenchy) DeMoisey hit the first shot he ever took in an organized basketball game.

He was in the sixth grade at Walton, Ky., and a scrub on the school's reserve team. In a game at Union with victory assured and only a minute to play, the coach waved DeMoisey into action.

Young DeMoisey was so excited he hardly knew which way to turn, but in the fading seconds a teammate tossed him the ball at the corner of the court. The tall youngster did what came natural—he tossed the ball at the basket. The ball swished through, the first of many bullseyes he would hit over the next 10 years.

DeMoisey played on the reserve team through the eighth grade, then moved up for four years on the high school varsity. By his junior year he was scoring around 20 points a game, and as a senior stretching 6 feet, 6 inches he averaged 22 points. His top game was against Butler when he scored 50 points, and he got 45 in a regional game at Paris.

Walton, coached by Ray Beverly, was one of the favorites for the state championship in 1930, DeMoisey's last year. The team appeared to be a cinch to advance to through the regional into the Sweet 16 of the state tournament. The script unfolded without a hitch until the finals of the regional when Walton played Corinth.

Corinth didn't figure to give Walton much trouble. Walton had whipped Corinth twice by sizable margins during the regular season. But Corinth, playing inspired ball for coach Ted Hornback (later to be Ed Diddle's assistant coach at Western Kentucky), upset Walton and went on to take the state crown.

A major factor in Corinth's win over Walton was the defensive work of forward Dave Lawrence, who harrassed Wal-

ton's ace guard, Jimmy Vest, from start to finish. Vest, usually second only to DeMoisey in scoring, got only one field goal. And more important, he was unable to get the ball to DeMoisey when the center was in scoring position.

Lawrence, a junior who eventually would follow DeMoisey to UK, had an extra incentive. Many of the Corinth rooters had offered him a dollar if he outscored Vest. Lawrence collected.

After graduation DeMoisey started making plans to attend Trinity College (later a part of Duke University) because as a son of a minister he was entitled to free tuition there. Athletic officials had promised him a job to pay other expenses.

In the summer of 1930, shortly after being named UK coach, Adolph Rupp visited DeMoisey. The coach found him working on the county roads outside Walton. Rupp asked the foreman for permission to talk to DeMoisey, and the two sat in the shade on the bank of a creek.

Rupp came straight to the point: did DeMoisey want to attend UK? DeMoisey explained his financial situation—he was one of eight children and he would have to work his way through school.

"I'll be back to see you again," Rupp promised.

Frenchy Sets a Deadline

A few weeks later Rupp went to the DeMoisey home. DeMoisey said he would like to attend UK but didn't have much money. This was before complete athletic scholarships at UK, but Rupp told him that tuition for the first semester was $31.50 and that he would try to find someone to pay the second semester. That clinched it.

As a freshman at UK DeMoisey found

out he didn't know much about basketball. He was woefully weak on defense and fundamentals. But he had two things in his favor: He was a shooter and he had a fierce desire to succeed.

His specialty was a hook shot from around the foul line, although he acquired a variety of shots before he finished at UK. He had learned the hook as a youngster in Walton. In playing against a husky cousin, Adolph Edwards, DeMoisey often was slammed completely off the court when going toward the hoop. So he learned to step away from the basket and shoot accurately.

Before he was through at Kentucky DeMoisey would make All-America, captain the team and become one of the South's greatest scorers. But if Rupp guessed that the awkward youth would be that good, he kept it to himself. From all the evidence, there was considerable doubt in Rupp's mind that DeMoisey would even make the varsity after a mediocre freshman year as a part-time starter.

When DeMoisey came out for the varsity as a sophomore in 1931, he told Rupp he had paid tuition, room and board through Christmas and would make the team by then or go home. After the second week of practice DeMoisey was so far down on the squad he wasn't even getting into the scrimmages. He spent most of his time working on fundamentals with freshman coach Len Miller.

Almost every day DeMoisey asked Rupp, "When are you going to let me get in there? I can't show you what I can do if I don't play."

Perhaps Rupp was priming DeMoisey with psychology. If so, the coach never admitted it. One day, though, he stopped scrimmage and told DeMoisey, "Frog, get in there at center against Aggie Sale."

In 10 minutes Frenchy popped in a dozen points. Rupp halted the workout again. "Move over to forward, Sale," he called. "I think I have me a new center."

After practice DeMoisey told Rupp, "You're not going to get me out of there now."

What transformed DeMoisey from a clumsy freshman to a varsity regular in one year? Mostly his own determination. After his freshman season he took stock of his weaknesses and decided to do something about them. He worked all spring on fundamentals.

As a sophomore DeMoisey proved he had the talent to be one of the South's top performers. His return as a junior, along with Sale, Ellis Johnson, Darrell Darby and George Yates (back for his final season of eligibility) had fans dreaming of a conference title for the 1932-33 campaign.

Up from the freshman team were Bill Davis, Jack Tucker and Dave Lawrence. Davis, a fast, clever guard from Hazard, soon nailed down a starting berth with Johnson in the backcourt. DeMoisey was at center, with Sale and Darby at forwards.

On Dec. 10, 1932, two days before UK's opening game with Georgetown, the old Southern Conference broke up and the Southeastern Conference was formed with 13 members. They were Kentucky, Ala-

Frenchy DeMoisey, one of the first players Adolph Rupp recruited.

bama, Auburn, Tennessee, Vanderbilt, Florida, Georgia, Georgia Tech, Louisiana State, Tulane, Mississippi, Mississippi State and Sewanee. UK President Frank L. McVey was named president of the new league.

While Rupp was getting off to a good start by beating Georgetown behind De-Moisey's 18 and Sale's 15 points, UK football coach Harry Gamage was under fire because his team had lost its last five games. The men's student council at UK recommended the firing of Gamage and assistant coach John Campbell, and reduction in the salaries of most coaches. There was one exception: no pay cut was asked for Rupp, then making $3,100 a year.

McVey ordered an investigation of the business and coaching affairs at UK, but

less than a week later the UK athletic council announced that Gamage would be retained for the remaining year of his contract and no action was taken on the other recommendations of the student council.

Meanwhile, Rupp's team was beating Marshall at Ashland, Ky., and downing Tulane twice in UK's Alumni Gym. In those first four games Rupp started his original combination, and he looked at reserves Howard Kreuter, Dave Lawrence, Maurice Jackson, George Yates, Ralph Yates, Ralph Kercheval, Jack Tucker and Evan Settle.

UK tuned up for a game with Big Ten power Ohio State by going to Chicago to down the University of Chicago 58-26. Talking to sports writers before the game, DeMoisey asked, "What's the scoring record for this gym?"

"Twenty-four points," a writer told him. "Why?"

"Because I'm going to break it," replied DeMoisey.

He probably would have, too, but Rupp pulled the cocky center out when he reached 24.

DeMoisey and UK came down to earth with a painful thud back home against Ohio State. The big Buckeyes, led by 6-foot-5 center Wilmer Hosket, defeated UK 46-30. Hosket scored 14 points and dominated the rebounding until he fouled out. Sale had 10 points and De-Moisey seven as UK hit only 11 of 52 shots. Ohio State hit 21 of 44. It was the worst defeat to that time for Rupp in high school or college coaching.

UK went to Omaha, Neb., for two games with Creighton, beating the Missouri Valley Conference champion the first night 32-26, but losing the next night 34-22 as Sale was held to six points and DeMoisey went scoreless. It was UK's second loss against six victories.

Rupp tried George Yates in DeMoisey's place in victories over South Carolina and Tennessee, then went back to the old lineup as visiting Clemson was beaten 67-18. Rupp used reserves Jack Tucker, Dave Lawrence, Evan Settle, George Skinner and Howard Kreuter in that one.

After a 12-day examination break, UK whipped Tennessee to increase its SEC record to 4-0. Vanderbilt, on top of the SEC with 8-0, was next. On the day UK left for Nashville, Jan. 30, 1933, events which would one day affect college basketball and all sports were taking place in Europe. German Field Marshal Von Hindenburg was placing the highest office of that nation in the hands of a former corporal. Adolf Hitler was named chancellor of Germany and two of his aides, Dr. Wilhelm Frick and Hermann Goering, were appointed to the cabinet.

But UK fans in Vandy's crowded gym weren't worried about foreign affairs. They watched Bill Davis limit Vandy's speedy forward, Skinny Huggins, to six points and score 11 himself as UK won 40-29. DeMoisey also scored 11 and Yates eight. Davis scored 12 as UK won at Clemson and 15 in a 44-38 loss at South Carolina. It was UK's first loss to a southern team.

DeMoisey bucketed 23 points and Sale 22 as the University of Mexico was crushed 81-22. Rupp paraded Yates,

Kreuter, Tucker, Lawrence, Settle, Jackson, Skinner, Joe Rupert and John Morris into the game. Georgia Tech fell 45-22 to make UK's SEC record 6-0, but Alabama was tougher before bowing 35-31. Only a return match with Vandy remained before the SEC tourney.

A few days before playing UK, Vandy coach Josh Cody named four UK players —DeMoisey, Yates, Johnson and Davis— to his all-opponent team. Cody must have wondered how he left Sale off as Aggie hit 26 points in a 45-26 UK romp. So UK went into the SEC tourney at Atlanta with an 8-0 league mark.

Sale Set Record

Rupp kept UK under wraps in beating Mississippi 49-31, with Sale scoring 17 and DeMoisey 16. Sale scored 20 as UK again coasted to victory, 48-24 over Florida, to gain the semifinals against Louisiana State. LSU had a fine little guard, Sparky Wade, and a powerful center, Jack Torrance (famous as a shotputter). But UK had Sale to outscore Torrance 20 to 2, and DeMoisey added 17 as UK won 51-38. Wade's 15 were high for LSU.

During the tournament, the presidents of the SEC schools voted to hold the tourney in Atlanta again in 1934 and agreed to limit the field to the eight teams with the best records.

UK breezed to the title 46-27 over Mississippi State, with Rupp clearing his bench. DeMoisey with 15 points and Sale with 14 led UK to its first championship in 12 years.

Atlanta writers described UK in glowing terms.

Ralph McGill reported that Mississippi State "saw more blue uniforms than their grand-dads did in 1861."

And Ed Danforth wrote: "Aggie Sale gave an Atlanta crowd the greatest exhibition of basketball in all the 13 annual tournaments (this included the Southern Conference). Sale swept through like a man inspired. He completely dominated the play of his own team, yet fitted into their plan of attack and defense perfectly. It may take 14 more tournaments to produce his like again, but at that it will be worth waiting for."

Many writers called UK "the greatest team in southern history." Sale, DeMoisey and Johnson were named on the All-SEC first team and Davis to the second team. Sale's 71 points were a new tournament record and DeMoisey's 59 also broke the old mark of 51.

Sale and Johnson later were named All-Americans and Sale was chosen national Player of the Year by Helms Athletic Foundation of California. Helms also named UK national collegiate champion, and UK was firmly established as the South's foremost exponent of top-flight basketball.

DeMoisey was picked by his teammates to be captain for the 1933-34 season, but Ashland was making the big basketball news by winning the state high school championship. A future UK player, Ralph Carlisle, starred on a Kavanaugh team that lost in the quarter-finals. Up in Indiana, a powerful youth named LeRoy Edwards was finishing up a brilliant career with Indianapolis Tech High. His next stop: UK.

Dave Lawrence made UK's starting lineup as a junior forward.

Dave Lawrence paints rosy future for self at UK

In the summer of 1931 the University of Kentucky had some fences in need of paint. Fortunately, there were some young men in the state—football and basketball players—eager to help with the job. One was Dave Lawrence, a forward who as a sophomore had led Corinth to the state high school basketball finals, and to the championship in '30.

He was working on railroad construction outside Corinth after graduation and he didn't like the job. The dynamiting gave him headaches. So when Adolph Rupp and UK freshman coach Len Miller came along that summer and offered him a painting job at UK, Dave took it gladly. And after making friends with other UK athletes that summer, he gave up the idea of following two brothers to Western

Kentucky College.

There never was much doubt, from his high school sophomore year on, that Dave Lawrence was going to make a college player. He was an excellent shooter, smart as a whip and aggressive on defense. He showed his ability to think quickly and produce under pressure in the 1930 National High School tournament in Chicago.

Corinth was playing St. John's Military Academy for third place and was leading by one point in the third quarter when a tip from center was chased down by Lawrence under his opponent's basket. He dribbled once and, though two teammates were open down the floor, fired the ball with two hands almost the length of the court at the basket.

The crowd groaned at the seemingly futile shot, but the ball dropped cleanly through the nets just as the gun went off ending the period. The alert Lawrence had spotted the timer raising his pistol and realized there was no time to work the ball down the floor.

Chicago sports writers called it "the greatest shot ever in a national tournament." Corinth won by two points.

Reached Finals Two Years

In the state tournament of '29, Corinth lost in the finals to Heath. In '30 the clever ball handlers from Corinth, playing their first year under coach Ted Hornback, won the state title by beating Kavanaugh in the final game. But in Law-

rence's senior year Corinth lost by a point to Newport in the district tourney although Dave hit a basket at the gun which didn't count.

Corinth's failure to get into the state tournament that year cost Lawrence a chance to make All-State for the third straight time (the All-State team was picked from state tourney players). He had the satisfaction, however, of averaging 16 points a game his final season and establishing himself as one of the leading young players in the nation (after graduation from UK he would go into education, becoming dean of men at the University of Louisville in 1952 and dean of students there in 1963).

He was a regular on a good UK freshman team and a reserve on the varsity national champions of 1932-33. He was ready for a starting position by his junior season, 1933-34. So was Jack Tucker of Cynthiana, who as a sophomore the previous season had played about the same amount as Lawrence. The third open position went to Milerd (Andy) Anderson, a sophomore guard from Covington.

Starters back from '33 were center John DeMoisey and guard Bill Davis. These five opened most of the games for UK.

In finishing strong in '33, UK had won four straight regular-season games and four more in the tournament to take a string of eight into the following season. The streak went to 23 before it was broken in one of the most stunning upsets in UK history.

DeMoisey Double-Teamed

Georgetown was mastered 41-12 in the opener as Rupp used 10 players. Besides his starters, the coach played Sam Potter, Herb Jerome, Evan Settle, Garland Lewis and Berkley Davis, DeMoisey scored 15 points but encountered a maneuver which would be used often by UK foes. The man guarding Andy Anderson dropped off to double-team the Wildcat center, and Anderson—never a good shooter—didn't take a single shot.

Tom Dandelot's Marshall team was beaten 48-26 as DeMoisey got 13 and Lawrence 10. Cincinnati was more troublesome. Coached by 21-year-old Ray Brown, believed to be the youngest head coach in the country, Cincy finally bowed 31-25 before 3,000 in UK's Alumni Gym.

Strong defense helped UK down Tulane 32-22, and UK held Tulane's highly-touted forwards, Grant Jancke and Ernie Beck, to five and three points, respectively. Bill Davis chipped in 11 and DeMoisey 10 for UK. UK beat Tulane again the next night 42-29, Davis getting 16 points but Tulane holding DeMoisey to one field goal.

Those five victories finished up the pre-holiday schedule and the Wildcats weren't due to play again until Jan. 12 at Sewanee. For a time it appeared that the team would be without Bill Davis—described by Dave Lawrence in later years as "as good a guard as any I ever saw"—for the rest of the season.

The Davis home in Hazard had burned and Bill's mother was seriously ill. Rupp got word that Davis would stay home to work. But three days before the Sewanee game, Davis called the coach.

"Everything's okay. I'll be back to school," he told Rupp.

"His return will make us unbeaten again in conference play," a jubilant Rupp said.

DeMoisey, ill with the flu, and Davis were used sparingly in a 55-15 rout of Sewanee. DeMoisey was back in good shape, scoring 20 as Tennessee was beaten 44-23. Chattanooga fell 47-20, and Lawrence scored 20 as Tennessee bowed again, this time 53-26.

UK's toughest game was at Birmingham against Alabama. The Wildcats had to come from a 28-16 deficit in the last five minutes to win 33-28 after DeMoisey had fouled out with nine minutes left. On the way home, UK stopped in Nashville to whip Vanderbilt 48-26, running the Kentucky Southeastern Conference record to 7-0 and the overall mark to 11-0.

About 4,000 squeezed into Alumni Gym to see UK down Alabama 26-21. Dave Lawrence scored 10 points, but the real hero was Bill Davis, who held leading

Bill Davis was the highest scorer of Adolph Rupp's early guards.

SEC scorer Zeke Kimbrough to three points while scoring eight himself.

UK Fans Claim Record

UK easily defeated Georgia Tech, Sewanee and Vanderbilt to finish 15-0 for the season and run the victory streak over two seasons to 23. UK fans claimed that as a national college record. Kansas had won 35 straight, but it was pointed out that it had lost to an athletic club during the streak. Rupp wasn't particularly concerned. He had a tournament to think about.

At the end of the previous season SEC school presidents had voted to limit the tournament to the eight teams with the best records. UK's first foe was Florida, one of the weaker teams in the SEC which had been invited only because some of the Ole Miss players had the flu. UK was rated co-favorite with Alabama, whose only losses in 15 games were to UK.

Georgia Tech coach Roy Mundorff angered UK fans when he said that Alabama was better than UK even though Bama had lost twice to Rupp's team.

"I think Alabama would have won those games if the team hadn't tightened up," he explained. "All Alabama has to do is relax and it can beat any team in the country."

Coach Ben Clements' Florida Gators played beautifully, displaying quickness and finesse, to defeat UK 38-32. UK tried desperately to gain control of the game and managed to take a 27-24 lead. But Welcome Shearer, a football center playing guard in basketball, hit two straight baskets to break the UK surge.

Lawrence Blames Nerves

DeMoisey scored 16 points but was far from his best. He missed repeatedly on his pivot shots and was handicapped with three fouls (four was the limit at that time) for the last third of the game. UK's forwards, Lawrence and Tucker, had a miserable time. Lawrence scored only three points, Tucker was shut out.

Lawrence was disconsolate over missing 11 close-in shots.

"We got behind, then got nervous," was his explanation of UK's loss and his own showing.

Florida went to the finals before Alabama made Mundorff a good prophet by winning 41-25. During the tournament SEC coaches were disgruntled by rumors that Rupp was working secretly to have the tournament discontinued. That was the first reported rift in Rupp's relations with his fellow coaches, and the gap was to widen over the years as UK's victories mounted.

DeMoisey and Davis were named to the all-tournament team and Frenchy also made All-American. Lawrence and Tucker were elected co-captains for the next season. Andy Anderson would also be back, but Bill Davis was to quit school and DeMoisey was to be graduated.

Rupp, who had a four-year record of 65-9, had help on the way in 6-foot-5 LeRoy Edwards and others off an unbeaten freshman team. Rupp knew what he was doing when he scheduled Eastern power New York University in Madison Square Garden for the next season.

Edwards' battering triggers rule change

New York's Madison Square Garden was buzzing with excitement as tipoff time neared for what the newspapers had billed as "the game to decide the national championship."

A crowd of 16,500 waited eagerly to see what their New York University Violets could do against the Southern upstarts from Kentucky, led by brawny LeRoy (Cowboy) Edwards. Adolph Rupp, coach of the Kentuckians, was confident. He thought he had the finest team and certainly the greatest center in Edwards, imported into Kentucky from bordering Indiana.

Rupp's only misgivings were about officiating. Would Eastern officials interpret the rules as officials did in the South and Midwest? Only a few days earlier Rupp had received a telegram from Notre Dame coach George Keogan urging UK to take a Midwest official to the Garden "or you won't have a chance." Notre Dame had lost 25-18 to NYU only a week before and a furious Keogan had blamed it on officiating.

Rupp's worst fears were realized from the opening whistle. Edwards and the UK players were unable to run their normal screening plays without drawing blocking fouls, and Edwards couldn't score against the defensive tactics of Irving (Slim) Terjesen and Irwin (King Kong) Klein. Edwards' foul enabled guard Sid Gross to drop in the winning point as NYU won 23-22. Only seconds before Gross had sunk a layup to tie the score.

A stunned Rupp wasn't at a loss for words.

"I can't understand why it's a foul when one of my boys moves toward the basket on a screening play and it isn't a foul when a New York boy drapes himself over the back of one of my country kids and hugs him around the arms."

Most of the New York sports writers agreed. The New York Post report was typical:

"The score says that NYU is the best college basketball team in the country and that the East still is supreme. But if Frank Lane, the ref from the Midwest, had worked the game, it's safe to assume big LeRoy Edwards would have been given a fantastic number of foul shots. Minor mayhem was committed on the person of Edwards by Terjesen and Klein. Something will have to be done or the game will become entirely too rough."

Something was done. This game as much as any single incident pointed up the need for a rule limiting the time a player can stay in the area under the basket. Eventual result was the three-second rule.

Despite what seemed to be a personal setback, Edwards' prestige was higher than ever after his appearence before the New York reporters. Most of them were convinced that he was, indeed, the nation's top center and potentially the best of all time. He went on his sophomore season to make All-America and followed in Aggie Sale's footsteps as Helms Foundation's Player of the Year.

Edwards first played basketball at the YMCA in his birthplace of Crawfordsville, Ind. His earliest instruction came there from former Wabash College players. Later his family moved to Indianapolis where he played for Tech High. As a sophomore at Tech he didn't have the shots to be a really high scorer. But when a touring pro team from Texas came through Indiana, LeRoy went to nearby Martinsville to watch them.

It was a profitable trip for young Edwards because from watching the pros he picked up the hook shot. By his junior year at Tech he was scoring with the hook, and it was one of his bread-and-butter shots until he quit pro basketball in 1947.

Keogan Tips Rupp

Had LeRoy shown more interest in attending college, it's doubtful if Rupp could have got him for UK. However, coaches in Indiana were convinced the happy-go-lucky youth never would attend college. Rupp's old friend at Notre Dame, George Keogan, tipped the UK coach off on Edwards.

"He's as big and tough as they come," Keogan told Rupp. "If you can just get him in school. . . ." As it turned out, keeping him was a bigger problem.

As a freshman at UK Edwards scored more than 400 points in 16 games, a terrific pace in those days of the center jump. Edwards, forward Ralph Carlisle and guard Warfield Donohue led coach Len Miller's freshmen to an unbeaten season and long-time UK rooters were certain it was the best frosh team in the school's history.

When UK opened the 1934-35 season with a tuneup against the Alumni, two

players up from the freshmen were in the starting lineup: 6-foot-5, 200-pound LeRoy Edwards at center and 6-2 Warfield Donohue, former Louisville St. Xavier captain, at guard. Returning regulars were Dave Lawrence and Jack Tucker at forwards and Andy Anderson at guard. This was the lineup that started most of the season as UK won 19 of 21 games.

UK quickly reeled off five victories. Edwards' best games were 24 points against Oglethorpe and 26 against Chicago. Bill Haarlow, Chicago scoring ace who later would become superintendent of Big Ten basketball officials, was limited to six points.

Then came the loss to NYU.

While in the big city Rupp proposed that the leading college teams from each section meet in a post-season tournament to decide the national championship. He believed it would do away with the conflicting claims for the "mythical" title and also do much towards standardizing officiating. Four years later, 1939, the National Collegiate Athletic Association (NCAA) would hold its first tournament along the lines suggested by Rupp.

Back home UK rolled by Tulane twice, Chattanooga and Tennessee. In those games Rupp was able to use most of his reserves, including Ralph Carlisle, Garland Lewis, Jim Goforth, Russ Ellington, Courtland Bliss, Bruce Davis, Ed Tierney, Bob Taylor, Charles Gates, Sam Potter and Jim McIntosh. Tulane had a good player, Monk Simons, who scored 10 points in one game against UK.

UK hit the road for its next three games, having its closest call in edging Alabama 33-26 Only a 21-point performance by Edwards saved UK. After the game in Birmingham, a woman walked up to Edwards and said, "You were wonderful. You never missed."

"Lady, I'm not supposed to miss," replied Edwards laconically.

UK swept by Vanderbilt and Xavier of Cincinnati before returning home to defeat Georgia Tech and Alabama.

Tucker Is Hurt

UK's second loss of the season came at Michigan State, 32-26, to a Spartan team which was beating most of the Big Ten squads. A broken hand suffered by Jack Tucker hampered UK. A stocky guard, Bob Herrick, scored 14 points for

All-American center LeRoy Edwards had a wrestling match in New York.

Michigan State. Dave Lawrence always called Herrick "the toughest player I ever paired off against."

Garland Lewis moved in at forward to replace Tucker against Tennessee and UK won 38-36 on Lewis' long shot from the sideline.

Creighton was defeated 63-42 and 24-13 on successive nights in UK's Alumni Gym. Edwards made headlines over the nation when he scored 34 points in 34 minutes in the first game, breaking the gym record held by Frenchy DeMoisey. LeRoy insisted it wasn't one of his better games.

"I missed too many shots under the basket," he complained "I never play a good game when I shoot that much, anyway."

Dave Lawrence also had a fine game in the opener, hitting most of his shots in scoring 17 points. Emil (Box) Engelbretson, greatest Missouri Valley scorer of his time, tallied 22 for Creighton.

In the rematch Creighton tried to stall and abandoned a pressing defense which had failed the night before. Edwards scored 14 points and Warfield Donohue 10 for UK. Donohue held Engelbretson to two points.

UK finished the season with easy victories over Vanderbilt and Xavier. Since the SEC had abandoned its annual tournament, UK had to share the conference title with Louisiana State on a basis of season records.

Edwards and Lawrence were named to the All-SEC team. Edwards made all the All-America teams, and referee Frank Lane picked both Edwards and Lawrence to his All-America. Andy Anderson was selected as the best guard to play that season in Madison Square Garden.

The 1934-35 campaign was important for Rupp and UK because it broke Kentucky out of the mold of being just a good Southern team. Rupp got together his toughest schedule for the next season, and he was looking forward to it.

He was losing Jack Tucker and Dave Lawrence, but the coach had Edwards for center, Warfield Donohue and Andy Anderson for guards, a good crop of reserves, plus Joe (Red) Hagan, Bill Spicer and J. Rice Walker moving up from the freshmen.

When school was out Rupp urged Edwards to stay in Lexington and make a tour of coaching clinics. The coach said he wanted to use Edwards to demonstrate playing techniques. More important, the coach wanted to keep an eye on the most valuable piece of basketball property in the country. Edwards declined and went home to Indianapolis.

Next word from him was that he was married and would not return to school.

Some of the players offered to chip in and pay living expenses for Edwards and his bride if he would come back to school. But Edwards got a job and played semi-pro basketball for a year. The following season he went into pro basketball with the Oshkosh (Wis.) All-Stars.

In ability there are strong cases to be made for several players as Rupp's best. But for sheer effectiveness against the opposition of his day, the Hoosier Cowboy stands below no one.

Donohue was almost overlooked

After five years of basketball prosperity, hard times came to Adolph Rupp. Truly great days were not to return for eight years although Kentucky always was respected and Rupp's reputation as one of the nation's finest coaches grew steadily.

As Rupp sent his Wildcats through their paces in the fall of 1935, he looked grimly ahead to playing Pittsburgh, New York University, Michigan State, Notre Dame, Butler and Creighton outside the Southeastern Conference and strong SEC foes Tennessee, Vanderbilt and Alabama.

Ironically, All-American center LeRoy Edwards had urged Rupp to schedule Notre Dame and Butler. LeRoy wanted a chance to perform "back home." But Edwards hadn't returned to UK after his sophomore year, and Rupp was left holding a stick of dynamite.

Not the least of the coach's worries was squad morale. The UK players realized they faced tough going without Edwards. Garland Lewis of Jeffersonville, Ind., was a good center, but he was no Edwards. For that matter, who was?

Ralph Carlisle moved into one of the vacated forward positions and sophomore Joe (Red) Hagan beat out another sophomore, J. Rice Walker of Lexington, for the other. Back at guards were Andy Anderson and Warfield Donohue.

Rupp must have shuddered at times over how close he came to not having Donohue. Donohue, from Louisville St. Xavier, was a steady though not spectacular high school player. Although a three-year regular, the slender 6-foot-2 Donohue was overshadowed as a college prospect by several other players in Louisville, notably Jim Goforth of Male and St. X, and Russ Ellington of Manual.

Donohue Is Walk-On

But Donohue, also an excellent tennis player, went out for basketball on his own. When practice was called his freshman year, he went to see Rupp. Donohue told the coach his background and said he'd like to try out. "Sure, come on out," Rupp said.

It took Donohue half a season to become a starter with the freshmen, but he finished that season as a regular and played in every game for three seasons with the varsity. Never a high scorer, he was the playmaker and floor general for the Wildcats and a good defensive player. One of the highlights of his career was the defensive job he did as a sophomore on Creighton's Emil (Box) Engelbretson.

Donohue's biggest thrills were in being named captain for his senior season and in making the All-Southeastern Conference team as UK won the SEC tourney his final year.

UK opened the 1935-36 season, Donohue's junior year, with its usual breather, Georgetown College. Even in the 42-17 triumph it was apparent Edwards would be sorely missed, particularly in rebounding. Behind his starting unit of Carlisle, Hagan, Lewis, Anderson and Donohue, Rupp used Jim Goforth, Russ Ellington, J. Rice Walker, Jim McIntosh, Bruce Davis, Nick Lutz and Charles Gates. Carlisle was in long enough to lead scorers with 10 points.

On Dec. 13, a week after the opener, SEC schools voted 11-2 to give athletic scholarships in the form of tuition, fees, books and board and lodging in a move to end the practice of under-the-table aid.

Lewis scored 19 points and Hagan 12 as Berea was buried 58-30, but Rupp was dissatisfied with UK's play. Then when Pittsburgh, the pride of the East, was battered 35-17, Rupp began to wonder if he hadn't underestimated his team. UK rolled to a 22-2 advantage and Pitt, using its famed "figure-eight offense" under H. C. (Doc) Carlson, never could get back in the game.

UK's impressive showing against Pitt was enough to convince New Yorkers that UK would be a handful again for powerful NYU. More than 18,000 turned out in Madison Square Garden in hopes of seeing another thriller like the years before. With Ralph Carlisle outshooting everyone on the court, UK was behind only 23-22 with eight minutes to play. Then NYU ran off and left UK to win 41-28. Carlisle finished with 17 points.

UK went to Xavier to start another winning streak, downing coach Clem Crowe's

team 36-32. Rupp and Crowe experimented with the foul rules, raising the foul limit to five. Even so, Carlisle, who scored 17 points, fouled out. Donohue and Anderson each drew four personals.

Beats Tulane Twice

UK defeated Tulane twice, Michigan State and Tennessee to raise its winning streak to five. Carlisle scored 16 as Michigan State was beaten 27-19. He had a bad night against Tennessee, but his running mate at forward, Joe Hagan, poured in 15 points as Tennessee fell 40-31. At this point Vanderbilt was leading the SEC with a 7-0 record, Mississippi State was 4-1 and UK 3-1.

Vandy handed UK its first regular-season loss in the four years of the SEC's existence on Feb. 1, 1936. Lewis and Carlisle both went out on fouls in the 32-23 loss.

UK bounced back to whip Alabama twice. After the second game against Alabama, in Lexington, Red Hagan grabbed the game basketball and ran to the locker room with it. Hagan wanted the new basketball for shooting practice. But Rupp followed him and demanded the ball.

Hagan handed it to Rupp with a little more force than necessary, along with an uncomplimentary remark. "That will be all for you," snapped Rupp, who had athletic director Chet Wynne suspend Hagan's athletic assistance. In short, no meals.

Being cut off meals didn't bother Hagan—a friend in Lexington saw that he got fed—but the fiery redhead hated to miss UK's next game. It was against powerful Notre Dame, at South Bend, Ind.

On Sunday Hagan walked to Alumni Gym with Jim Goforth and Russ Ellington to see the team off for the Monday night game.

"What are you doing here?" Rupp demanded of Hagan. Then the coach added, "Well, as long as you're here, you might as well make the trip because it'll be the last one you'll make anyway."

Hagan was on the bench at the start of the game, but UK fell 14 points be-

Warfield Donohue was the floor general and defensive ace for three years as a starting guard. He was All-Conference as a senior.

hind in the first half. Rupp pulled a piece of paper from his pocket, waved it down the bench at Hagan, and said, "I just got a telegram. Your suspension has been lifted and you can go in now."

Hagan hit six field goals in the game—no one else on UK had more than one—but UK was thumped 41-20. Notre Dame's super sophs, forward Johnny Moir with 17 points and center Paul Nowak with 11 were the winners' top scorers. But the Irish got great defensive work from guard Frank Wade, who held Carlisle scoreless. One of the Notre Dame subs was Johnny Jordan, eventually a good player who would one day coach Notre Dame teams against Rupp.

On the way home UK stopped in Indianapolis to beat Butler 39-28. Then came a trip to Tennessee and a 39-28 loss as Floyd (Biggie) Marshall hurt UK

badly with 17 points. Alvin Rice, former Ashland, Ky., star, hit three straight goals for Tennessee near the end to kill off UK comeback hopes.

Home Streak Ends

Carlisle scored 20 points as Xavier was beaten and 18 in a romp over Creighton. But the next night UK went cold and lost at home for the first time since Ohio State turned the trick on Jan. 2, 1933. Creighton, coached by Ed Hickey, who in future years would be one of Rupp's keenest rivals at St. Louis, broke UK's home court victory string at 38 by a 31-29 score.

A victory over Vanderbilt left UK atop the SEC standings with a 6-2 record. Vandy was close behind at 9-4.

Because of the difficulty of narrowing

the field to eight, 10 teams were invited to the SEC tourney in Knoxville and UK opened by trimming Mississippi State. But coach Blair Gullion's Tennessee squad laced UK 39-28, although Carlisle scored 17 points. Tennessee went on to win the title by clipping Alabama in the finals.

Carlisle was the only UK player voted to the All-SEC team.

The overall 15-6 record was Rupp's worst in six years at UK, but he was hopeful of improving the next season. Coming up from a good freshman team were Walter Hodge, Bernie Opper and Homer (Tub) Thompson.

Corbin High School, coached by Nick Denes, was winning the state tournament, and the talk of the tournament was Corbin's 6-8 Marion Cluggish, who would enter UK in the fall.

Carlisle was started on his way by top high school coaches

A lanky black-haired youth walked disconsolately to the sidelines in the University of Kentucky's Alumni Gymnasium. He and his Kavanaugh teammates had just lost 22-17 to Danville in the quarter-finals of the 1933 state high school basketball tournament.

"I guess now we'll have to go home without seeing the rest of the tournament," the boy said.

"No, I think they'll let you stay in the hotel for the rest of the tournament because you didn't lose in the first game," he was told by a husky man standing at the edge of the court.

Those were the first words Adolph Rupp ever spoke to Ralph Carlisle, who would become one of UK's great players and a two-time All-Conference forward.

A few months after the state tournament, Rupp sent former UK guard Jake Bronston and freshman coach Len Miller to Lawrenceburg to recruit Carlisle out of the middle of a tobacco patch. Carlisle later sold his small crop for $238 to help pay his expenses to school.

UK provided him with tuition, but he had to pay for his room and worked in a downtown drug store for three meals a day. Before he finished at UK, though, the Southeastern Conference approved full scholarships to athletes.

If Carlisle had any advantage over other basketball players entering UK, it was the coaching he received in high school. He played two years at Kavanaugh Academy, in Lawrenceburg, under Earle D. Jones, later to make a great record at Maysville, and two years for Paul McBrayer, who went on to become Rupp's assistant coach and later head coach at Eastern Kentucky State.

Those were great years for Kavanaugh and Carlisle. As a freshman he teamed with Fred (Buzz) Borries, later an All-American halfback at Navy, to lead Kavanaugh to the state tournament finals. When Carlisle was a sophomore in 1931, Kavanaugh got to the semifinals of the

Sweet 16, where the team lost 20-13 to Covington.

The next season Carlisle had the mumps and Kavanaugh couldn't get out of the district without him. He had one great satisfaction that season. In one game he scored 18 points, outscoring the entire Hazard team as Kavanaugh won 33-17. Hazard went on to the state championship, and Kavanaugh fans felt their team might have been champs except for a case of mumps.

By his senior year Carlisle was scoring 19 points a game and again took Kavanaugh to the Sweet 16 before the loss to Danville. Carlisle's 10 points were high for the game and he was named All-State center.

Carlisle was well prepared for a college career when he entered UK in the fall of 1933. He was a deadly shooter, had a beautiful drive-in shot on which he seemed to hang in the air, and was full of competitive fire. He always maintained that he developed his layup style of necessity.

"In our gym at Kavanaugh the basket was almost right against the wall," he explained. "When I went for a layup, I had to jump high for the basket, which is the best way to shoot a layup, instead of broadjumping."

Carlisle and Rupp never were close. There were times when their personalities clashed. As a sophomore, Carlisle felt that he didn't play enough and that Rupp played favorites.

All-SEC as Junior

In spite of what he considered obstacles Carlisle was rated a coming star by UK fans, and he lived up to his notices by playing regularly as a junior and making All-SEC.

Seniors Carlisle and Warfield Donohue and junior Joe Hagan were returning starters as Rupp got his Wildcats ready for the 1936-37 season. In addition, he had

experienced reserves from the previous season in J. Rice Walker and Louisvillian Jim Goforth, and a promising group of sophs headed by Walter Hodge (who had played for Blanton Collier at Paris, Ky.), Bernie Opper, Homer (Tub) Thompson of Jeffersonville and Fred (Cab) Curtis of Nashville, Tenn.

Carlisle, Hagan and Donohue were regulars all season, but Rupp never could decide between Walker and Thompson at center, and it took Hodge a few games to finally beat out Opper at a guard.

Opper, a New York City boy, and Walker of Lexington were in the opening lineup as UK trimmed Georgetown behind Carlisle's 17 points. Berea was even easier as Carlisle got 14 points and Thompson 13. Rupp also used Walker, Hodge, football star Bob (Twenty Grand) Davis, Elmo Head, Jim Goforth, Fred Curtis, Charles Combs, Jim McIntosh, Walt Hatcher and Robert Strohm.

The first real test came at Xavier. Carlisle's free throw sent the game into overtime and UK finally won 34-28, with Carlisle scoring 18. Centenary and Michigan State were beaten, giving UK five straight victories and bringing up the Notre Dame game. It was played in Louisville, UK's first appearance in Louisville since Rupp had become coach.

The UK players were nervous that afternoon of Jan. 5, 1937, as they waited for game time. Carlisle was especially jittery, pacing the floor and thinking, "Those guys are going to beat us into the floor."

"Settle him down," ordered Rupp. "Some of you guys get a deck of cards and play a game with him."

Carlisle didn't play well that night. Neither did most of the boys from the Louisville area, or perhaps the Notre Dame defense was just too tough. Thompson got only four points. Goforth three and Donohue was scoreless. Only Hagan had any kind of game, scoring eight points as UK lost 41-28.

A crowd of 6,352, largest ever to see a game in the state, packed the Jefferson County Armory. Conditions were anything but ideal. The floor was slippery and players slid into each other for 33 fouls. The floor also was a dark hue, making it difficult for viewers to follow the ball.

Walt Hodge, a great defensive player, was assigned to guard Notre Dame's high-scoring forward, Johnny Moir. But Moir scored 12 points and Irish center Paul Nowak 16.

UK beat Creighton, then lost at Michigan State, before racking up four straight victories. Most of the headlines in those weeks were about the great 1937 flood which had put areas of the state, including Louisville, under water. Donohue, Hagan and Goforth were under considerable mental stress since their families lived in the flooded part of Louisville.

UK lost to Tulane, then beat Tulane and Mexico University before losing to Alabama 34-31. It was the first win for Alabama, coached by Hank Crisp, over Rupp. Perhaps inspired by Alabama, Tennessee edged UK 26-24 to make UK's conference record 4-3. Georgia Tech at this time was 7-0 and Mississippi 8-1.

UK clinched a berth in the SEC tournament by ripping Vanderbilt 51-19. Carlisle, Hagan, Walker, Donohue and Hodge started the game, then Rupp called on Tub Thompson, Bernie Opper, Cab Curtis, Jim Goforth, Bob Tice, Elmo Head, Bob Davis, Jim McIntosh and Charles Combs.

UK finished the regular season with a 14-5 record after beating Xavier. Carlisle was ill with the flu and missed the game.

Rupp started Curtis in place of Carlisle in UK's tournament opener against Louisiana State at Knoxville. Carlisle started the second half and hit five of seven one-handed push shots as UK won 57-37. Carlisle was back in good shape, scoring 16 as Georgia Tech was ousted 40-30.

Tennessee, which had lost only once (to UK), tumbled before UK 39-25 in the title game. Goforth came off the bench when Donohue fouled out and got six points, two of his goals coming at crucial moments. Floyd (Biggie) Marshall kept Tennessee in the game with 15 points.

Carlisle and Donohue were given first-team All-SEC berths, while Hodge and Walker were on the second team.

At the end of seven seasons Rupp had a 116-22 record. At the rate the fellow was going, he could wind up with three or four hundred victories before he was through.

Ralph Carlisle of Lawrenceburg made All-Conference two years at UK.

48-foot, 2¼-inch shot made Hagan a UK immortal

By his senior year, Louisville's Joe (Red) Hagan had built a reputation as one of the University of Kentucky's finest all-round athletes. An end, he had captained the football team his final season and had played as a regular for basketball coach Adolph Rupp for two years.

But even without the solid performances in two sports, Hagan would have carved a special place for himself in UK athletic annals with just one shot—Feb. 14, 1938.

It came against a Marquette team which was considered vastly superior to UK. Marquette had whipped Notre Dame, which had beaten UK and many other strong teams. But Rupp had his Wildcats keyed up, and they played one of their best games before 4,000 spectators in UK's Alumni Gym.

With 12 seconds to play, the score was tied and UK in possession of the ball. When the ball was thrown back into play, UK made a couple of passes before the ball went to Hagan. Standing behind the center line, the redhead lofted a two-hand shot which swished through cleanly to give UK the game 35-33.

The crowd carried Hagan off the court. Governor A. B. Chandler came down from the stands, and called for a hammer and nail to mark the spot of what was the longest shot up to that time in UK basketball history. It measured 48 feet, two and a quarter inches.

Like another Louisville product, Warfield Donohue, Hagan just wandered into Rupp's clutches. Hagan went to UK to play football and went out for basketball without an invitation from Rupp.

UK almost missed getting Hagan altogether. Hagan started in sports at Southern Junior High, playing football and basketball for coach Butch Charmoli. He went to Male High in the 10th grade and to St. Xavier his last two years. He was a terrific athlete at each school. After graduation he went to Cincinnati Xavier and was in football camp there for a week.

He came home on a Friday night to get his clothes and other belongings, and was to report back to Xavier on Monday. But on Saturday morning a UK alumnus, Reed Miller, came by Hagan's home.

"Get in the car. We'll go for a ride," he told Hagan.

"Where are we going?" asked Hagan.

"Get in. We're just going up the road a piece," was the answer.

Joe did, and the next stop was the UK campus in Lexington. He decided to stay on a football scholarship.

"Rupp may have heard of me," Hagan said later, "but I don't think he cared particularly whether I came out for basketball or not. I guess I really turned out to be better at basketball."

He made Rupp's starting team as a sophomore forward, and stayed at forward except for a couple of times when he moved his 6-foot-2 frame to center.

Hagan started his final season, 1937-38, as college basketball was getting a new look: the center jump after every basket had been eliminated to the consternation of the game's inventor, Dr. James A. Naismith. He complained that the new rule would turn the sport "into a game of racehorse."

Rupp was at home with a cold when the '37-'38 campaign opened. Freshman coach Paul McBrayer guided the team and used 16 players in smashing Berea 69-35. Three UK sophomores started the game. They were Jim Goodman of Paris and Harry Denham of Maysville at forwards, and Layton (Mickey) Rouse of Ludlow at guard. With them were holdovers Homer (Tub) Thompson of Jeffersonville, Ind., at center and J. Rice Walker of Lexington at guard. Walt Hodge, the sophomore starting guard of the previous season, didn't come out for basketball after injuring his knees in football.

The starters didn't click, however, and McBrayer soon had to go to the veterans. Hagan went in and scored 14 points to tie Thompson for scoring honors. The 6-8 Marion Cluggish went in to score 11 points. Other reserves included Fred (Cab) Curtis, Ralph Jackowski, John Trivette, Charles Combs, Elmo Head, Bob Davis, Ed Gough and Larry Spears.

In a victory over Cincinnati, Rupp started Hagan and Goodman, forwards; Thompson, center, with Rouse and Bernie Opper, guards. Rupp started Curtis, Hagan, Thompson, Rouse and Opper in beating Centenary, and this was as close to a regular lineup as Rupp got. Rupp juggled his starters all season.

Rupp had only a week to get UK ready for its first trip to the Sugar Bowl to play Pittsburgh. Although it was referred to as a tournament, only two teams were invited in the event's early years to compete for the title.

UK took an early lead as Pitt, still operating Doc Carlson's "figure eight" offense, kept trying to break through UK's defense for layups. When the Pitt players couldn't get layups, they refused to shoot. UK managed to get possession of the ball often enough to build up a 28-13 halftime lead.

Pitt Finishes Strong

Pitt became more effective in the second half as Ed Spotovich and Bob Johnson started scoring, but Joe Hagan connected several times for UK. Hagan finished with nine points and was presented with the game ball after a 40-29 UK victory. Tub Thompson scored 11 points and Cab Curtis 10 for UK.

After the game a disgruntled Doc Carlson gathered up a bunch of sweat clothes, rushed up to Rupp and dumped them at the UK coach's feet. "Here, take these, you've taken everything else," Carlson said.

UK came back to earth quickly by losing its next three games, the first time in Rupp's tenure at UK he had lost three in a row.

All the defeats came on a trip north: 43-38 at Michigan State, 34-26 at Detroit and 47-37 at Notre Dame. Hagan scored 14 points at Michigan State and was even better with 16 at Detroit. He tried desperately to rally UK near the end of the loss at Detroit.

"We need four baskets," he told his teammates during a timeout. "I'll get three of them if you guys will just get one."

But Rupp's Wildcats, tired and off in their shooting, couldn't catch up.

Johnny Moir, who had been recently benched by coach George Keogan for

Adolph Rupp and Assistant Coach Paul McBrayer. McBrayer was with Rupp for seven years, 1935-1942. His freshmen teams won 64, lost 9.

Joe Hagan of Louisville went to UK to play football and became a star on Adolph Rupp's basketball team.

"indifferent play," was at his best for Notre Dame, scoring 20 points against UK. About the only consolation for UK was that Tub Thompson snapped out of a shooting slump with 15 points.

Back home UK opened Southeastern Conference play by beating Tennessee 52-27 with Curtis scoring 16 and Rouse 11. Bernie Opper held Tennessee ace Wilton Putnam to seven points.

Rupp, who said he was wearing out his fourth brown suit since coming to UK, took his team on its first SEC swing. UK tripped Vanderbilt and Alabama to equal Georgia Tech's 3-0 SEC record.

UK's shooting was erratic in a 39-32 loss at Xavier, but Hagan hit 11 points, Opper 14 and Rouse nine as UK avenged its loss to Michigan State 44-27. After Alabama was beaten, Hagan's 48-foot shot downed Marquette (he scored 11 points for the game) and ran UK's season record to 10-4.

Tulane Pulls Upset

UK scored a revenge victory over Xavier, then beat Vanderbilt and Tennessee to run the Kentucky SEC record to 6-0.

UK, Mississippi, Georgia Tech and Auburn were seeded for the SEC tourney to be held in Louisiana State's 8,000-seat coliseum. Tulane was the surprise of the tournament, upsetting UK 38-36 in the opener. Paul Pare hit the winning field goal in the final seconds.

Hagan with 13 points and Opper with seven played fine games for UK and Opper was named All-SEC. The title eventually went to Georgia Tech, which beat Ole Miss 58-47 in the finals despite a 23-point performance by the losers' Bonnie (Country) Graham.

Opper was chosen to captain UK for the next season. Meanwhile, Sharpe was winning the Kentucky high school championship behind the play of center Jim King, another future UK player.

Opper wanted to play
far away, so he chose UK

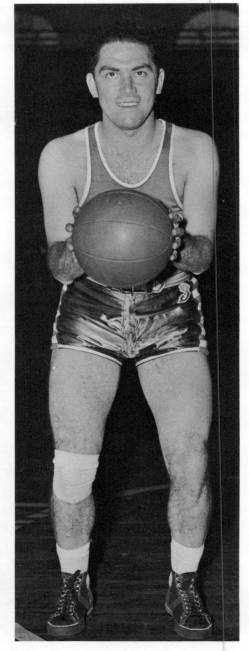

Bernie Opper, from New York, became Adolph Rupp's second All-American guard.

In the three seasons following the 19-2 record which LeRoy Edwards helped fashion in 1934-35, Adolph Rupp's teams won 45 and lost 16. While that was a good record, it wasn't up to the 84-11 pace of Rupp's first five years at the University of Kentucky. And the Baron of the Bluegrass hadn't had an All-American since Edwards.

Bernie Opper helped take care of both departments in 1938-39. The stocky 5-foot-10 guard made All-American and was a key man as UK won 16 of 20 games and took its third undisputed Southeastern Conference championship.

Opper had been a high scorer at Morris in New York's Bronx and later at a New York City prep school. He could have gone to Long Island, coached by Clair Bee, and one of the nation's best at the time. However, Opper wanted to go away to school and he wanted to play with a strong team.

Rupp Has 'Lost Battalion'

"I knew Rupp always had a good record," Opper once said, "and I saw Kentucky play in 1935 against NYU in Madison Square Garden. I didn't talk to Rupp at the time, but I wrote him a letter and told him I'd like to attend UK. I had recommendations from Clair Bee and Nat Holman (then City College of New York coach). Rupp wrote back and said to come on down."

Opper played part time as a sophomore at guard and forward, was a regular guard as a junior when he made All-Southeastern Conference, and reached his full potential as a shooter, playmaker and leader as a senior in 1938-39.

He teamed with Layton Rouse at guard although sophomore Lee Huber started several games at guard. Rupp's regular front line consisted of senior Fred (Cab)

Curtis of Nashville and Keith Farnsley, a sophomore from New Albany, Ind., at forwards, and Corbin junior Marion Cluggish at center. Tub Thompson played almost as much as Cluggish at center, and was a better scorer.

Rupp added something new for the '38-39 season: the Lost Battalion. In later years these players would have been called "redshirts"—players being held out of games, but practicing with the team. The idea was to give them a chance to develop while preserving their year of eligibility.

On Rupp's Lost Battalion were Waller White, Carl Staker, Don Orme, Carl (Hoot) Combs and Marion Cluggish's brother, 6-6 Stan (Little Clug) Cluggish.

In the opener UK breezed by Georgetown 39-19 as Rupp used 12 men. Besides his starters, Rupp played Jim Goodman, Tub Thompson, Lee Huber, Ernie Jefferson (the left-hander from Midway's 1937 state high school champs), Elmo Head and Harry Denham.

Kentucky Wesleyan also was an easy mark. One of the reserves used by UK in this game was Walter Hodge, the fine defensive guard of two years previous who had missed a season with injured knees. He wore braces on both knees when he ran onto the court.

After beating Cincinnati and Washington & Lee, UK went to New York's Madison Square Garden to meet powerful Long Island U. With Irving Torgoff giving the UK guards a lesson in outside shooting, the LIU team trounced Kentucky 52-34. LIU was bigger than UK and had a good fast break.

"Long Island was the best team I played against in college," Opper said years later, "including the great Notre Dame teams."

After beating St. Joseph's in Philadelphia, UK returned home to play Notre Dame at Louisville. UK made a strong effort to beat the Irish for the first time behind Mickey Rouse's outside shooting, but Notre Dame won 42-37.

Rupp began to worry when he lost to Tennessee and Alabama, making three straight losses for the second season in a row for UK. He would have felt a lot better, though, if he had known UK would win its next 11 to finish with a 16-4 record and the SEC title.

UK tuned up for its important game with Marquette by downing Vanderbilt. Now Rupp had to get ready for one of his toughest games. UK assistant coach

Paul McBrayer scouted Marquette in its win over Northwestern and brought this warning back to Rupp: "I have seen Notre Dame at its best, I saw Marquette last season and Long Island this year, but this Marquette team is the best I have ever seen."

Rupp had his Wildcats keyed perfectly for the game and the seven men he used gave beautiful all-round performances to win 37-31. Rouse, one of the smoothest and smartest guards Rupp ever had, popped in 10 points and Cluggish seven.

Rupp got word that Ernie Jefferson had been declared scholastically ineligible and would not be in school the second semester.

Thompson came into the next three games as a substitute to boost UK by Xavier, Alabama and Mississippi State. Then Keith Farnsley hit a shot from the foul line midway of the second overtime to beat Johnny Mauer's Tennessee Vols 36-34. After Xavier and Vanderbilt were beaten, Rupp was feeling pretty good about the SEC tournament in Knoxville.

"It'll take a smart team to beat us," he said. He was a little worried, though, about Tennessee and Alabama.

Opper Rallies UK

Rupp had a scare in the tourney opener, trailing Mississippi by three points at halftime before winning 49-30. Louisiana State was an easy 53-34 victim.

Then Tennessee was beaten 46-38 for the championship. Opper scored 13 points in the title game and scored three baskets to get UK moving after it trailed 18-11 eary in the game.

Opper, an almost unanimous choice for All-SEC, got a big hand from the crowd of 3,000 when he left the court. Later Opper, who would remain an admirer of Rupp and follow UK's fortunes closely after settling in California, was named to an All-America team.

UK would miss Opper, Cab Curtis, Elmo Head and Tub Thompson the next season, with a trip to the Sugar Bowl to play Ohio State coming up, but as usual Rupp had more talent in the pipeline from the freshman team.

Bernie Opper was captain of this 1938-39 UK team. Front row, from left, are: Ernie Jefferson, Don Orme, Elmo Head, Waller White, Carl Combs and Lee Huber. Middle row, from left: head coach Adolph Rupp, Walt Hodge, Mickey Rouse, Opper, Keith Farnsley, Harry Denham and assistant coach Paul McBrayer. Back, same order: trainer Frank (Skipper) Mann, Jay Nelson, Carl Staker, Stan Cluggish, Marion Cluggish, Homer (Tub) Thompson, Fred Curtis, Jim Goodman and student manager J. B. Faulconer.

Rouse pleasant surprise for UK

When Layton Rouse showed up on the University of Kentucky campus in the fall of 1936 to play basketball, his prospects were anything but bright.

He wasn't exceptionally tall, about 6 feet 1, and that wasn't big for a boy who had played center and forward in high school at Ludlow, Ky.

His high school coach, Ted Hornback, hadn't been impressed enough with him to try to steer him to Western Kentucky College, Hornback's alma mater.

UK coach Adolph Rupp hadn't beaten a path to Rouse's door, either. Rouse came in contact with Rupp when the coach spoke at the Ludlow basketball banquet. "I recruited myself for Kentucky," Rouse always insisted.

Rouse did have some things in his favor. He had made All-Northern Kentucky and All-Little Six Conference. He was a good shooter, too, preferring to fire the ball up one-handed after watching Frenchy DeMoisey play a few years earlier. Rouse wasn't a sensational player, though, for the simple reason that he wasn't really hungry for points.

He didn't care who scored as long as his team won, and Ludlow had good teams his last two years there. They advanced to the regional tournament both seasons.

Rupp invited Rouse to Lexington in the spring of 1936 for a tryout, perfectly legal in those days. Rouse, playing against Red Hagan and the rest of the UK varsity, threw in three or four baskets. Rupp offered him a partial scholarship, with the assurance that if he proved himself, he'd get a full ride.

Rouse never started a game as a freshman. He was second-team forward behind Harry Denham of Maysville. But there was something about Rouse that Rupp liked. Rouse figured it was "because I always tried to do exactly what he told me." So Rupp put him on full scholarship for the second semester.

Rouse was convinced he'd never do much in basketball at forward. Rupp expected his forwards to get off the mark quickly—those first two steps were vital —and Rouse simply wasn't a fast starter.

But he got a break in his sophomore year. Walter Hodge, the second-team All-Southeastern Conference guard and defensive specialist of the previous season, couldn't play because of "football knees."

Rupp promptly shifted Rouse to guard, and the poised youth, who always seemed to know exactly what his coach was thinking, stayed there as a regular for three years.

It Rhymes With Mouse

Rouse had picked up a nickname as a freshman. One of his teammates, Ed Gough, had decided that since Rouse rhymes with mouse, Rouse would have to be called Mickey.

Rouse's career overlapped with two All-American guards at UK—Lee Huber and Bernie Opper—and he was on a par with both.

Mickey Rouse would have many memories of his days at UK. . . .

His first day of freshman basketball practice when frosh coach Paul McBrayer said, "You fancy-dans save those one-hand shots for the alumni games." . . .

Playing in a losing game against Louisville Manual High School as a UK freshman, watching Manual's Junie Jones pass to Bob King in the final seconds, King miss the basket and Fred Davis (later a football All-American at Alabama) rebound the winning basket. . . .

His first SEC tournament, as a sophomore, when he fouled out in only two minutes of playing time as UK was upset by Tulane in Baton Rouge, La. And scorekeeper William (Big Six) Henderson coming back on the train with the UK team afterwards. . . .

Playing in three losses to Notre Dame, and as a soph guarding 6-4 All-American Johnny Moir and knocking him off the court three times, and fouling out. . . .

Notre Dame athletic director Elmer Layden, one of football's famed Four Horsemen, coming in the UK locker room to compliment the Kentuckians after a loss to the Fighting Irish. "Congratulating us for losing," Rouse said. . . .

Seeing Red Hagan hit the 48-foot shot which beat Marquette in 1938, then watching helplessly as a Marquette player brought the ball across midcourt, stop, and fire a high archer that dipped into the basket and popped out into Rouse's arms. "The longest three seconds of my life," Rouse said. . . .

Going up for a rebound with teammate Lee Huber in an SEC tournament game

as a senior and scoring for Tennessee as the ball popped out of their grasp, tying the score and sending the game into overtime (UK later won it). . . .

Teaming with Lee Huber in the backcourt to make what was probably the best pair of guards UK had had until then. . . .

Making All-SEC in his final season. . . .

And the greatest thrill of all, hearing Adolph Rupp announce after the 1939-40 season that no other player would ever wear Rouse's jersey. No. 10 would be retired, the first time Rupp had ever done this.

(The number would show up again 15 years later, worn by a junior from Maysville, Gerry Calvert, and has been used ever since.)

Rupp Hunts a Lineup

Rupp was still experimenting, trying to find a regular lineup, when UK beat Berea in the 1939-40 opener. Rupp had Stan Cluggish (from off the previous season's Lost Batallion) and junior Keith Farnsley at forwards, Marion Cluggish at center, with senior Mickey Rouse and junior Lee Huber at guards.

But Stan Cluggish, at 6-6 second only to 6-8 brother Marion in height on the team, wasn't mobile or quick enough for Rupp. In succeeding games the coach tried Don Orme, Waller White, Ermal Allen and Harry Denham at the forward position. By February Allen, a football halfback, was starting most of the games, although White also got some starts and was a valuable relief man.

UK lost its second game of the season 39-30 at Cincinnati in what Rupp called "one of the worst exhibitions a team of mine ever put on." After Clemson was beaten, UK traveled to New Orleans to play unbeaten Ohio State in the Sugar Bowl tournament. OSU coach Harold Olsen had three starters back from a team which had lost to Oregon in the finals of the 1939 National Collegiate (NCAA) tournament.

Rouse and Huber were superb. "We just ran our plays and they seemed to work," Rouse said. Rouse scored 14 points and Huber nine, combining for 23 points as UK won 36-30 before 7,000 fans.

Three more victories—over Kansas State (its first year under coach Jack

Mickey Rouse (center of the front row) is wearing his road uniform instead of the No. 10 so familiar to UK home fans. Hamming it up on one of UK's trips in the 1939-40 season are, front row (from left): Carl (Hoot) Combs, Keith Farnsley, Rouse, Lee Huber and Jim King. Back row (from left) are: Ermal Allen, Waller White, Marion Cluggish, Don Orme and Carl Staker.

Gardner), Xavier and West Virginia—gave UK a five-game winning streak going into its game at Notre Dame.

Rouse scored 13 and Huber nine, but overall UK's shooting—mostly at long range—couldn't match Notre Dame's. The Irish did a better job than UK at working the ball inside, and won 52-47 behind Ed Riska's 17 points.

Marquette Loses Star

UK beat Tennessee in Lexington, then went on the road to lose to Alabama and Vanderbilt. That brought UK up against another good Marquette team at Milwaukee, but just before the game star Marquette guard Bill Womenich was

declared ineligible. UK won 51-45 as Keith Farnsley scored 18 points and Rouse 12. Huber, ill with the flu, played only five minutes and never was able to play regularly the rest of the season. His place was taken by Carl (Hoot) Combs, the football halfback.

UK lost two of its remaining six games, losing to Tennessee and Georgia Tech, then went to Knoxville for the SEC tournament. Vanderbilt was easy, 44-31, but the Huber-Rouse inadvertent tip-in sent a semifinal game with Tennessee into overtime. With only a few seconds to play in the overtime, UK had the ball out of bounds. "Call my play, I'll make it," Farnsley pleaded. UK did and he hit to win the game 30-29.

After Georgia was defeated 51-43 in the finals, Rouse was the only player chosen on the All-SEC first team. However, Farnsley made the second team.

There was talk that UK would get a bid to the NCAA tournament (this was before the SEC champ got an automatic bid), but UK athletic director Bernie Shively announced that "Kentucky won't compete. It's not in condition."

UK's freshman team, with brilliant play from forwards Cliff Barker and Milt Ticco and center Mel Brewer, finished unbeaten. However, Barker would not return until after World War II, then he would become a part of UK's most famous team—the Fabulous Five.

Huber only stabilizing influence
in 'bleak' season

If Lee Huber hadn't been such a good tennis player, he might never have played basketball at the University of Kentucky.

When Huber was graduated from Louisville St. Xavier High School in 1937, his reputation in tennis was perhaps better than it was in basketball. There was considerable doubt as to who was the best basketball player in the state, but there was no question whatsoever in tennis.

Huber won the state high school singles championship his sophomore and senior years, and probably would have made it three in a row if the tournament hadn't been rained out his junior year.

So Huber had two inducements to attend UK: Adolph Rupp wanted him for basketball, and professor H. H. Downing, a kind, elderly man who seemed to regard every player as his son, wanted Huber for tennis. Making the decision even easier, Lee had a brother, Harold, ahead of him at UK.

Huber had been a fine basketball player at St. X, All-State as a senior and a starter for two years among several future college players. In his senior year, 1937, St. X lost to eventual champion Midway in the semifinals of the state tournament. A fellow who later became better known for football at Notre Dame, Bernie Crimmins, also was All-State for S. X. Two other good players were Billy Gates and Bert Robben, both of whom attended Xavier University at Cincinnati and played against Huber.

Huber's two-hand shot, which he fired anywhere from the center of the court to the free throw circle, was a thing of beauty. Hands to the rear and slightly atop the ball, the ball held chest high; then Huber would dip slightly and loft the ball effortlessly, high and soft, toward the basket. Short, you'd think; then, swish—two points.

It was apparent his freshman year, when he and Keith Farnsley were the stars of Paul McBrayer's frosh squad, that Huber would be a great UK player.

But when he was a sophomore, he had to be patient and wait. Two other great guards, Mickey Rouse and Bernie Opper, were ahead of him on the varsity. It wasn't a wasted year by any means, though. As the No. 3 guard, Huber got valuable experience and acquired the feel of playing guard the way Rupp wanted it played.

Rupp's ways were simple: play the percentages, which meant no shots from the corners; don't throw the ball away, or you might find yourself sitting on the bench, and apply a physically rough defense to the opposition.

Rupp's Hopes Are High

As a junior Huber was ready to start alongside Rouse, and the two of them were an ideal pair of guards for the Rupp system. Both could hit from long range, over the defense; both were excellent passers, and they played intelligently. No wonder Rupp called them "the best pair of guards in the U.S."

Huber had some excellent games as a junior. He scored 17 points in a victory over Clemson, a remarkable total for a guard in those days. Two of his better games were against Ohio State (Sugar Bowl) and Notre Dame. His junior season was marred only by influenza, which handicapped him the second half of the season.

When practice started for Huber's senior season, 1940-41, Rupp expected great things from the guard and was looking forward to a good season. UK had lost Mickey Rouse, Marion Cluggish and Harry Denham by graduation, but some good players were coming up from what had been one of UK's finest freshman teams. It had been the only unbeaten frosh team at UK since LeRoy Edwards, Ralph Carlisle and company had accomplished it six years before.

Rupp didn't get all he anticipated. First, Cliff Barker, the leading freshman scorer, didn't return and wouldn't be back until after World War II. Second,

Rupp had trouble getting consistent play at Cluggish's center position.

What Rupp finally got was a great season from Huber, until flu slowed the guard late in the campaign, and the worst record of any UK team since Rupp had been at Kentucky. The final 17-8 mark, a .680 winning percentage, would stand as Rupp's worst mark for another 20 years.

Rupp had a difficult time deciding on a regular lineup. In the beginning he leaned toward seniors Keith Farnsley of New Albany and Waller White of Lawrenceburg as forwards, junior Jim King of Sharpe, Ky., at center, with Huber and sophomore Ken England of Campbellsburg, Ky., in the backcourt.

Rupp never did decide on a starting lineup. Before the season was over Rupp would start five different forwards: Farnsley, White, Ermal Allen, Lloyd Ramsey and sophomore Milt Ticco. King and sophomore Mel Brewer shared the pivot all season. Sophomores Marvin Akers and Ken England and junior Carl Staker shared the guard spot opposite Huber. In addition, Rupp had available Don Orme, Hoot Combs, Louis (Bud) Robertson, J. S. Robertson, and Frank Etscorn.

The season didn't get far along before Rupp knew he was in trouble. After beating the UK Alumni, West Virginia and Maryville, Kentucky went on the road to lose to Nebraska and Creighton. Sid Held scored near the end of the game to beat UK by a point at Nebraska. Creighton coach Ed Hickey scouted UK in that one and saw what he had to to to beat UK—stop its fast break. He did, too, and won 54-45.

After beating Kansas State and Centenary, UK faced an awesome task in the Sugar Bowl—playing a veteran Indiana University team which had won the NCAA championship the previous season. It started as if it would be a lop-sided affair, with Herm Schaefer and Bill Menke leading the IU charge. But Huber began

hitting from outside and UK closed the margin to 48-45 before time ran out.

That performance and the one the year before against Ohio State earned Huber a high honor—a berth on the all-time Sugar Bowl team. On it with him are Bob Cousy (Holy Cross and pro Boston Celtics), Paul Arizin (Villanova and Philadelphia Warriors), Bob Davies (Seton Hall and Rochester Royals) and Ed Macauley (St. Louis U. and several pro teams).

Next came Notre Dame in the Armory at Louisville. Huber was in the hospital with the flu for several days before, but got out of bed the day of the game to play. It was one of the strangest games he was ever in. The scoreboard showed the score tied 48-48 at the end of regulation time, and 4,600 fans settled back in their seats for an overtime.

But the scorer called the officials over and said the game was over and that Notre Dame had won 48-47. It seemed that a UK player had stepped over the foul line while shooting a free throw, nullifying the point. The scoreboard operator had missed the referee's call. Despite being weak from the flu, Huber scored nine points. Waller White was even better with 15.

UK lost three of its next five games before closing the regular season with a seven-game winning streak. Included in the string were road victories over Vanderbilt, Vandy's Pinky Lipscomb scoring 21 points, and over Hank Crisp's Alabama team. Rupp was ill and had to turn the team over to assistant Paul McBrayer for the trip.

UK, which finished with the best Southeastern Conference record, 8-1, had to share the favorite's role with Tennessee for the SEC tourney. It was held for the first time in Louisville after years of financial failure in other cities.

The tournament was a success in Louisville, but a failure for UK. After beating Mississippi, Tulane and Alabama, UK lost to Tennessee 36-33 in the finals.

A brilliant performance by Lee Huber (12 points) kept UK in the game. Tennessee placed forward Bernie Mehen, center Frank Thomas and guard Gil Huffman on the All-SEC team. UK got center Jim King and guards Marvin Akers and Lee Huber on it.

And Huber was chosen All-America, the seventh Rupp player to be so honored.

Lee Huber's specialty was a smooth two-hand shot from long range.

UK scores upset, but no title in NCAA bow

The National Collegiate Athletic Association, the regulatory body for college sports, was formed in 1905, fourteen years after Dr. James A. Naismith nailed his peach basket on the side of a gymnasium wall in Springfield, Mass.

But it wasn't until 1939 that the NCAA conducted its first basketball tournament to choose a national champion. It was no overnight decision or stroke of genius by one man. Several coaches, including Kentucky's Adolph Rupp, had suggested it. No one, though, is on record as foreseeing the impact the tournament would have.

In addition to providing a major source of income for operation of the NCAA offices, the tournament pushed basketball from what New York sports writer Paul Gallico once called a "mildly exciting game," to the front ranks of the nation's sports. The NCAA tournament did for basketball what the World Series did for pro baseball—provided a goal and a stimulus for participants, and a focal point of interest for fans.

UK had a chance for a tournament berth in 1940, but athletic director Bernie Shively withdrew the school from consideration because several members of the squad had been ill with the flu. Two years later, the fourth time the tournament was held, the opportunity came again. This time UK jumped at the chance.

UK didn't win the national championship, but it scored the biggest upset of the tournament by knocking off Big Ten champion Illinois.

Adolph Rupp knew he would have a good team in 1941-42. Although his Wildcats were about to tackle what he called "the toughest schedule in the country," Rupp said before the first game that he expected to have the best squad since his 1933 national champs. He had experience at all positions and two teams of about equal ability.

Rupp had trouble arriving at a starting lineup. By the end of the season he was starting Ermal Allen, Morristown, Tenn.,

and Waller White, Lawrenceburg, Ky., forwards; Mel Brewer, New Albany, Ind., center and Marvin Akers, Jeffersonville, Ind., and Carl Staker, Maysville, Ky., the team captain, guards.

Off and on throughout the season Milt Ticco, Jenkins, Ky.; Lloyd Ramsey, Lexington, and Vince Splane, Flemingsburg, Ky., were starters at forward. Jim King, Sharpe, Ky., drew several starts at center, as did Ken England, Campbellsburg, Ky., at guard.

The day after UK defeated Miami (Ohio) in the opener, the nation was stunned by the news that Japan had attacked the U.S. Naval base at Pearl Harbor, Hawaii. Like all college teams,

Mel Brewer of New Albany, Ind., was starting center in 1941-42.

UK would be affected, but not drastically for two years.

Six days after Pearl Harbor, Rupp took UK to Columbus, Ohio, and lost 43-41 to Ohio State. Ticco, UK's leading scorer with nine points, missed a shot underneath the basket near the end of the game. Rupp sarcastically suggested that Ohio State award him a varsity letter.

UK had little trouble piling up victories over Nebraska, South Carolina, Texas A & M and Washington and Lee. Vince Splane started and scored well in several of those games. Rupp also had a chance to give experience to reserves Ed Lander, Adrian Back, Bruce Boehler, Frank Etscorn, Louis (Bud) Robertson and Jim Mathewson.

Xavier of Cincinnati was a lot tougher. Ermal Allen hit two free throws with five seconds to go to give UK a 40-39 edge over coach Clem Crowe's team. Former Louisville St. Xavier High star Bert Robben scored 20 for the losers.

Tennessee, coached by Johnny Mauer, ran its record to 9-1 by downing UK 46-40 at Knoxville. Forward Bernie Mehen, one of the South's great players of that period, hit 13 points for Tennessee.

UK put together a four-game winning streak before losing at Alabama 41-35 and to Notre Dame at Louisville 46-43. UK led Notre Dame 27-21 but faded after Carl Staker fouled out. The series was becoming embarrassing for Rupp. This was the seventh straight time UK had lost to the Irish.

UK won its next four games, in the process avenging the losses to Alabama and Tennessee.

Tennessee finished first in the Southeastern Conference standings and was a slight favorite to capture the SEC tourney title in the Armory at Louisville. Referee Bowser Chest said fans "will see one of the best games in America this year if UK and Tennessee meet in the tournament."

The game never came off. Alabama upset Tennessee 21-18, then UK edged Alabama 36-34 for the championship.

Carl Staker, captain of the team, was a key man in UK's upset of Big Ten champion Illinois in the NCAA tournament.

Ermal Allen was the only UK player named to the all-tourney team.

Immediately after the final game, Louisville Courier-Journal sports editor Earl Ruby approached Rupp with a proposition to play a post-season game in Louisville for Navy relief. The newspaper had been asked to sponsor the charity game.

Rupp said he would be willing to play "the champion of the Big Ten, the Southern Conference champion or the Great Lakes Naval Training Station."

So Great Lakes was invited by The Courier-Journal and the Navy League to meet UK. The Navy team promptly accepted.

Great Lakes had a powerhouse, with such top-flight players as Junie Andres (Indiana), Lee Huber (UK), Bob Menke (Indiana), Dick Klein (Northwestern), Bob Calihan (Detroit) and Frank Baumholtz (Ohio University). Great Lakes already had beaten Western Kentucky 64-37 at Jeffersonville and had won 31 of 36 for the season.

Meanwhile, UK was hoping to play in the Eastern eliminations of the NCAA tournament at New Orleans. Kentucky,

Duke, George Washington, Tennessee and Alabama were under consideration from the NCAA's district 3.

At that time all NCAA tourney teams were chosen by invitation. There were eight districts—four in the Eastern half of the country, four in the West—and a committee from each district picked a team to represent it. The districts were set up more along conference lines rather than any regard to population or number of states.

There were 11 states—Kentucky, Maryland, Virginia, North Carolina, South Carolina, Tennessee, Mississippi, Louisiana, Georgia, Alabama and Florida—and the District of Columbia in district 3. The two main conferences included were the Southeastern and the Southern.

District 6, however, took in only three states—Texas, Arkansas and Arizona—but included the Southwest and Border Conferences. District 5 was composed of Missouri, North Dakota, South Dakota, Kansas, Nebraska, Iowa and Oklahoma, covering basically the Big 6 (later the Big 8) and Missouri Valley Conferences.

Once eight teams were selected, the four Eastern teams would meet in a two-

night tournament to select an Eastern champion. The West would follow the same foremat. The two survivors would play, then, for the national title.

Thus, a team needed to play only three games to win the national championship.

The tournament system had one major flaw—too many good teams never got a chance to play for the NCAA title. There were years that the NCAA's tournament rival, the National Invitation Tournament in New York, had a stronger field than the NCAA. If the Big Ten champ got the NCAA district 4 (Midwest) tourney berth, there was DePaul with George Mikan playing in the NIT. If Missouri got district 5 NCAA bid, there were Bob Kurland and Oklahoma A & M headed for the NIT.

To make matters worse, some teams accepted NIT bids without waiting to see whether they'd get an NCAA spot. Eventually, the NCAA tourney setup would be changed to give automatic berths to 16 conference champions, plus a number of at-large bids for independents, but the eight-team limit would continue throughout the 1940s.

After UK got it's 1942 NCAA invitation, Rupp felt fortunate to be playing Great Lakes in the charity exhibition. The SEC tournament had ended on Mar. 1 and the NCAA playoffs didn't start until Mar. 20. Rupp knew his team could use some tough competition to get ready for its first-round game with Illinois. UK got off to a slow start, but lost to Great Lakes by only 58-47 as more than 9,000 spectators squeezed into the Armory. The game netted $5,800 for Navy relief.

Four nights later UK met mighty Illinois (18-4 record) in one-half of the NCAA Eastern Regional double-header at New Orleans. Penn State and Dartmouth played the other game. Three of the teams stayed at one hotel in New Orleans, but Illinois coach Doug Mills housed his team at another hotel. Mills' aloofnes. got under the UK players' skins. They were determined to beat him.

UK played a beautiful game, with Milt Ticco scoring 13 points, Carl Staker nine and Marvin Akers eight, to edge Illinois 46-44. Three of those Illinois players—Ken Menke, Andy Phillip and Gene Vance—were only sophomores, but they would become legends at their school as the Illinois Whiz Kids. They played one more season (with a 17-1 record), left to go to war, and didn't return until the 1946-47 season

Beating Illinois took everything out of UK. The next night Dartmouth handled UK easily, 47-28, but lost to Stanford by 15 points in the national championship game the following week.

Sharpshooting of Akers, Ticco snip '43 Irish victory string

The University of Kentucky's annual basketball game with Notre Dame was following a predictable pattern.

Notre Dame had pulled out to a 10-point lead and appeared to be well on the way to its eighth straight victory over UK. Not even the staunchest UK fans expected anything different. Notre Dame was unbeaten in six games and Irish coach George Keogan had said this was one of his greatest teams.

Just when a sizable number of the spectators in Louisville's Jefferson County Armory had resigned themselves to Kentucky's defeat on this night of Jan. 23, 1943, a brawny UK guard, Marvin Akers, dropped in a two-hand shot from midcourt. Then Milt Ticco, a loose-jointed forward who pushed the ball at the basket from up in front of his eyes, hit from the side for UK.

Akers and Ticco continued to connect, and suddenly the trend of the game changed. Now it was Notre Dame struggling to regain its poise. Another Akers long shot tied the score 49-49 with nine minutes to play, and although Ticco, Akers and sophomore guard Kenny Rollins fouled out, UK outplayed the Irish in the remaining time to win 60-55.

Akers finished with 17 points in what he would always consider his finest hour as a UK player. Ticco was close behind with 16, giving the two of them 33 of UK's 60 points.

Akers came close to not playing basketball. When he first started to Jeffersonville (Ind.) High School, he was too busy playing the trombone in the band to think much about sports. But Frank Barnes, Jeff's basketball coach, saw Akers playing basketball in physical education class and asked him to come out for the team.

As a sophomore, Akers played on the junior varsity. After four games as a junior he moved into the varsity starting lineup, although about half of the team's games were canceled because of the 1937 Ohio River flood.

As a senior, 6 feet 3, the dark-haired youth developed into an All-Sectional tournament player. One of his best games was against New Albany, which had a slender 6-5 senior, Mel Brewer, playing center.

Akers knew all about UK basketball. Two other Jeff players, Tub Thompson and Garland Lewis, had played for UK coach Adolph Rupp. Barnes took his entire Jeff team down to see UK play, and Rupp made a trip to Jeffersonville to talk to Akers.

Akers had a hangup, however, about whether he was good enough for big-time college basketball.

"I was overshadowed in high school by some other boys," he would say in later years. "I think I had a complex built up. Rupp gave me a lot of confidence, but he also could irritate me and make me play better, just to show him I could."

Rupp was in good shape for guards when Akers was a sophomore, so the player was held out of action to save his year's eligibility.

In the beginning Rupp had one complaint—Akers wouldn't shoot enough. It was that lack of confidence coming through. So Rupp kept urging Akers to take his shots in scrimmages, even from far out. The broad-shouldered guard had strong hands and wrists and could snap the ball to the basket quickly and accurately.

Akers started about half the games as a sophomore—he, Lee Huber and Carl Staker could all be considered regular guards—and made All-Southeastern Conference with a good tournament performance. He was a fulltime starter the next two years, making All-SEC again as a senior.

Ticco, also 6-3, had played his high school basketball in the small town of Jenkins, Ky. He was all set to attend Western Kentucky College on a scholar-

ship when he got word that UK was interested in him if he wanted to come to Lexington for a tryout.

Ticco was an athlete who did everything his own way. As a baseball first baseman, he used a glove with no padding which he flipped about as casually as a cow swishing her tail to drive flies away. He gathered up low throws from the dirt with consummate ease.

He played center in basketball for coach Jim Lauder at Jenkins. His best shot was a two-hander facing the basket. He'd hold the ball up, dip it back over his head slightly and shoot it. He was accurate, too, averaging about 14 points a game as a senior at Jenkins.

But he wasn't big enough or rugged enough to be a college center, and when he went to UK for his tryout, he soon saw, by watching the other boys, that he'd have to adjust his shot. So he moved the ball forward, holding it in front of his eyes, and pushing it to the basket. He soon learned to get the shot off quickly and became a good outside shooter.

Ticco was only 16 years old as a freshman at UK, but he and Cliff Barker were starting forwards on the 1940 frosh, which went unbeaten.

Ticco wasn't able to move in as a full-time starter his first two years on the varsity, but he gave some of the most exciting exhibitions of shooting on the squad. As a sophomore he scored 26 points in a 48-43 victory at Xavier of Cincinnati.

One of his best games as a junior was in the 46-44 upset of Illinois' Whiz Kids in the NCAA tournament, when he scored 13 points.

Ticco, Akers and Mel Brewer were the senior starters for UK as the 1942-43 season began. Rupp went with two sophomores, 6-1 guard Kenny Rollins, Wickliffe, Ky., and 6-1 forward Mulford (Muff) Davis, Elwood, Ind., at the other two spots. Main reserves were freshman Paul Noel, Midway, at forward; Lexing-

The 1942-43 UK team was captained by center Mel Brewer. Front row, from left: Carl Althaus, Ray Turley, Bob Atherton, Art Fish, and Tom Moseley. Middle row, from left: head coach Adolph Rupp, trainer Frank Mann, Wilbur Schu, Clyde Parker, Muff Davis, Kenny Rollins, Bill Barlow, Bill Hamm and assistant coach Paul McBrayer. Back row, same order: Milt Ticco, student manager Bob Landrum, Marvin Akers, Brewer, Jim Weber, Tom Moore, Ed Lander, Everett Penick and Paul Noel.

ton Lafayette's Ed Lander, center, and Clyde (Ace) Parker, Chrisney, Ind., and Bill Barlow, North Vernon, Ind., guards.

Rupp had lost Jim King, Carl Staker, Waller White and Ermal Allen by graduation while Ken England and Lloyd Ramsey had entered service.

UK ran into difficulty early. After beating Cincinnati and Washington of St. Louis, UK lost to Indiana 58-52 in the Louisville Armory and Ohio State 45-40 in Kentucky's Alumni Gym. UK led IU for the first 29 minutes, but tired against the Hoosiers' constant fast-breaking. Ralph Hamilton scored 18 points for IU, Brewer and Ticco 10, and Lander 9 for UK.

Ohio State wasn't an impressive team. Two of its players, Jack Dugger and Gene Fekete, were better known for football. But UK didn't get a sharp performance from anyone unless it was from Akers, who hit 12 points. By beating UK, Ohio State carved a special niche for itself in Kentucky history. It was the last home court defeat for UK in Alumni Gym, which was UK's home court through the 1949-50 season. After switching to Memorial Coliseum, UK would continue the streak until Jan. 8, 1955, setting a national record of 129 straight home-court victories.

UK got back on the right track after the loss to Ohio State by winning the next seven games. Included were two-point decisions over Tennessee and Georgia Tech, the grueling battle with Notre Dame and a 39-38 squeaker over Vanderbilt. Vandy almost beat UK because a little forward, Dave Scobey, poured in 14 points. In later years Scobey would become an SEC referee.

Among the reserves Rupp used in some of UK's easier games were Jim Weber, Wilbur Schu, Tom Moseley, Carl Althaus and Bill Hamm.

Bart Avery scored 14 points to help Alabama hand UK its first SEC loss 41-32, but it was the only conference loss of the season for Kentucky. After five more victories, four in the SEC, UK went to Chicago Stadium to play strong dePaul.

Notre Dame played Great Lakes the same evening as part of the stadium Saturday double-header, but Irish coach George Keogan wasn't there. He had died the previous Wednesday.

A crowd of 16,000 watched UK lose to DePaul 53-44 and Notre Dame bow to Great Lakes 60-56. UK certainly would have won except for a 6-foot-10 DePaul center, George Mikan, who batted about 20 Kentucky shots away from the goal. It was a perfectly legal maneuver in those days.

In the second half, UK began to solve DePaul's defense and break through for layups, but a 14-point DePaul halftime margin was too big.

Next, the SEC tournament in Louisville. UK had beaten Tennessee twice in the regular season but three times were too many. They met in the finals and Tennessee won 33-30 as center Dick Mehen tallied 13 points for Johnny Mauer's squad.

Marvin Akers and Mel Brewer were placed on the All-SEC team, and Ticco made the second team.

UK had one more game, against Great Lakes at Louisville. The Sailors, with Bob Davies (Seton Hall), Ed Riska (Notre Dame) and Dick Klein (Northwestern) and coached by Butler University's Tony Hinkle, were too tough. They beat UK 53-39.

Rupp didn't know what to expect for the next basketball season. He was certain of one thing: the war would make great changes in college basketball.

Brannum blossoms for UK's NIT-bound kindergarten kids

Bob Brannum was an All-American center a strong war-time team.

Gloomy old Alumni Gym was almost deserted, and quiet except for the steady thud-thud of basketballs bouncing on the court.

Adolph Rupp stood on the sidelines this late spring day watching four rangy players take practice shots.

Two of the boys, Bob and Clarence Brannum, were twin brothers. They had turned 17 years of age only a few days before, on May 28, 1943, and they had come all the way from Winfield, Kan., to try out for the University of Kentucky basketball team.

Someone suggested a half-court game, the Brannums against the other two. For about 15 minutes Bob and Clarence, who had become overly foul-conscious in high school, were shoved all over the court. Bob stopped play for a minute and walked over to his brother.

"Look, there's nobody calling fouls out here," he said. "Let's go."

As Bob would recall the incident in later years, "We started cleaning house. We bounced those other guys around good. I looked over at Mr. Rupp, and he was smiling."

After Rupp stopped the workout, he offered both Brannums scholarships to UK. Clarence became ill that summer and didn't attend college until after World War II, when he went to Kansas State.

But Bob Brannum accepted and gave Rupp many occasions to smile in that wartime season of 1943-44. The 6-5 center, whose style of play, as he put it, "was to get the ball," was an All-Ameri-can on the youngest team UK ever had. In aggressiveness, he was the closest thing to 1935 All-American LeRoy Edwards that Rupp had found.

Gained Notice as a Senior

Surprisingly, Brannum didn't become an exceptional player until his senior year in high school. Even as a junior he still played parttime on the junior varsity and parttime on the varsity. He did get to play, though, and was high man with seven points when Winfield lost to Newton for the state championship.

In Brannum's senior year, he began to get some notice and led Winfield to the state finals again, and again Newton won the title. The sister of Bob's girl friend (later Mrs. Brannum) worked for a Major Boxley at a nearby Air Force base. Boxley, who had gone to UK, took note of her talk about the Brannums' basketball ability. He asked the Brannums if they were interested in playing at UK. When they said yes, he wrote Rupp.

Rupp, on a visit with relatives at his home town of Halstead, Kan., talked with the Brannums and invited them for a tryout. Rupp was delighted when Bob Brannum made the team. At 17, Brannum was safe from the draft until after the season.

From the start it was obvious that Brannum was the key man on the 1943-44 squad, as a scorer and rebounder. Rupp had other able players, but all were freshmen except guard Tom Moseley of Lexington and forward Wilbur Schu of Versailles, both sophomores.

"It's like running a kindergarten," Rupp said. But he said he enjoyed working with his Kindergarten Kids, "Teaching them the simplest fundamentals."

When the season opened Rupp had Don Whitehead, only six feet tall but fast and smooth, at one forward. Whitehead had played for Evansville (Ind.) Bosse High School and had been directed to UK by his cousin, Clyde (Ace) Parker, a guard on Rupp's '42-43 team. Like Brannum, Whitehead had made the team in a tryout.

At the other forward Rupp had Schu, 6-3. The guards were 6-3 Moseley, who had played on Maurice Jackson's Lexington Lafayette state championship team of 1942, and Walter Johnson, a 6-footer from Mt. Sterling, Ky.

Navy Takes Two Players

Jack Tingle, a 6-3 one-hand shooter from Bedford, Ky., improved rapidly and after a few games took over from Whitehead at forward. Johnson and Whitehead were both called into the Navy before the season was over. Jack Parkinson, 6-0, from Yorktown, Ind., moved into Johnson's spot.

Whitehead later was a starter for two other schools while in the Navy—Bowling Green of Ohio, where he was No. 3 scorer behind big Don Otten and Wyndol Gray in the '44-45 season, and at Rensselaer Poly in Troy, New York. After the war Whitehead played at Evansville College, where his high school coach, Arad McCutchan, was head coach.

UK was pushed to win the '43-44 opener with Berea, which was blessed with naval trainees. Two of the best were Ken Wulfemeyer, who had played against UK the previous season as a member of the Washington of St. Louis team, and Joe Holland, from Benton, Ky. Holland scored 12 points but Berea lost 54-40. Rupp took special notice of Holland's rebounding ability. Rupp would have a scholarship waiting for him when he got out of the Navy.

Rupp substituted liberally during many of UK's games. Among his reserves were Nate Buis, George Vulich, Glen Parker, Rudy Yessin, Bill Cravens, Harry Gorham, Ed Allin, Red Bell and Truitt DeMoisey (brother of 1934 All-American John DeMoisey).

UK beat Harry Good's Indiana University team 61-41 as Johnson scored 12 points and Brannum 11. Ohio State wasn't much trouble either, although coach Harold Olsen had three players who would develop quickly: Don Grate, Arnie Risen and Jack Dugger. UK beat the Buckeyes 40-28, but Ohio State would come on later in the season to win the Big Ten title.

After Cincinnati was defeated easily, UK went to Illinois and lost 43-41 on a goal by Howie Judson (a major league baseball pitcher after the war) with 40 seconds to play.

Then UK went on a nine-game winning streak to close its regular schedule. A 44-38 victory over strong St. John's was an important game in the streak. Brannum played a fine game, rebounding strongly and scoring 12 points.

After St. John's came Notre Dame, in Louisville's Armory. The UK players dressed at the Kentucky Hotel and headed across the Fifth and Walnut intersection at the Armory. Don Whitehead laughed aloud. Rupp turned to him and said sharply, "Don't you realize we're playing Notre Dame?"

Brannum was the hero of the game, or thought he was. With the score tied 52-52, Notre Dame center Mark Todorovich got the ball. He wheeled toward the basket and scored on a layup as Brannum, instead of cutting off the path to the basket, followed the Irish center in.

A few seconds later Notre Dame got possession of the ball again. Johnny Lujack (the football quarterback) passed the ball toward Todorovich. Brannum knocked the ball free, pounced on it and dribbled the length of the court for a layup. This time Todorovich trailed him to the hoop, and fouled Brannum. Brannum sank the free throw to win the game 55-54.

Everyone but Rupp made over Brannum in the locker room. The UK coach jumped on him about the defensive lapse which had allowed Notre Dame to take the lead.

As the season passed the halfway mark, Rupp became more impressed with the ability and determination of a guard from Lexington University High, Harry Gorham. Rupp was counting on Gorham as a valuable relief man in the Southeastern Conference tournament. However, several games before the regular season ended, Gorham was called to duty with the Marines.

Rupp was fortunate, though, to have Ed (Buddy) Parker of Lexington join the squad after receiving a discharge from the Navy. Parker took Gorham's place on the traveling squad.

UK Avenges Defeat

UK, by now playing without Johnson and Whitehead, still had one other job to do before the schedule ended—beat Illinois. UK trailed at the half, but rallied

Wilbur Schu was one of two sophomores among UK's Kindergarten Kids.

behind Brannum (he finished with 16 points) to beat the Illini 51-40.

UK wasn't pushed in winning the Southeastern Conference tournament in Louisville. Only six teams competed, and UK beat Tulane 62-46 for the title. Tulane had a naval trainee, Alex Athas, who scored 19 points. He made the All-SEC team along with Wes Paxson of Georgia Tech and Kentucky's Brannum, Tingle and Parkinson

UK had accepted a National Invitational Tournament bid even before the regular season ended. Rupp looked forward to the NIT, but the challenge was imposing when the records of the other contenders was considered: DePaul 20-3, Muhlenberg 20-4, Oklahoma A & M 26-4, Bowling Green 22-3, Canisius 15-5, Utah 17-2, and St. John's of New York 15-4. UK's 17-1 mark was the best in the field.

Four players in the tournament would make All-American—Arnold Ferrin of Utah, Bob Kurland of Oklahoma A & M, George Mikan of DePaul and Brannum, all selected on the 10-man Helms Foundation team.

UK's first NIT game was against Utah in Madison Square Garden. Brannum rebounded well but was astonished at the leaping ability of the smaller Utah center, Fred Sheffield. With Jack Parkinson hitting from out for 20 points and Brannum scoring 11, UK won 46-38. No one knew it at the time but that wasn't the end of coach Vadal Peterson and his Utah Blitz Kids, an all-civilian team averaging 18 1/2 years of age.

Two nights later UK was eliminated by St. John's 41-38 in as tense a struggle as Garden fans had seen all season. The score was tied eight times and twice UK led by eight points. Wade Duym hit a free throw with 1:40 to play and when UK went to a pressing defense to gain possession, Don Wehr slipped in for a final layup.

UK beat Oklahoma A & M and 7-foot Bob Kurland 45-29 for third place, but Brannum had the unsettling experience of going scoreless. Kurland played under the basket and batted Brannum's shots away, so the UK center contented himself with passing off to his teammates, who had practiced banking the ball to avoid Kurland's goaltending (it was legal then).

St. John's defeated DePaul and 6-10 George Mikan 47-39 for the NIT title. Next for the NIT champs was the Red Cross benefit game with the NCAA tourney winner. St. John's opponent? The Utah team UK had beaten.

Utah had gotten a second life when Arkansas, co-champion of the Southwest Conference, had abandoned plans to play in the NCAA after two star players had been hurt in an auto accident. Utah by now was being called the Live Five with the Jive Drive, the Squeeze Kids, Wonder Boys and almost anything else you care to add. They gave a Cinderella twist to the whole tournament business by beating St. John's in the Red Cross game 43-36.

UK would see more of Arnie Ferrin and Wat Misaka of the Utah team, meeting them again in the NIT three years later.

Snubbed Groza was ready for Ohio State

As Alex Groza took his warmup shots in the University of Kentucky's packed Alumni Gymnasium, two thoughts kept running through his head: "We've got to beat these guys. . . . I've got to play a good game."

Groza wasn't vain enough to think that UK couldn't win without an exceptional performance from him, though it was true. His motivation was more personal— UK was playing Ohio State.

Ohio State. Groza had longed to follow his brother, football star Lou Groza, to the big state university at Columbus. After Alex's senior season at Martins Ferry, Ohio, when he set a one-season individual state scoring record, he expected Ohio State to offer him a scholarship.

Ohio State didn't contact him. No college coach did except Kentucky's Adolph Rupp.

"No one else wanted me, no one," Groza would say many times in later years. "No one but coach Rupp."

So here was Groza, a 6-foot-5, 167-pound freshman, ready to play against Ohio State and "show them they were wrong about me." It also was Groza's toughest test as an individual. Ohio State's center was experienced and able Arnie Risen, a future pro player and ironically a Williamstown, Ky., boy.

Rebounding Is Even

UK and Ohio State both were unbeaten, and the winner would be recognized as one of the nation's top basketball powers.

From the start, Groza and Risen went at each other with grim determination. It was just about an even match in rebounding, although Risen was three inches taller, and Groza had a slight edge in scoring, 16-14. UK won 53-48 in overtime.

Groza had a little more support in scoring from teammates than Risen. Forward Jack Tingle and guard Jack Parkinson each scored 15 points for UK, while Don Grate, a terrific fast-breaking forward, was the only other big Ohio State scorer with 14.

Later, in the shower area near the basement locker rooms, Ohio State head coach Harold Olsen walked up to Groza. "Son, why didn't you come to Ohio State?" he asked.

Groza shook his head. "You didn't want me. It's too late now."

How could a talented player like Groza be ignored by recruiters? Blame it on World War II. Coaches couldn't be certain from one week to the next who would be on the team and who would be catching a train for an Army camp. So it's not surprising that most coaches were lax in rounding up players.

In later years Groza would have been hounded from his sophomore year to his final game. He was that good.

He always credited one of his older brothers, Frank, with teaching him to play basketball. Alex was playing grade school basketball and after practice would hurry home in time to go with Frank to the high school to pick up Lou, a star player with the Martins Ferry varsity. While Lou was showering and dressing, Frank would get a basketball and teach Alex fundamentals.

When he was a freshman, already a shade over 6 feet, Alex played freshman basketball and also suited up with the Martins Ferry varsity. The next season he had grown to 6-4 and was a varsity starting forward. Lou, a senior, played center on the team, which advanced to the regional tournament before being eliminated.

Alex was the leading scorer his last two years at Martins Ferry, an Ohio River town of 16,000 on the eastern border of Ohio. He carried the team to the state tournament semifinals both years, twice making All-State, and scored 628 points as a senior to set a state record.

After Groza's final season, Martins Ferry coach Floyd Baker invited a friend, UK's Adolph Rupp, to speak at the basketball banquet. Baker gave his skinny center a big buildup to Rupp. The UK coach, who knew he might need a new center to replace Bob Brannum the next season, invited Groza to Lexington for a tryout.

"I worked out on a Saturday morning with about 30 or 40 other guys," Groza would recall later. "I was picked and invited back on scholarship. I accepted right then. Heck, it was the only offer I had."

Groza learned more about Rupp when he reported for practice prior to the start of the next season. The impression that stayed with Groza was this: "Even with a bunch of good players, he was still demanding. I think that's why he has been successful."

Rupp must have been lucky, too. How else could a coach get a player like Groza so easily? A player who not only would become one of UK's greatest, but also one of the finest college players of all time.

He would make All-American three times, twice make All-NCAA and earn a place on the all-time All-NCAA squad. He would be a superb player on two UK national championship teams, and in 1948 would be a member of Rupp's most renowned team, the Fabulous Five.

When Groza was a freshman the 1944-45 season, Rupp knew he would have a good team if "the big boy" came through. Rupp had four starters back—all except center Bob Brannum, who had gone into the Army—from the team which had won 19 and lost 2 the previous season.

Back to play forward were sophomore Jack Tingle, Bedford, Ky., and junior Wilbur Schu, Versailles, Ky. The returning guards were sophomore Jack Parkinson, Yorktown, Ind., and junior Tom Moseley, Lexington. Before the first game, though, Moseley was dismissed from the squad for failing to report one night for extra practice. That moved Johnny Stough, Montgomery, Ala., freshman, in as a starting guard.

Groza almost passed up the season entirely. He had been examined and accepted for the Army a few days before UK's opener. He decided he would spend his remaining three weeks with his parents. "No," his mother said. "You owe those people something. They took you when no one else would."

Groza wasn't spectacular the first few games, getting nine points twice, then 11, and up to 15 against Indiana. After the Ohio State game, Groza's induction was delayed. He went east with UK. After scoring 14 points against Wyoming at Buffalo, N.Y., he broke out with 27

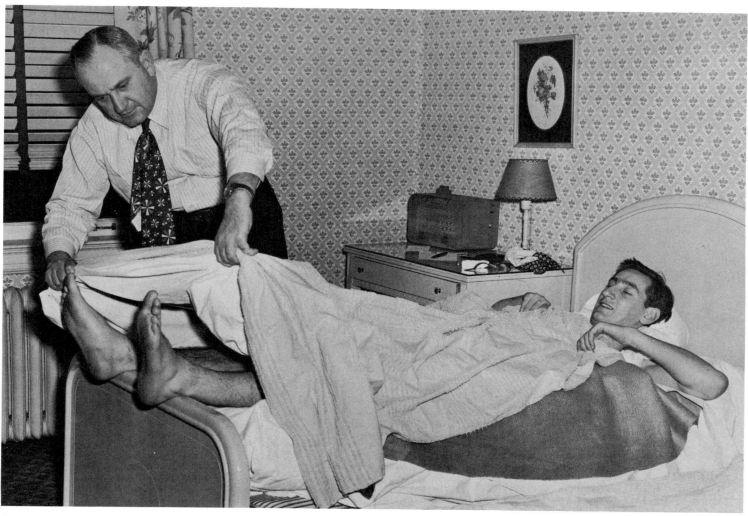

Gagging it up is Kentucky basketball coach Adolph Rupp as he tucks his star center, Alex Groza, into bed. Groza, from Martins Ferry, Ohio, was picked by Rupp for a scholarship after trying out with other prospects.

in a 45-44 win over Temple at Philadelphia. He followed with 25 as UK beat Long Island 62-52 in Madison Square Garden to stay unbeaten. UK, down by 15 points against Long Island, got a big lift from Ed (Buddy) Parker, whose hustle and fire got the team moving.

Back in Lexington, he scored 25 against Ohio University. Then he went home for a visit and skipped UK's game with hapless Arkansas State. UK won 75-6.

Rupp had a large squad and used many players in some of UK's easier games. In addition to his starters, in various games Rupp played Parker, Ed Allin, Clyde Cooper, Lonnie Nelson, Bill Sturgill, Jim Durham, Dick Derrickson, Sing Yeary, Kenton (Dutch) Campbell, Deward Compton, Jim Howe, Ernest Sparkman, Al Reynolds, Chester Duff, Jack Schiffli and George Vulich.

Groza Late for Game

After his trip home, Groza arrived at Alumni Gym only two minutes before his final game—against Michigan State. The opening half was 10 minutes old by the time he dressed and entered the game. Cold, he scored only two points

in the half and UK trailed. At halftime, the UK student president presented him with a key to the university in a farewell ceremony.

Groza came back in the second half with 12 points as UK broke loose to win 66-35. It ran UK's record to 11-0.

Two days later, Jan. 15, the big center reported to the Army, and five days after that UK lost at Tennessee 35-34. "Why should Rupp miss one player when he has 30?" asked Tennessee coach Johnny Mauer, who had to be joking.

Rupp already had answered that when he said, "You don't replace a Caruso with a barbershop singer."

Dutch Campbell, 6-4 freshman from Newark, Ohio, became UK's starting center.

Ed Allin's prospects improved steadily as the UK season unfolded. After an exceptional performance by the 6-1 guard in scrimmage, Rupp commented, "Allin was great today." The coach considered Allin, who had played for John Heber at Lexington Henry Clay High, as one of UK's steadiest reserves the second half of the season.

Notre Dame edged UK 59-58 in Louis-

ville, with Vince (Bullets) Boryla and Johnny Dee (a future Notre Dame coach) each scoring 16 points for the Irish. UK's final loss of the regular season was 66-50 at East Lansing, Mich., to a Michigan State team which had won only six games.

UK won the Southeastern Conference tournament in Louisville's Armory and avenged the Tennessee loss by beating the Vols 39-35 in the finals. Stough held Vol ace Paul Walther to one field goal. Groza's replacement at center, Dutch Campbell, played well during the tournament. So well that he made All-SEC, along with two other UK players, forward Jack Tingle and guard Jack Parkinson.

After the tournament UK accepted a bid to the NCAA tournament, and a rematch with Big Ten champ Ohio State in the Eastern Regional in New York. Campbell held Risen to nine points, but no UK player had a big scoring night and Ohio State won 45-37. UK beat Tufts 66-56 the next night for third place.

This wasn't one of Rupp's greatest teams, but it was excellent for that war year and had Groza been able to stay the whole season UK might have gone far.

Everyone knew Harlan's 'Wah-Wah'

UK won two championships in Wallace (Wah-Wah) Jones' first season.

Wallace Jones' teammates on the University of Kentucky basketball team always marveled that no matter where UK played, there were at least a few fans yelling, "Wah-Wah, Wah-Wah."

It was difficult for the players to accept, but Wah-Wah Jones was a national sports figure even before he enrolled at UK in the fall of 1945.

He had played four years of football, four years of baseball and five of basketball at Harlan (Ky.) High School. He had played in the state basketball tournament his last four seasons and had set a national high school four-year scoring record of 2,398 points.

UK coach Adolph Rupp didn't mind the cheers for Jones, but Rupp didn't appreciate it when the fans tried to help coach the team. Jones played football at UK and always got a late start in basketball, so Rupp liked to give the 6-foot-4, 205-pound athlete plenty of time to make the transition.

Although he never complained to Rupp, Jones felt he didn't need much time to make the changeover. Some of the spectators were impatient, too. The football players and many of the students would chant, "We want Wah-Wah, we want Wah-Wah." Jones would squirm, mildly embarrassed, on the bench. Rupp, his face set in stern lines, would ignore the yelling.

One year, though, Rupp didn't make Jones wait long for a starting job. That was 1945-46, Jones' first season at UK. Rupp needed the strong, mobile Jones at center, and after only two games the big freshman moved in as a regular.

He was UK's No. 2 scorer that season with 290 points, second only to long-shooting guard Jack Parkinson's 339. Parkinson's total was not a school record, however, as many persons thought at the time. LeRoy Edwards had scored 345 points in '34-'35.

Without Jones it's safe to say UK never could have gone on to a 28-2 record that season or to UK's first national tournament championship—the National Invitation Tournament title. He was a great player for four years (all the while playing football and making All-Southeastern Conference end in 1946), making All-SEC in basketball four times, becoming one of the celebrated Fabulous Five as a junior and going to the

Olympics that same year (1948), playing on two National Collegiate (NCAA) championship teams, and making All-American as a senior.

With all that, though, he had to take third billing his last three years at UK. "Groza, Beard and Jones," the phrase went, or "Beard, Groza and Jones." Always third, until after his final game in the UK uniform.

He and his All-American teammates were invited to play for the College All-Stars that fall against the professional Minneapolis Lakers. When the game was over in Chicago Stadium, the Most Valuable Player was announced. This time Jones' name led all the rest. He had scored 22 points against the finest pro team in the land.

Jones had always been something special in athletics, even as an eighth grader back in Harlan. He made the starting team in basketball that season. He and brother Hugh (Dean Eagle, then writing for the Harlan Daily Enterprise and now sports editor of The Courier-Journal, called Wah-Wah Whirlwind and Hugh Hurricane) led Harlan to the state tournament in '42 and '43.

All-State Three Times

After Hugh was graduated and in the Navy, Wah-Wah and Harlan were back in the state tournament two more years. The only one of the four years Wah-Wah failed to make the all-tournament team (then considered All-State) was in 1943. That year Kentucky tried the Indiana system of splitting the Sweet 16 into four semi-state tourneys, with four winners moving into the finals. Only five players were chosen All-State and they were all from the final four teams. Harlan wasn't one of the four, having lost in the second round at Richmond.

When Jones was a senior, there was an awesome struggle between the University of Tennessee and UK for his athletic services. Harlan County is on the Kentucky-Tennessee border and there are many alumni and fans of both schools in the area.

If Wah-Wah's girl friend, Edna Ball (later Mrs. Jones) hadn't been attending UK, Jones probably would have gone to Tennessee. A Tennessee alumnus took Wah-Wah and a guard on the Harlan basketball team, Humzey Yessin, to Knoxville for a look at the campus. Jones and Yessin were just about sold on Tennessee, but they said they'd have to go home and get their belongings.

"Here, take my car," one Tennessee grad offered. On the way home, the boys stopped off in Middlesboro to see Edna Ball. A sophomore at UK, she wouldn't hear of Wah-Wah going to Tennessee. He signed to attend Kentucky. Humzey had the unenviable task of driving the car back to Knoxville, then didn't stay himself. He went to UK and was student manager of the basketball team for four years.

Little Sister Names Him

UK was a young team when Wah-Wah (he got the nickname when a baby sister couldn't quite say Wallace) was a fresh-man. The starters with Jones were freshman Ralph Beard, from Louisville Male, and junior Jack Parkinson, from Yorktown, Ind., at guards; freshman Joe Holland, Benton, Ky., and junior Jack Tingle, Bedford, Ky., forwards. Wilbur Schu, a senior from Versailles, Ky., started at times in place of Holland.

Others who played that season were Malcolm McMullen, Buddy Parker, Darrel Lorance, Ed Allin, Sam Zeaman, Jim Weber, Bill and Barkley Sturgill, Deward Compton (he would later transfer to the University of Louisville and become an excellent center), Dutch Campbell, Muff Davis, Zeb Blankenship, Bob Hehl and Johnny Crockett.

Guard Jack Parkinson was leading scorer on the 1945-46 team.

It wasn't a great team and it lacked a strong bench, but no UK team ever wanted to win more and no UK team ever got more out of its ability.

UK won its first seven games before losing to Temple 53-45 in Philadelphia's Convention Center. Then UK won six straight games before Notre Dame broke the string 56-47 in the most humiliating experience of Ralph Beard's life. Beard, playing for the first time in his home town of Louisville as a college player, was held scoreless. Johnny Dee guarded Beard most of the time.

"I felt like jumping off the bridge," Beard said later.

The game also provided Wah Jones with a rather humbling lesson. Irish center Vince (Bullets) Boryla scored 18 points off Jones, although Jones salvaged close to an even break by scoring 16 himself. It wasn't as bad as an earlier game

in New York's Madison Square Garden when taller Harry Boykoff outscored Wah-Wah 27-7.

Only a week before the Notre Dame game, football crowded into the news when UK signed a 32-year-old coach, Paul (Bear) Bryant, to a five-year contract. He seemed to have promise; at least he'd done a good overhaul job in one year at Maryland.

The loss to Notre Dame was UK's last of the season. With Parkinson the most frequent high scorer UK won 15 straight.

Parkinson, 6 feet 1, had been steered to UK by his high school coach, Kenneth Sigler. Parkinson was only a high school freshman when he first visited UK. He went along with Cliff Barker and Louis (Bud) Robertson when those 1939 graduates of Yorktown (Ind.) High School tried out for the UK team. So the idea of attending UK was with him early.

After that early visit, he became an All-Delaware County center for three years. Too small for the pivot, he shifted to guard his freshman year at UK and by the middle of that first season, 1943-44, had become a regular. He was a starter again the next season, and as a junior had the kind of backcourt experience and poise Rupp wanted to go with freshman Ralph Beard.

Parkinson had great range with his two-hand shots. It wasn't unusual to see him take the tap from center, then shoot the ball immediately if the defense fell back. He also had an accurate driving one-hand shot from 12 to 15 feet which he used if his man played him too tight.

UK's 1946 post-season play started at Louisville with the SEC tourney title—four victories, all fairly easy. UK placed four men on the All-SEC team—Parkinson, Jack Tingle, Wah Jones and Ralph Beard. It was the third time on the all-tourney team for Parkinson and Tingle.

UK avenged one of its two losses by beating Temple 54-43 in Louisville's Armory, and a week later, Mar. 16, played its first NIT game in New York.

Jones with 16 points, Parkinson with 14 and Tingle with 13 led UK over Arizona 77-53. West Virginia was tougher, bowing 59-51, with Tingle scoring 16 points and Beard 15.

Rhode Island was almost too tough.

"If we hold Rhode Island to 45 points, we'll win," Rupp predicted before the game. It was an amazing prophecy.

With the score tied 45-45 and only 40 seconds to play, Beard drove down the right side of the basket with Rhode Island's Ernie Calverley right behind. Beard stopped, and Calverley fell over the UK guard.

"I was scared to death," Beard would say later of his walk to the free throw line. But his nerves didn't show. He dropped the free throw through cleanly, and UK was the NIT champion.

Beard also guarded Calverley, a great player, and held him to eight points.

Parkinson, who was chosen All-America after the season, would depart for a year in the Army, but a flood of skilled players was on the way. The 1945-46 record of 28-2 was the start of a four-year period in which UK would win 130 of 140 games.

Kenny Rollins brought leadership to the Kentucky team.

Too much talent was Rupp's '46-47 postwar problem

The war was over and the boys were coming back to Adolph Rupp.

They brought one problem with them to the University of Kentucky in the fall of 1946: too much talent.

That's not the worst trouble that can beset a coach, but it's something which can be deadly to a team shooting for high national honors.

How can I keep them happy? Rupp asked himself every time he looked down a roster which included two All-Americans, four others who had made All-Southeastern Conference, three more players who had been starters in recent years at UK, plus probably the finest group of sophomores in the nation.

The answer was that Rupp couldn't keep everyone happy. All-Americans don't like sitting on the bench, and first-stringers aren't satisfied to play half a game, then sit down so the coach can give everyone some playing time. Yet, that's exactly what happened.

Consider the situation facing Rupp.

At center he had four former UK regulars: Bob Brannum, All-America on the 1943-44 team; Alex Groza, the stringbean who was on his way to All-America honors the following year until called into the Army; Kenton (Dutch) Campbell, who had taken over when Groza left and had made All-SEC, and Wallace (Wah-Wah) Jones, the 1945-46 All-Conference center. Campbell was a junior

and the rest sophomores since they had played their year of varsity basketball as freshmen.

The guard positions weren't quite as crowded, but Ralph Beard was back after a good season with the '46 National Invitation Tournament champs; Kenny Rollins, a sophomore starter for Rupp in '42-43, had returned, experienced and mature after three years of service basketball, and there was one notable newcomer. He was Jim Jordan, who twice had made All-America during the war as a naval trainee at North Carolina.

Freshmen were still eligible and Rupp had a good one at guard, All-State Al Cummins from Brooksville, Ky.

There was depth at forward, too: Jack Tingle, three-time All-SEC; sophomore Joe Holland, a part-time starter the previous season; sophomore Cliff Barker, who had been a freshman seven years before; Mulford (Muff) Davis, a regular with Rollins in '43 and a reserve in '46, and two freshmen with bright futures—Dale Barnstable and left-handed deadeye Jim Line.

There were so many good players that Rupp could have split the squad into two teams, one for himself and one for assistant coach Harry Lancaster, and each would have won most of its games. Lancaster, a former high school basketball coach, had taught physical education and assisted Rupp on the side during the

'43-44 season until called into the Navy. Now he was back at both jobs and also would coach baseball.

If there is one word which described the 1946-47 team, it is "unsettled." Rupp made a mistake right off when he appointed Jack Tingle captain. Tingle was a good forward, but his image was not that of a leader.

Nothing was said about Rupp's choice as UK won its first 11 games. UK starters were the 6-foot-3 Tingle and 6-3 Holland, forwards; 6-7 Groza, now a well-built 220 pounds, center, and 5-10 1/2 Beard and 6-foot Rollins, guards.

Then UK went to the Sugar Bowl tournament in New Orleans and lost to Hank Iba's Oklahoma A & M team 37-31.

Afterwards Rupp asked some of his more mature players what was wrong. "For one thing you don't have any leadership," he was told. Rupp said, "Maybe you're right. What do you think we should do about it?"

The players suggested that the team vote on a captain. Rupp agreed. A few days later UK made the announcement that Kenny Rollins, a junior from Wickliffe, Ky., had been elected captain. It was a wise choice. The players respected Rollins' intelligence, his coolness in tough games and his inspirational qualities.

Rollins might never have attended UK if Western Kentucky coach Ed Diddle had wanted him. Rollins had been a

center at Wickliffe and the leading scorer his fourth and final year on the varsity. His greatest game had been against favored Heath in the 1941 district tournament. He had fouled out before the half, but he had scored most of his team's points to give Wickliffe the lead.

Watching was Waldo Page, who had attended Western Kentucky and UK. He said to Rollins, "I believe you're good enough to play major college basketball." Page wrote Rupp and Diddle to get Rollins a tryout.

Rollins was too late for Western's regular tryout camp. However, he went to Bowling Green for several days and worked out against some of the varsity players who were in summer school. Diddle told him that he was a little small for Western's style of play, but suggested that Rollins come to Western on his own for a year. If Rollins made the

team, then he'd get a scholarship. Rollins wasn't financially able to accept.

Four Survived Tryout

About a month later he received a letter from Rupp, inviting him for a tryout. He went to Lexington in August. Out of about 35 players there, Rupp picked Rollins, Muff Davis, Clyde Parker and Bill Hamm.

Rollins was switched to guard, a change he made easily. "I used to bring the ball up the court most of the time in high school, anyway," he said later. "The change wasn't difficult."

He was a regular as a sophomore, teaming with Marvin Akers at guard. Then he went into the Navy and played for three years. He spent one season with national service champion Great Lakes, along with a couple of other Kentuckians, Johnny Oldham (later to be Western

Kentucky coach and it's athletic director) of Hartford and Jack Coleman of Burgin.

"The service basketball helped me a great deal," Rollins said. "I gained confidence and developed whatever defensive ability I had."

After the Sugar Bowl loss to Oklahoma A & M, UK put together a 10-game winning streak. Included was a 60-30 victory over Notre Dame in Louisville. It was a great personal triumph for Beard, who made up for his failure against the Irish of the year before by scoring 17 points and holding star Notre Dame guard Kevin O'Shea to two. Groza dominated the rebounding and scored 18 points.

Rupp Leaves Brannum Home

DePaul broke the UK streak in Chicago 53-47, and only Groza had a good game offensively. He scored 21 points, but DePaul center Ed Mikan hit 18.

UK finished its regular schedule by winning the last six games. Among the reserves Rupp used were Barker (a starter in several games), Muff Davis, Jim Line, Bob Brannum, Dutch Campbell, Dale Barnstable, Buddy Parker, Jim Jordan, Malcolm McMullen and Al Cummins.

When Rupp had to pick 10 men for the SEC tournament in Louisville, he surprised the fans and players by leaving Brannum and Jordan, the All-Americans, off in favor of freshmen Jim Line and Dale Barnstable. "We needed speed, not height," Rupp said. When Brannum made known publicly his dissatisfaction, Rupp offered the player's phone number to any coach who was interested.

One coach was—even before Rupp made the offer. While UK was getting ready to play in the National Invitation Tournament—after easily winning the SEC tourney and beating Temple in a post-season game—Brannum announced he was leaving UK to attend Michigan State.

Brannum enrolled at Michigan State to start the spring quarter. By going to summer school he would be eligible for the next basketball season.

Five UK players—Jones, Beard, Rollins, Tingle and Holland—were picked to the All-SEC team. Groza was used only for short periods in each tourney game because he had an injured back.

Wah Jones got his second start of the season and his first at forward against Temple, a warmup game for the NIT. He stayed there through the NIT, replacing Jack Tingle.

UK beat Long Island 63-62 and North Carolina 60-42 to gain the NIT finals against Utah. Utah guard Wat Misaka, Utah-born of Japanese parentage, held Ralph Beard without a field goal as the now veteran Cinderella Kids slowed the game to a walk. Arnold Ferrin and Vern Gardner took care of the scoring with 15 points apiece and Utah won 49-45.

Despite falling a little short of expectations, UK got its share of individual honors. Beard and Groza each made All-America, and Beard was selected by the Metropolitan Basketball Writers as the outstanding player to appear in Madison Square Garden all season.

Since it had played 20 games away from home, UK's 34-3 record was remarkable. Even bettter times were just ahead.

Joe Holland was a starting forward for the 1946-47 UK team.

Even as a freshman Jim Line was a deadly one-hand shooter.

The fabulous five: Kentucky's perfect fit

The birth of a legend went unnoticed. Not even Adolph Rupp, the midwife of the event, attached any particular importance to it on the night of Jan. 5, 1948. There was no reason he should have. The basketball season was 11 games old and he had tried several lineups without being completely satisfied.

So he stood in front of his University of Kentucky team in the locker room at Miami University, in Oxford, Ohio, and named a new lineup.

Alex Groza was All-America for the second straight year in UK's Olympic season.

Wallace (Wah-Wah) Jones and Cliff Barker would start at forward, Kenny Rollins and Ralph Beard at guard, and Alex Groza at center.

The Fabulous Five were born.

They would live a short, spectacular life and would play only 28 games together, but in that brief span of less than a season they would become Rupp's most famous team.

They would win the NCAA championship, play in the 1948 Olympics in London, England, and earn such a reputation for perfection that they would be the yardstick by which every good team Rupp would have in the years to follow would be measured.

Rupp could have assembled the Fabulous Five a full year earlier, in the 1946-47 campaign. All the players were available. He did start Barker several times that season at forward, but the usual forwards were Joe Holland and Jack Tingle. Jones was backup man to Groza at center and played some forward, but he didn't become a regular forward until the final four games.

Jones Is Injured

Jones had started the fifth game of the season, against Idaho, in place of Groza. However, Wah-Wah limped off early with a twisted ankle and didn't start again until he took over Tingle's spot in a postseason game with Temple at Louisville, just before the National Invitation Tournament. Jones stayed in the lineup for the three NIT games—with Beard, Rollins and Groza—but the Fabulous Five weren't together as a starting unit because Holland still was a regular forward.

When the '47-48 season got under way, Rupp has moved Barker into the starting lineup with Groza, Beard, Rollins and Holland. Jones might have been there, too, but as usual Rupp was giving him plenty of time to make the change from football to basketball. To make matters worse, Jones had come out of football with a foot injury.

Jones didn't get his first start until Jan. 3, against Western Ontario. Again one of the Fabulous Five was missing. Beard had been troubled with an injured hip and didn't start. Jack Parkinson, back after a year of Air Force basketball, took his place.

Two nights later Rupp finally fitted all the pieces together in that game at Miami.

While it seemed that fate was reluctant to let the Fabulous Five get together as a starting unit, it must also be pointed out that fate—or history—made it possible for them to ever play together. Without World War II, the five players would not have been in school at the same time.

Rollins, a sophomore in '43, would have finished at UK in 1945 while Beard and

Adolph Rupp (right) receives his first national championship trophy from Kenneth L. (Tug) Wilson, representing the NCAA, at Madison Square Garden. Enjoying it are (from left) Johnny Stough, Joe Holland, Ralph Beard (barely visible), Wallace Jones, Kenny Rollins, Roger Day, Cliff Barker and assistant coach Harry Lancaster.

Jones were completing their high school careers.

Barker, a freshman in '40, would have been graduated in '43 had he continued straight through. Beard and Jones, though, would have been together throughout their UK playing days and Groza would have been with them for two years if the war hadn't intervened.

They Worked Together

What made the Fabulous Five great? Basketball ability, of course, was part of it. But there was something else, too: they complemented each other. Jones, for example was a good long shooter from the side of the court—as a forward should be—but he retained some of the attributes of a pivotman. Strong, aggressive and agile at 6 feet 4, he could go inside and help Groza with the rebounding.

Barker's greatest asset was passing the ball, either on the fast break or in UK's pattern offense. But the 6-1 forward's skill would have been wasted if he had been at all selfish on the court.

Groza was exceptionally quick for a 6-7 player, able to go around anyone who played him tightly. Marvelous timing around the basket made him a strong rebounder. He had a delicate touch on his shots.

Rollins, 6 feet tall, had fine speed with a deceptive change of pace. Like Barker, he was completely unselfish. He was a good shooter, and got enough points to keep the defense honest, but he usually was content to start the plays and let someone else score. He was a superb defensive player.

Beard was a super-quick starter who could pick up a loose ball and be 20 feet upcourt before the opposing players could get started. A slashing driver, a deadly two-handed shooter and able to use his speed effectively on defense, Beard hadn't reached his peak at UK. Beard would go into pro basketball, where he was a better guard than Holy Cross All-

American Bob Cousy. An unforgettable moment for Beard in pro ball would be going head-to-head with Cousy, then with the Boston Celtics, and outscoring him 24-2.

Beard Hurt in Football

UK came awfully close to losing Beard a couple of times. The first was in the summer of 1945 when the 5-10 1/2 guard played in the Kentucky-Indiana high school all-star game. Ed Diddle of Western Kentucky was the Kentucky stars' coach and practices were held in Bowling Green. Beard was greatly impressed with the friendliness shown him at Western.

But he did enroll at UK after he and Wah-Wah Jones helped the Kentucky stars beat Indiana for the first time in the summer series. Beard was never sure he began at UK on a football or basketball scholarship. It didn't matter because he planned to play both.

He played three games of football in

Continued

Ralph Beard, UK's All-America guard, gets off a shot against Georgia Tech as Alex Groza (15) and Wallace Jones (27) get in position to rebound. Beard played one of his finest games later against the Bartlesville (Okla.) Oilers.

Continued

the fall of '45. With both shoulders hurt —and "disillusioned," as he put it—he went home to Louisville. He was thinking seriously about transferring to the University of Louisville.

Two of his coaches at Male High, Paul Jenkins and Harry (Pap) Glenn, persuaded him to return. Beard went to see Rupp.

"Coach, I've made a mistake. I want to come back and play basketball for UK," Beard said.

Rupp said, "Ralph, that's fine."

In his first UK scrimmage, shortly after that, Beard raced through and around everyone to score 25 points. No one

watching the scrimmage could doubt that UK had another great player on the way.

Beard was born in Hardinsburg, Ky. He played basketball in the eighth and ninth grade at Breckinridge County High School—the same school which would produce Alfred (Butch) Beard, an All-State player and U of L star, nearly 20 years later.

Before his sophomore year, Ralph moved 75 miles to Louisville, where he was a two-time All-State guard at Male High. Counting the tournaments, he scored 509 points his senior year as Male won its first state basketball championship. An all-round athlete, Beard played

halfback on the football team, was an infielder in baseball and managed to work in enough track to win the state half-mile championship as a senior.

Beard's Scoring Picks Up

He considered his first season at UK ('45-46) "a learning year." He would remember two games most keenly: the 46-45 victory over Rhode Island in the finals of the NIT, when he dropped in the winning free throw; his failure to score a point in his home town in UK's loss to Notre Dame.

"I was tight as a fiddle string," he

would say later of the Notre Dame game. "I wanted to do well so badly."

He finished as the team's No. 3 scorer for the season, with 279 points, behind Jack Parkinson and Wah-Wah Jones.

The 1946-47 season was a good one for Beard. His 392 points was only one behind Alex Groza's team-leading total, he was named to the All-America team with Groza, and he was chosen the outstanding player to appear in Madison Square Garden.

Beard's outside shooting had improved over his first two years when the '47-48 season began. With he and Groza leading the scoring, UK raced easily by its first seven opponents.

On the way to New York to play St. John's, UK stopped off in Philadelphia to meet Temple, and lost 60-59. Rollins, UK's best free throw shooter, had a chance to tie the game near the end but missed the second of two free throws. Beard, who had an injured hip, played only 10 minutes as a substitute. Jones, still bothered by a sore foot, didn't play at all.

After the game someone mentioned to Rupp that Jones could have played. Rupp didn't take too kindly to the advice. The next day in New York he sent Jones through a gruelling scrimmage (the injury had improved amazingly). Two nights later he used Jones extensively in a 52-40 victory over St. John's. Jones with 10 points was third high scorer behind Rollins' 16 and sophomore Jim Line's 11.

It was three games later that Rupp moved Jones into the lineup to form what came to be known as the Fabulous Five. That game at Miami was the start of six straight games on the road.

Notre Dame Breaks String

One of those road games was at Michigan State. The center for Michigan State was Bob Brannum, burning to hit Rupp right where it would hurt the most—smack on his coaching record. He almost did, outscoring Groza 23-10 as Michigan State lost by only 47-45.

UK's home fans didn't get to see the new lineup until Jan. 24 against Cincinnati. Students were taking most of the seats in Alumni Gym, and even the students weren't able to see all the games. The students were issued "A" and "B" ticket books. The "A" tickets were good for one game, the "B" good for the next.

UK took an 11-game winning streak to South Bend to play Notre Dame. With their student fans giving ear-splitting support, the Irish defeated UK 64-55. Then UK won its next 18 games, including the Southeastern Conference tournament and the NCAA title in Madison Square Garden.

Rupp's key reserves were sophomores Jim Line, Dale Barnstable, Joe Holland and Johnny Stough (back after a year in service). Rupp also played Dutch Campbell, Jack Parkinson, Al Cummins, Jim Jordan, Walt Hirsch, Garland Townes, Roger Day, Will Smether, Bob Henne and Mike Homa.

UK whipped Columbia 76-53 in the NCAA opener, sort of a case of Rupp beating his alma mater because he had earned a master's degree in school administration there in 1929.

Next was defending champion Holy Cross, coached by Alvin (Doggie) Julian and starring George Kaftan and Bob Cousy. Someone had painted, COUSY—THE GREATEST, on a bed sheet and hung it from a Garden balcony.

After the game someone brought the sheet to Kenny Rollins as a souvenir. He deserved it. He had held Cousy without a field goal and to only three points as UK won 60-52. Cousy had got his only field goal after Rollins left the game near the end. Groza with 13 points, Beard 13 and Jones 12 did most of UK's scoring.

The championship game with Baylor three nights later was anticlimatic. UK beat the Western tiltist 58-42.

UK wasn't through. This was an Olympic year. The NCAA champ and runner-up, the NIT winner, the NAIB (National Association for Intercollegiate Basketball) champion and several AAU teams were to compete in the Olympic Trials at New York. NIT champ St. Louis declined and was replaced by runner-up New York University.

UK Plays U of L

UK played the University of Louisville, which had won the NAIB title in Kansas City, in the first round. U of L had a good team—with Jack Coleman, Glenn Combs, Johnny Knopf, Dee Compton and Kenny Reeves—but it was no match for UK. With Beard scoring 22 points, Jones 19, Barker 14 and Groza 12, UK won 91-57.

Next UK won a rematch with Baylor, 77-59, to advance to the finals against the professional-quality Bartlesville (Okla.) Oilers.

Beard played perhaps his finest game in a UK uniform, scoring 23 points, but UK lost 53-49. UK was hurt badly when Barker suffered a broken nose midway of the first half and missed the rest of the game. With Barker out, UK's fast break declined. Jones sat out five minutes of the first half after drawing three fouls, and went out for good with 11 minutes left in the game.

UK tried a strategy of playing Groza farther from the basket than usual in an effort to pull Oiler center Bob Kurland away from the hoop. The scheme seemed to deprive Groza of the chance to score without bothering Kurland much. The 7-foot Kurland outscored Groza 20-4.

"Kentucky is the greatest team we faced all year," Oiler coach Bud Browning said. "Bob (Kurland) was the difference. Beard is absolutely the best I ever saw."

Rupp said simply, "Losing Barker so early was a tough blow."

The Olympic selection committee picked the five UK starters, plus the five from the Oilers—Jesse Rennick, Lew Beck, R. C. Pitts, Gordon Carpenter and Kurland—to the Olympic team. Browning was head coach and Rupp his assistant.

During the summer, prior to leaving for London, UK and the Oilers played three exhibition games. One drew 13,000 into UK's football stadium. All were close games—less than 10-point margins —but the Oilers won two of the three. The UK players never were convinced, however, that they wouldn't have won the one that counted, in New York, if Barker hadn't been hurt.

Jones, Beard and Rollins had been selected on the All-SEC team after the conference tournament back in early March, and Groza and Barker to the second team. The honors were complete when Beard and Groza were named All-America for the second straight year. Groza won the team scoring title from Beard 488 to 476.

Johnny Stough was an important reserve for the Fabulous Five.

Cliff Barker had a hatful of tricks to use against UK's opponents.

Barker's nifty passes gave Groza more scoring punch

The game which college basketball fans had wanted to see at the end of the 1948 tournaments—NCAA king Kentucky against National Invitational Tournament champion St. Louis—was played in the Sugar Bowl tournament the following season.

The match might have come about in the Olympic Trials, but St. Louis had declined to take part. That left the Olympic tournament berth to NIT runner-up New York University, which lost to Baylor. UK then beat Baylor easily.

UK vs. St. Louis. It was a natural. Attention centered on what was supposed to a historic battle of All-American centers. St. Louis had Easy Ed Macauley, a 6-9 smoothie who had been voted Most Valuable Player in the NIT and Player of the Year by the Helms Athletic Foundation.

Kentucky had 6-7 Alex Groza, who had been voted MVP in the NCAA tournament and had been chosen Player of the Year by a special committee of sports writers headed by Grantland Rice.

Like so many heralded duels, this one fell a little flat. The two centers played each other about even: Groza scored 13 points, Macauley 12. But a little-known St. Louis player who hadn't started a game during the NIT of the previous season, Lou Lehman, made seven points in the last five minutes to give St. Louis a 42-40 victory.

The loss broke a 26-game winning streak against college teams for UK, extending back to the Notre Dame game of Feb. 2, 1948.

Jones Held to One Goal

Ed Hickey, in his second year as coach at St. Louis, said the key to his team's triumph was Marv Schatzman's defensive work on Wah Jones, holding the UK forward to one field goal. "That was the difference because Jones is their greatest player," Hickey said.

Rupp looked at the box score and took a slightly different view. He felt that 13 points weren't enough for a center of Groza's caliber, regardless of the opposition. He made a change in the UK lineup.

Dale Barnstable, a 6-3 junior from Antioch, Ill., had replaced the graduated Kenny Rollins in the UK lineup. For eight games all went well, although Barnstable wasn't quite as adept at getting the ball out on the fast break. The St. Louis game pointed to a flaw: Neither Ralph Beard nor Barnstable was the feeder-type guard UK needed to best take advantage of Groza's impressive and growing skills.

"Can you get the ball into Groza?" Rupp asked Barker. When Barker said yes, Rupp moved him to guard for the next game and shifted Barnstable to forward. With Barker at guard, UK's offense became more and more center oriented.

Barker was another player who had come to Rupp via the tryout route. Some of his teammates thought Cliff was better at baseball than basketball at Yorktown, Ind., High School. As a pitcher he had once won two games in the Delaware County tournament with a broken arm (not his pitching arm). He might have gone on to a pro baseball career except

that he was hooked on basketball.

He was the leading scorer his last two years in high school, helping Yorktown win two county championships and reaching the finals of the sectional tournament against Muncie Central his last year. His coach, Kenneth Sigler, was convinced Barker would make a college player. The question was, where?

Barker Flops in Tryout

Sigler took Barker to UK for a tryout. Nervous perhaps, Barker didn't perform well. Rupp wasn't interested. But Sigler was stubborn. He asked the UK coach to reconsider and give Barker a scholarship. Rupp yielded to Sigler's pleas.

It didn't take UK freshman coach Paul McBrayer and Rupp long to realize they had a future college star in Barker. His crisp passes, his defensive quickness which led to frequent steals, and his consistent scoring at forward made him a star on an unbeaten freshman team. With him on that team were Mel Brewer and Milt Ticco.

Barker didn't return after his freshman year, eventually entering the Air Force in World War II. On his fifth raid over Germany as assistant engineer and gunner on a B-17, Barker was shot down and taken prisoner.

For the first six months of a 16-month imprisonment, Barker had plenty of opportunity to play basketball.

"We could play about all we wanted," he said later. "We'd go from one camp to another, playing other teams."

Something happened to Barker's play-

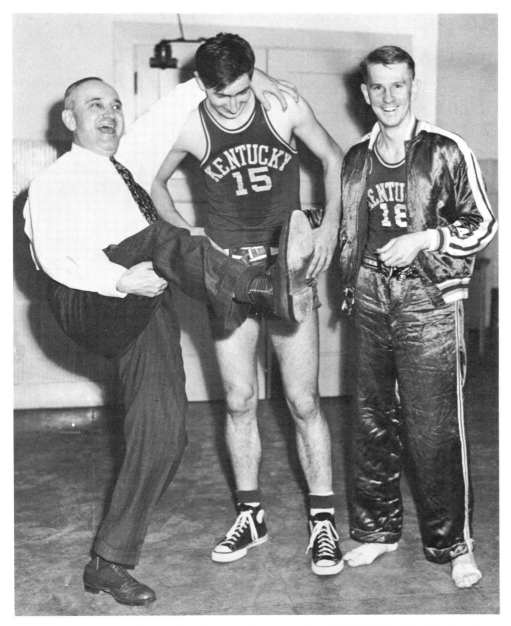

When your basketball team has just won its second straight NCAA title, it's time for a victory dance. Hanging on to Alex Groza's shoulder, Adolph Rupp tries a high kick. Enjoying it all is Dale Barnstable.

ing style. No longer were his passes just straight and a little harder than those of other players. He began to work more on trick passes—behind the back, looking one way and passing another, putting spin on the ball so that it would bounce around a defensive player's reach.

"I gained confidence in my passing, but I lost confidence in my shooting," Barker once said.

The change made Barker a more valuable player to UK, which had plenty of scoring in Groza, Beard and Jones. After Barker was moved to guard in the 1948-49 season, Groza's scoring began to climb. He scored 31 points against Vanderbilt, 23 at Alabama, 21 against Mississippi, 30 in a victory over Bradley and 34 (tying LeRoy Edwards' Southeastern Conference one-game record) against Tennessee.

"Usually I didn't even look at Groza," Barker said. "I knew he'd catch the ball."

Late in February, Groza broke the SEC record with 38 points against Georgia.

Barker had one memorable personal thrill during a 21-game winning streak leading up to entry in both the National Invitation and NCAA tournaments. In the last minute of a game with Vanderbilt at Lexington, Barker took an inbound pass and dribbled up court. As he passed Rupp on the bench, Barker yelled, "Can I shoot it from here?"

"Hell no," Rupp yelled back.

The next time up court, Barker didn't ask. With 15 seconds left, he fired the ball two-handed 63 feet, 7 1/2 inches for a field goal. It broke the Alumni Gym record of 53 feet, 9 1/2 inches set the previous season by Ralph Beard against Tennessee. Beard's long shot had broken the mark Red Hagan had set with a shot of 48 feet, 2 1/4 inches against Marquette in 1938.

Barker the passer also got a kick out of becoming Barker the scorer in a game at Xavier in Cincinnati late in the season. He scored 15 points in a tough 51-40 UK win while Groza was scoring only eight and Beard seven.

After the game Rupp said, "If it hadn't been for the old man (Barker was 28), this might have been a different game."

Groza bounced back the next game — the last on UK's regular schedule — to score 23 against Vanderbilt. That gave him 508 points, breaking the SEC one-season record of 504 set by Bonnie (Country) Graham of Mississippi in 1937-38.

Walt Hirsch and Jim Line at forward and Johnny Stough at guard were Rupp's most-used reserves throughout the season. Rupp also played Roger Day, Garland Townes, Bob Henne, Joe Hall and Al Bruno.

Hall, a 6-1 sophomore guard from Cynthiana, would finish his playing career at Sewanee, but would return to UK as an assistant coach in 1965.

UK had little trouble winning the SEC tournament in Louisville. Tulane gave UK the closest game in losing 68-52 in the final. Jones, Groza and Beard made the All-tourney team, and Barker was placed on the second team again.

Nine days later UK played Loyola of Chicago in the first round of the NIT in New York. UK, 29-1, was a heavy favorite although Loyola had won 25 of 30 games and had the reputation of running hot-and-cold. Beard scored 15 points to keep UK in the running, but Groza was outplayed by Jack Kerris, finally fouling out as Kerris outscored him 23-12. UK lost 67-56 and with it missed the chance of becoming the first team ever to win both big tournaments.

Lancaster Spots Weakness

UK approached the NCAA Eastern Regional in New York with steely determination. Villanova and Paul Arizin were polished off 85-72 with Groza scoring 30 points. Groza poured in 27 as Illinois was routed 76-47.

That left Western champion Oklahoma A & M between UK and a second NCAA title. Rupp's assistant coach, Harry Lancaster, had scouted A & M, and his report put the burden squarely on Groza.

Oklahoma A & M coach Hank Iba had said his own center, 6-8 Bob Harris, was the best defensive center in the nation. Lancaster said, "Get the ball to Groza. Harris can't handle him."

Wah Jones did an especially good job of feeding Groza, driving across the circle to lure Harris out, then passing to Groza breaking under for layups. Groza scored 25 points and UK won 46-36.

UK placed three players on various All-America teams: Jones, Groza and Beard.

Groza was honored for the second straight year as the Most Valuable Player in the NCAA tournament.

An era had ended.

NCAA snub, loss to CCNY marred season

Adolph Rupp was angry.

His University of Kentucky basketball team had been snubbed by the National Collegiate Athletic Association's district 3 tournament selection committee. The committee had picked North Carolina State to represent the district in the tournament which would decide the 1950 national champion.

Rupp pointed out that UK had placed fourth in the most recent Associated Press poll, and North Carolina State ninth.

"We defeated Bradley, the No. 1 team in the nation, and Villanova on a neutral court (the Sugar Bowl tournament in New Orleans)," Rupp said, "and Villanova beat North Carolina State on State's floor."

Gus Tebell of the University of Virginia, chairman of the selection committee, said the records of the teams were nearly identical (UK, 25-4; NC State, 24-5) and that the committee had recommended a playoff.

"North Carolina State agreed to play Kentucky anyplace, anytime," Tebell said, "but Kentucky declined and asked to be selected outright."

Rupp, who felt that as defending champion UK should have been given the benefit of any doubt, denied that there had been a formal request for a playoff. This probably meant that had Rupp known it was a case of playoff or nothing, he would have accepted.

As it turned out, UK might have fared better playing North Carolina State. UK accepted a bid to the National Invitation Tournament and drew City College of New York in the first round in Madison Square Garden. It was a game Rupp would never forget.

CCNY, coached by Nat Holman, had won 17 and lost 5, and had failed to impress the voters in the AP poll. CCNY was down in the also rans, not even in the top 20, of the ratings which came out just prior to the start of the NIT.

Kentucky, meanwhile, had moved up to third behind Bradley and Ohio State.

Rupp was in an expansive mood when he arrived in New York. He couldn't resist bragging a little on his team. He told reporters that his sophomore crop was better than the Fabulous Five "at this stage." And he said his sophomore center, 7-foot Bill Spivey, was going to

Guard Bobby Watson started at UK without a scholarship.

be better than three-time All-American Alex Groza.

Then the UK team went out on the Garden court and was humiliated 89-50—the worst defeat Rupp had ever endured. With 6-6 Ed Warner pumping in 26 points, CCNY was devastating, an unstoppable basketball machine. Spivey scored 15 points and Shelby Linville 13 for UK; no one else could find the range.

After the game Rupp, who had been named College Coach of the Year by the Metropolitan Basketball Writers, said disgustedly to his players, "Thanks a lot, boys. You get me named Coach of the Year, then embarrass the hell out of me."

Rupp said flatly that CCNY would win

the tournament. CCNY did more than that. After defeating Bradley in the NIT finals 69-61, CCNY played in the NCAA tournament and won that, too. Along the way to the NCAA title, CCNY had to struggle to beat North Carolina State 78-73.

The loss to CCNY proved that Rupp hadn't rebuilt entirely after the loss of his 1949 superstars. But the margin of the defeat obscured to some extent the progress Rupp had made in fitting the pieces together for another national championship team.

Just three of those players would be a good start: a 6-6 forward, Shelby Linville, one of the best players Middletown, Ohio, High had ever turned out; Spivey, a still slightly awkward giant who could give Rupp inside scoring and control of the backboards; and Bobby Watson, an outside shooter who could keep defenses from backing up around Spivey.

Watson Deadly Long Shooter

Watson, 5-10 and boyish in appearance, could have been mistaken for a student manager—until he picked up the basketball. He was another one of those players who wound up at UK through his own persistence rather than through UK's diligence.

Watson learned a good bit of his basketball, at least the shooting part of it, playing at the YMCA in Owensboro, Ky. Even after he got on the Owensboro High team, he kept practicing and playing at the YMCA on weekends.

He was a starter as a junior on a good Owensboro team, one which had J. M. Gipe, Dwayne Morrison and Roscoe Foster. The team advanced to the semifinals of the state tournament before losing to Maysville. The next season Owensboro lost out again to Maysville, this time in the quarter-finals. By now Watson had acquired quite a reputation as a shooter. He made the Courier-Journal All-State team.

UK's coaches still weren't completely sold. Rupp's assistant, Harry Lancaster, suggested that Watson come to UK on his own. If Watson made the team, then he would be put on scholarship.

Watson decided to accept a scholarship offer to Alabama, and boarded a train for Tuscaloosa. No one met him at the

train and he had difficulty finding out where to go. Discouraged, he left for Lexington without ever seeing the Alabama coach.

It didn't take long for Lancaster, who was coaching the freshmen, to see that Watson was one of the better players on a large squad. Watson was granted a scholarship for the second semester, made the starting team and was elected captain by his teammates. With Guy Strong, Bill Spivey, Lucian (Skippy) Whitaker, Len Pearson and C. M. Newton, it was one of UK's finest freshman teams. It was unbeaten in 15 games.

With only three experienced players returning, it was obvious that Rupp would have to get plenty of help from his sophomores when practice for the 1949-50 season started.

It was quickly apparent that four of the positions would go to 6-4 junior Walt Hirsch, Dayton, Ohio, and 6-2 senior Jim Line, Akron, Ohio, at forwards; Spivey, Warner Robins, Ga., center, and 6-2 Dale Barnstable, Antioch, Ill., at one guard.

Barnstable, a fine two-hand set shooter, had been sent to Rupp by Milt Ticco, a senior on Rupp's '43 team. Ticco had spotted Barnstable playing Army basketball in Europe. Barney played as a reserve for two years and was a starting forward as a junior. Rupp moved him back to guard for his senior season, confident that Barney would be a steadying influence.

The question was: who would be the other guard. At times Rupp started Len Pearson, a 6-1 Chicagoan. Guy Strong, 6-2, from Irvine, Ky., got a crack at it after dropping in 14 points on long shots in a loss to St. John's in Madison Square Garden. So did the 6-foot Whitaker, from Sarasota, Fla.

The job finally went to the smallest of all, Bobby Watson. He did it with a 20-point performance, 16 of them in the second half, as UK beat Arkansas at Little Rock on Jan. 2.

But that's getting a bit ahead of the story.

UK started the season well, considering the lack of experience. After a couple of easy victories, it lost 69-58 to St. John's but played well in beating DePaul 49-47 and Purdue 60-54, both on the road. That gave UK a 4-1 record to take into the Sugar Bowl tournament at New Orleans, against Paul Arizin and Villanova in the first round. UK won 57-56 in overtime, Whitaker scoring two baskets and Jim Line one in the extra period.

Spivey Scores 22 Points

That put UK against Bradley for the title. Bradley, with Bill Mann, Paul Unruh and Gene (Squeaky) Melchiorre. "Look out for Bradley next year," UK's national championship team of '49 had warned after beating Bradley by only 10 points at Owensboro.

Well, next year was here and UK didn't seem strong enough to handle Bradley. Melchiorre scored 20 points, but Spivey got 22, Line 19 and Whitaker 13, and UK won 71-66.

"Boys, I'm proud of you," Rupp said. "You did something the Fabulous Five never did."

Actually the Fabulous Five as a starting unit never played in the Sugar Bowl. However, three of the Fabulous Five were starters on the '46-47 squad which lost to Oklahoma A & M in the Sugar Bowl. And four of the five—Kenny Rollins was gone — were playing when UK lost to St. Louis in the Sugar Bowl during the '48-49 season.

UK had a seven-game winning streak by the time it met coach Emmett Lowery's Tennessee Volunteers at Knoxville. With center Art Burris outscoring Spivey 28-12, Tennessee won 66-53.

Two games later UK lost another road game, at Georgia 71-60. Again Spivey had trouble. This time 6-8 Bob Schloss outscored him 28-8. Spivey scored 16 points as DePaul was beaten a second time, and hit 27 in a 64-51 loss at Notre Dame. Kevin O'Shea, in his final season, was high for the Irish with 18.

UK wound up its regular season by winning the next 11 games. Spivey began to score more consistently and made 34 points as UK got back at Tennessee 79-52 at Lexington. This time Burris got only 12.

Spivey evened the score with Georgia's Schloss, hooking in 18 points and holding Schloss to four.

Groza's Record Broken

Spivey's biggest output was against Georgia Tech. He scored 40 points to break Alex Groza's Southeastern Conference single-game record of 38.

Rupp substituted often during many of UK's games. Besides key reserves Shelby Linville (he became eligible the second semester because he was a transfer from Miami, Ohio), Guy Strong, Len Pearson and Skippy Whitaker, Rupp also used Read Morgan, C. M. Newton, Roger Layne (transfer from Magnolia, Ark., A&M Junior College), Garland Townes, Arlan King, Walter Whittaker, George Lambros, and Roger Day.

UK breezed through the SEC tournament at Louisville. The only surprise was that Spivey, after scoring 37 points in the 95-58 victory over Tennessee in the finals to tie Groza's one-game SEC tourney record, had to settle for second place on the All-tourney team. Tennessee center Art Burris was placed on the first team. Jim Line was the only UK player in the top five.

The Associated Press, however, picked Spivey to its All-SEC team and to third-team All-America.

With Spivey and Watson returning, plus Frank Ramsey, Lou Tsioropoulos and Cliff Hagan (to be eligible after the second semester) coming up from the freshman team, Rupp knew there were happy days in sight for next season.

Dale Barnstable was sent to UK by one of Adolph Rupp's former players.

Skippy Whitaker played well in both Sugar Bowl games.

Kansas one of many 'disasters' caused by 7-foot Spivey

Bill Spivey, who had to play some high school games in his stocking feet, found the size 15 shoes he needed at UK. He also found a center position left vacant by the graduation of Alex Groza. Like Groza, Spivey became an All-America player.

One afternoon when 7-foot Bill Spivey walked into the dressing room to get ready to practice basketball with the University of Kentucky, he found a newspaper clipping pasted on his locker door.

The clipping told of a wonderful 6-9 sophomore, Clyde Lovellette, at the University of Kansas. Averaging 23 points a game, he was already being talked about as this season's All-American center.

For several straight days Spivey found new clippings on the locker, all on the same theme: how good Lovellette was, how good Kansas was. There was no doubt in Spivey's mind as to who was wielding the scissors. He knew Adolph Rupp was applying a bit of psychology for Saturday's game.

"I was ready to jump through the ceiling," Spivey said later. "I knew how much it meant to coach Rupp and to me."

Memorial Coliseum was overflowing the night of the game, Dec. 16, 1950. In three previous games UK hadn't filled the new arena's 11,500 seats.

But Kansas. This was different. Rarely had UK played a regular-season game so packed with drama.

✔ Kentucky vs. Kansas—a battle for the No. 1 national ranking in college basketball.

✔ Clyde Lovellette vs. Bill Spivey, with the winner of this personal duel an almost sure shot for All-America.

✔ Adolph Rupp against his old coach, Dr. Forrest (Phog) Allen.

At least 13,000 fans—some estimates were higher—jammed into the Coliseum. Fans stood several rows deep around the walkways separating the two levels of stands. Hundreds of others sat in the aisles. They had come to see Spivey and UK show Lovellette and Kansas a thing or two.

A 'Disaster,' Says Lovellette

They weren't disappointed. Lovellette later described the game as a "disaster." It was—for him and for Kansas as UK won 68-39.

Spivey tried to keep Lovellette from getting the ball. Eleven times Spivey slapped away passes into the Kansas center. The play that brought the loudest roar from the frenzied crowd came in the first half when Spivey stole the ball, dribbled the length of the court and dunked in a goal.

"I played him position," Spivey said. "I knew in advance where he'd like to be, depending on where the ball was, and I'd beat him there."

Lovellette took 17 shots over the barrier of Spivey's long arms, and hit only four. Spivey shot 16 times, hit nine. Spivey finished with 22 points, Lovellette with 10.

Tears in his eyes, Lovellette fouled out with 13:33 to play. Rupp promptly pulled Spivey, and refused to heed the big junior's pleas to "let me go back in."

"I wanted them (the centers) to have exactly the same amount of playing time," Rupp said afterwards.

Three days after the game, UK was voted No. 1 in the first Associated Press rating of the season. Kansas was rated 11th. UK would prove it belonged on top by winning the NCAA tournament in March.

Lovellette, from Terre Haute, Ind., would go on to a fine season and career at Kansas. He would set many scoring records, lead Kansas to one NCAA title (1952) and become a top professional with Minneapolis, Cincinnati, St. Louis and Boston.

Both Made All-America

He also would make the All-America team his sophomore season, even after

Regular UK forward Walt Hirsch had to sit out the NCAA tourney.

his losing battle with Spivey. All-America selectors from some teams would find room for both players.

Spivey had come close to All-America as a sophomore. He was disappointed that he had to settle for second and third-team. Still, considering the improvement he needed to make after enrolling at UK to be even a good center, second and third team was a remarkable achievement.

Spivey had come to UK from Georgia, where the caliber of basketball was a few notches below the Kentucky-Indiana area in which Rupp had always recruited so heavily.

Spivey was born in Lakeland, Fla., and moved to Georgia when he was two years old. He played his first school basketball at Jordan High in Columbus, Ga. (his

father was a civil service worker at nearby Ft. Benning).

In his first game, as a freshman, he scored 19 points in only half the game. That convinced his coach, B. F. Register, that Spivey would be able to take over at center the following season in place of a graduating senior. Spivey always credited Register with "teaching me the fundamentals of defense. He was probably the best coach in Georgia."

Before the next season, however, Spivey's dad went to work at an air base near Warner Robins, Ga., which didn't have a high school. Spivey had to go by bus 10 miles to Bon Air, Ga., where he played basketball.

There were problems. The gym was only a barn, with a coal stove in each end, and Spivey couldn't find any size 15 basketball shoes. So he played in his sweat socks—three pair.

"I couldn't stop when I'd run," he'd recall years later, "and I'd get called a lot for traveling. The next season I got smart and got a size 12 and cut the toes out."

He stayed only half a season at Bon Air. The military personnel and civilian workers at Warner Robins had complained so much about not having a school that a barracks-type building was put up to serve as a high school. Spivey, by now at least 6-7 in height, enrolled there and a basketball team was formed. The team played its games on the USO dance floor.

By the time his junior year rolled around, Spivey's parents had decided to send him to Lanier High, in Macon, Ga., about 18 miles away. They wanted him to have qualified teachers, instead of the officers' wives filling in at Warner Robins.

Bill didn't stay long. When he didn't make the basketball team, he returned to Warner Robins. That put the Macon coach in a rare class. Not many coaches get a chance to cut a future All-America.

Spivey was 6-9 that junior season and averaged about 22 points in the class B (small school) competition. The next season his average was up to 29-plus and he was getting known around the state. Ed Danforth, an Atlanta sports writer, wrote an article about him, which someone sent to Rupp.

Rupp sent a former UK player, Buddy Parker, down to see Spivey—probably to make sure he was really 7 feet tall—and invite him to UK for a tryout. Spivey had had several offers from other schools, but this was the chance he had waited for.

Among the players Rupp kept out of a large group trying out that day were Bobby Watson, Guy Strong and Spivey. One of the players Rupp didn't keep was Mark Workman, who would become an All-America and one of the nation's leading scorers at West Virginia. Rupp didn't care for Workman's attitude.

After offering Spivey a scholarship, Rupp asked him to stay in Lexington all summer. "I did, and Harry Lancaster (Rupp's assistant) spent all summer throwing me the ball so that I could practice a hook shot," Spivey would remember. "I didn't get vacations like the

Continued

other boys all through my career at UK."

As a freshman, Spivey got some other valuable training. He was the only freshman allowed to scrimmage against the varsity, which gave him the experience of playing against the best college center in the country—Alex Groza. "He was the cleverest pivotman I ever saw," Spivey said of Groza.

He Breaks Groza's Record

Spivey had an excellent sophomore season, although it was obvious he still was far from his peak. Scoring 40 points against Georgia Tech to break Groza's Southeastern Conference record was a high spot. So was outplaying Bradley center Paul Unruh in the Sugar Bowl. Spivey couldn't understand it at the season's end when Unruh was picked ahead of him on most All-America teams.

He did get one unsual honor as a sophomore. He made the Ukranian All-America team. "What's a Ukranian?" he asked his roommate, C. M. Newton. They looked it up and were more puzzled than ever. "I'm not a Russian. I'm Scotch-Irish and English," Spivey said.

There wasn't any question about UK's strength in Spivey's junior season, 1950-51. Dale Barnstable and Jim Line were gone, but Rupp had 6-3 senior Walt Hirsch returning as a regular forward and 6-5 junior Shelby Linville ready to become a starter. At guard, Bobby Watson was back and a 6-3 sophomore, Frank Ramsey of Madisonville, was ticketed for a starting berth from the beginning.

On the freshman team, Rupp had a 6-4 hook shooter, Cliff Hagan of Owensboro, who would move up to the varsity at midseason.

With Hirsch, Linville, Spivey, Watson and Ramsey starting, UK moved easily by five opponents. St. John's was more difficult, though, holding UK to a 43-37 margin in Madison Square Garden. Spivey saved the day by holding St. John's center 6-7 Bob Zawoluk to six points.

Then it happened, as it had two years before—St. Louis beat UK in the Sugar Bowl tournament. This time the score was 43-42. UK led 41-39 with 20 seconds left on Spivey's free throw and field goal, but Hirsch threw the ball away and St. Louis scored to send the game into overtime.

In the extra period, Spivey hit a free throw and Hirsch missed two. Ray Sonnenberg got the only basket to win it for St. Louis.

The defeat dropped UK to second in the polls behind unbeaten Oklahoma A&M. In early February, however, after A&M had lost and UK had won 11 straight—including victories over DePaul and Notre Dame—Kentucky regained the No. 1 position. Hagan started playing on Jan. 27 and added scoring and rebounding to the UK team as a reserve forward.

Hagan and Lucian (Skippy) Whitaker were the most useful members of a splendid crop of reserves. Rupp had depth at every position with Read Morgan, Lou Tsioropoulos, Guy Strong, Dwight Price, Lindle Castle, Paul Lansaw and C. M. Newton.

By the time the finals of the SEC tournament in Louisville rolled around, UK had won 21 straight and was considered a cinch to brush Vanderbilt aside in the title game. UK had beaten Vandy twice by big scores. With Bob Smith scoring 15 points, substitute Gene Southwood 14 and Dave Kardokus 13, Vandy upset UK 61-57.

Nashville Banner writer Dudley Green called it "the greatest victory ever in Vanderbilt athletic history—football or basketball." Tom Siler of the Knoxville News-Sentinel wrote that Vanderbilt "had poise . . . Kentucky was outfought and it failed to move the ball."

The loss didn't knock UK out of the NCAA tournament. This was the first time the SEC championship was decided on the basis of regular-season records, and it was the first year the SEC champion received an automatic bid to the NCAA tournamet. Perhaps partly as an outgrowth of Rupp's fussing about being passed over the previous season, the NCAA had doubled its tournament field to 16.

UK went into the tournament without Hirsch, ineligible because he was in his fourth season of varsity play. His place in the lineup was taken by Hagan.

Guy Strong was a good long shooter on two Kentucky teams.

One of the independent teams invited as an at-large entry was the University of Louisville, which played UK in a first-round game at Raleigh, N.C. UK trailed 64-60 with 9:35 to go, but some clutch baskets by Skippy Whitaker pulled UK to a 79-68 victory. "Whitaker beat us," a glum U of L head coach, Peck Hickman, said.

Adolph Meets Al McGuire

UK got by St. John's in Madison Square Garden without difficulty, 59-43. Afterwards one of the St. John's players, Al McGuire, told Rupp, "We stopped Spivey but we couldn't stop Watson or Ramsey." The losers held Spivey to 12 points, but they didn't anticipate Ramsey scoring 15 and Watson 12.

(Apparently analyzing a game came natural for McGuire. He would go into coaching and send his Marquette University teams against Rupp's teams in the 1968, 1969 and 1971 NCAA regional tournaments.)

UK needed extraordinary performances by Spivey and Shelby Linville to get by Big Ten champ Illinois in the Eastern final. Spivey scored 28 points and hauled down 16 rebounds. Linville scored 14 points, three of them in the last hectic two and a half minutes of the game. He got free under the basket to score the deciding goal in a 76-74 victory with only 12 seconds left.

Three days later UK played Kansas State for the national championship at Minneapolis. Both teams ate their pregame meal in the same hotel dining room. While the Kentucky players sat quietly waiting to be served, the Kansas State players were laughing and talking, apparently relaxed.

"They're just whistling in the graveyard," the confident Rupp told his team.

Skippy Whitaker started at forward for UK in place of Cliff Hagan, who had the flu. Spivey was ailing, too, with a bad cold. For the first half UK looked like anything but the No. 1 team in the nation. When Rupp took his players to the locker room at halftime, they trailed 29-27.

The second half was all Kentucky's. Playing savagely, UK took control of the game in the first few minutes and went on to win 68-58. Spivey scored 22 points and finished with 21 rebounds, Hagan scored 10 points, Whitaker nine and Linville eight.

Spivey and Linville were named to the all-tournament team. Spivey was ushered into select company when the Helms Athletic Foundation of California selected him as All-America and Player of the Year.

As for Rupp, he looked forward to having perhaps the greatest team of his career. All his stars were due back next season; there wasn't a cloud in the sky. Or was there?

It was a time for cheers and arm-waving after Kentucky defeated Kansas State 68-58 for the 1951 NCAA championship in Minneapolis, Minn. Kneeling on the court, from left, are: Lou Tsioropoulos, student manager Bobby Moore, C. M. Newton, Bobby Watson, Cliff Hagan and Skippy Whitaker. Standing, from left, are: trainer Smokey Harper, Walt Hirsch (in street clothes), Dwight Price, Bill Spivey, Guy Strong, assistant coach Harry Lancaster, head coach Adolph Rupp, Roger Layne, Shelby Linville and Frank Ramsey. It was UK's third NCAA title.

Fix scandal was an agonizing time for Adolph

Adolph Rupp, one of the wittiest speakers in all of sports, turned serious as he talked to the Chicago Herald-American Quarterback Club in the fall of 1951.

Rupp talked about the "fix" scandal rocking college basketball.

The University of Kentucky coach urged leniency in public opinion for college players involved in the gambling cases. He said it was unfair to bracket the basketball players with the 1919 Chicago "Black Sox," who lost the World Series to the Cincinnati Reds.

"The Black Sox threw games," Rupp said. "These kids shaved points. There's a difference. Why forever condemn a boy for his one mistake of a lifetime?"

Rupp was in Chicago to coach the College All-Stars against the professional Rochester Royals. Three days after his speech, his All-Stars lost 76-70.

Watching from the stands were several of Rupp's former players, then player-owners of the professional Indianapolis Olympians. They were on their way to Moline, Ill., to play an exhibition game.

As they left Chicago Stadium that night after the All-Stars-Royals game, Ralph Beard and Alex Groza were taken into custody. The next day the news broke that the two former All-Americans had admitted to a conspiracy with gamblers to "fix" a basketball game in 1949.

The game involved was the UK-Chicago Loyola in the National Invitation Tournament. Another ex-UK player, Dale Barnstable, also admitted being in on the conspiracy.

UK Upset By Loyola

UK had been a 10-point favorite over Loyola. The idea was to go under the point spread, thus enabling the gamblers who arranged the fix to win money. As it turned out, UK was in trouble from the start of that game and was upset 67-56.

Soon it developed that there were other games involved, and other UK players. Eventually Walt Hirsch and Jim Line were implicated. Line had finished at UK in the 1949-50 season, Hirsch's last year was the national championship season of '50-51.

Rupp didn't know it at the time, but the gambling scandal which began breaking in the summer of 1951 was the start of the most agonizing two years of his career. It was apparent that he had no idea any of his players were involved

Shelby Linville was a returning starter at forward for UK.

when he spoke in Lincoln, Neb., on Aug. 15.

"The gamblers couldn't touch my boys with a 10-foot pole," he said. Eastern sports writers had a ball kicking that remark around as the fix cases spread to UK.

Rupp shook off the bad news and began thinking about the 1951-52 season. With 7-foot Bill Spivey, Cliff Hagan, Frank Ramsey, Bobby Watson and Shelby Linville back, and many others, UK could have its best team ever. Then Rupp lost Spivey. The big center injured his knee making a movie for Rupp to use in basketball coaching clinics, and had to have an operation.

When Spivey's knee was slow to heal, Rupp began to wonder if the big boy would play at all. Cliff Hagan, only 6 feet 4 but a super jumper, was shifted back to his old high school position to center.

Rupp found out quickly what UK's main problem would be without Spivey defensing a tall center. UK went to Minnesota and lost 61-57 when the Big Ten team started to get the ball into husky Ed Kalafat after Hagan and Ramsey got into foul trouble. Kalafat ended with 30 points.

UK did have one thing in its favor: an offense which on a given night could blast any team off the court. That's just what happened when UK went home from Minneapolis to play St. John's. With Hagan and Watson scoring 25 points apiece, UK crushed St. John's 81-40.

The Associated Press poll which came out the following day did not include, of course, that result. It showed St. John's second in the nation behind Illinois, UK third. The next week UK moved to the top.

Meanwhile, rumors were about that there was some reason other than his injured knee keeping Spivey from playing. When New York assistant district attorney Vincent O'Connor came to Lexington late in December to investigate UK's part in the fix scandal, Spivey withdrew from the team's eligibility list. He said he wanted to clear his name.

He never played another game for UK.

Six weeks after withdrawing, Spivey asked to be put back on the eligibility list. However, the directors of the UK Athletics Association told him he could not be on the list "as long as there is a question" of him being involved in the scandal.

Spivey was tired of waiting. He took an aggressive attitude and agreed to go to New York to testify before the grand jury. "I'm not afraid of any question they might ask," he said.

Walt Hirsch and Jim Line also testified before the grand jury. It was reported that their testimony was somewhat contradictory and Spivey's was different from both. Spivey never wavered in denying any part in fixing basketball games. His only admission of wrong was that twice a man named "George" (later identified as gambler Eli Kay) had contacted him about fixing games and Spivey had not reported it to the authorities. The fixer had told Spivey others on the team were involved, and Spivey said he didn't want to get them in trouble.

Before the season was over, Spivey lost his scholarship and was suspended from school.

In Knoxville to play in an independent tournament, a bitter Spivey said, "Instead of getting behind me and trying to help me out after my name had been pulled into this awful fix case, university officials went against me and suspended me from school without bringing any charge whatsoever."

Dr. Leo Chamberlain, vice president of UK and a member of the athletic board, answered Spivey: "The public will have to await the verdict. I have no fear of what the verdict will be."

Later, Spivey went to New York to stand trial on a perjury charge. Spivey was accused of falsifying his testimony when charged with conspiring to fix UK's games with Arkansas, Jan. 2, 1950 (UK

won 57-53); St. Louis, Dec. 29, 1950 (UK lost 43-42 in the Sugar Bowl when Hirsch made a bad pass to put the game into overtime, then missed two free throws which would have won the game in overtime); DePaul, Jan. 8, 1951 (UK won 63-55), and Notre Dame, Jan. 15, 1951 (UK won 69-44).

The jury in New York voted for acquittal, by 9-3, according to reports. After many tortured months, Spivey was vindicated.

(The professional National Basketball Association refused to accept Spivey. But in 1959 the Cincinnati Royals signed the big center to a $10,000 contract. When league officials still refused to permit him to play, Spivey planned a court suit. Spivey was paid the $10,000 settlement in an out-of-court settlement.

(Spivey later played pro basketball with the Los Angeles Jets of the American Basketball League after taking a lie detector test which indicated he was not involved with fixing games at UK.)

While Spivey's tribulations were taking place, UK was having a good basketball season without him. It lost only twice during the regular season—to Minnesota and to St. Louis 61-60 in the Sugar Bowl.

UK was leading by a point with 12 seconds left. Bobby Watson, guarded closely by Pat Partington, had the ball. Watson lost the ball to Partington, who shot, and substitute Tom Lillis tipped it in.

Back in Lexington Rupp held his customary critique of the game, discussing each player's performance.

"Well, Bobby, you'll always be remembered as the boy who lost the Sugar Bowl," Rupp said to Watson.

UK won its next 23 games. Hagan, playing the pivot as though he had never been out of it, hooked in 37 points against Mississippi. Bob Jarvis (he would become Ole Miss head basketball coach) scored 24 of his team's 58 points in the 116-58 loss.

Bob Pettit, while not the polished player he would become later with the pro St. Louis Hawks, scored 22 for Louisiana State against UK although Rupp's Wildcats won 57-47.

Rupp's usual starters were 6-5 Shelby Linville and 6-6 Lou Tsioropoulos at forwards, Hagan at center, with 6-3 Frank Ramsey and 5-10 Bobby Watson at guards. As the season progressed, sophomore Billy Evans, from Berea, drew some starts at forward in place of Linville. Ramsey also played some forward, and the versatile Skippy Whitaker was valuable as a switch man between both positions.

Guy Strong. the good shooter from Irvine, had not returned this season. He had enrolled at Eastern Kentucky and after a stint in service would finish his eligibility at Eastern, where he later would be head coach.

But Rupp had plenty of reserves: Gayle Rose, Dan Swartz, Willie Rouse, Gene Neff, Cliff Dwyer, Houston Nutt, Jim Flynn, George Cooke, Don Clark, Browne Sharpe, Charles Keller and Woodrow Preston.

UK's winning streak became almost frightening to Rupp. The season before UK had lost to Vanderbilt in the finals of the Southeastern Conference tourney, then won the NCAA title.

UK almost lost in the finals of the SEC tourney again, squeezing by LSU 44-43 as Pettit outscored Hagan 25-19.

Lou Tsioropoulos' layup with 1:43 left won it.

UK had no trouble with Penn State in the first round of the NCAA Eastern Regional at Raleigh, N.C. winning 82-54, although a 6-5 freshman, Jesse Arnelle, scored 25 points for the losers.

St. John's didn't figure to be much trouble the next night. After all UK, which had improved steadily as the season progressed to finish No. 1 in the polls, had polished off the New York team easily back in December.

The UK players got the idea that St. John's players expected to lose. Both teams stayed in the same North Carolina State dormitory, and UK players suspected that some of the St. John's team had drunk a few beers. They could hear the St. John's players laughing and yelling and having water fights well past a normal curfew.

The next night St. John's beat UK 64-57. Bob Zawoluk, the 6-7 center who always had so much trouble scoring against Spivey, tallied 32 points and Jack McMahon (later a pro coach with Kansas City, Chicago, Cincinnati, San Diego and Pittsburgh) scored 18. Hagan scored 22 points, but he, Billy Evans and Lou Tsioropoulos fouled out.

St. John's coach Frank McGuire apparently didn't know about his team's casual attitude of the night before. "Our boys hadn't forgotten that game (at Lexington in December) and were determined to make up for it," he said.

Both Hagan and Ramsey made various All-America teams. They'd rather have had a national championship trophy, though, and no UK player doubted that they would have got it with Spivey.

This UK team was rated No. 1 in the nation in the final poll. Front row, from left: coach Adolph Rupp, Gayle Rose, Bill Evans, Bobby Watson, Skippy Whitaker, Willie Rouse and student manager Bob Moore. Back, from left: Gene Neff, Cliff Hagan, Shelby Linville, Ron Clark, Lou Tsioropoulos, Frank Ramsey, Jim Flynn. Several squad members were missing from the photo.

1952-53 Suspended

In wake of scandals, UK is suspended for season

Athletic director Bernie Shively planned non-conference schedule.

His title was judge, but there was more than a little of the crusader in the character of Saul S. Streit.

The New York judge had blistered college athletic policies and practices in November and December of 1951 when sentencing players and fixers in the college basketball scandal.

He wasn't through. On April 29, 1952, he had another job: deciding on the penalty for three University of Kentucky players involved in the scandal. Ralph Beard, Alex Groza and Dale Barnstable had cooperated in the investigation so no one expected their punishment to be severe.

It wasn't. But before announcing a suspended sentence for the three, Streit had a speech to make. It would start a chain reaction which would rock the University of Kentucky to its foundations, result in the cancellation of UK's entire basketball schedule for the forthcoming season and test the mettle of Adolph Rupp to the fullest.

Streit's speech lasted 80 minutes. It ran for 63 pages.

One paragraph of it contained the gist of his message:

"The present athletic scandal at Kentucky and the plight of these defendents can be traced directly to the inordinate desire by the trustees and alumni of Kentucky University (his phrasing) for prestige and profit from sports."

The 53-year-old Streit charged:

✔ Cribbing by some UK players was "encouraged and tolerated by university officials."

✔ UK subsidized athletes in violation of amateur rules.

✔ Unqualfied students got into school through athletic scholarships.

✔ The coach, alumni and people of Lexington, Ky., all shared in "demoralizing" the athletes.

UK president Herman L. Donovan defended coach Adolph Rupp.

The judge said angrily that Rupp "failed in his duty to observe the amateur rules to build character and protect the morals and health of his charges." He charged Rupp with "openly subsidizing the players."

The judge disclosed the following testimony by Rupp in an appearance before the grand jury:

Asked if it was true that $50 was given to Walt Hirsch after the Kansas game in 1950, Rupp said, "Yes, sir."

Q. "And where did the money come from?"

A. "This money was left over from the money that was raised to send these boys to the Olympics."

And so the reports by Streit went, mercilessly flaying UK's conduct of athletics. It was obvious to many persons close to athletics that many of Streit's statements were unfair and based on misleading information. However, it was equally obvious that there had been violations of the rules against paying college athletes.

UK officials prepared an answer to Streit's blast and were able to refute some of his points, at least to the satisfaction of many UK alumni. In explaining the source of money given out to players in small amounts ($50 for some players after a Sugar Bowl tournament), UK officials said the money was donated to send three UK players to England on the 1948 Olympic trip. These were players not among the five selected to the Olympic basketball team.

Then UK sent telegrams to three organizations—the National Collegiate Athletic Association, the Southeastern Conference and the Southern Association of Colleges and Secondary Schools—asking that athletics at the university be investigated.

The SEC started its investigation promptly, though it didn't announce the shocking result until three months later, in August: UK was, indeed, guilty of violations in the area of subsidizing players and would be barred from playing basketball within the conference for a period of one year.

A tough penalty, yes, but UK was still in business. Rupp, who already had scheduled eight games outside the SEC, began to plan with athletic director Bernie Shively for a complete schedule outside the SEC.

UK president Herman Donovan said UK would make no appeal of the penalty. However, he said the university "is not admitting anything that hasn't been the practice in other schools and confer-ences . . . The thing that hurt us was the fact that some of our former players took bribes."

Meanwhile, the NCAA was investigating UK, and three months after the SEC ruling, dropped the final bombshell: All NCAA member schools were being asked not to play UK in basketball in the 1952-53 season.

The specific violations listed were virtually the same as those cited by the SEC:

✔In 1948, members of the basketball team were given $50 each by sports enthusiasts not connected with the university when the team left for the NCAA tournament.

✔In 1949, team supporters again gave the players $50 before they went to the NCAA tournament.

✔In the winter of 1950, six players were given $50 each before they left for New York and the St. John's game.

✔In January, 1951, several players were given $25 to $50 after the Sugar Bowl games.

UK officials announced they were accepting the NCAA verdict without appeal and were canceling a 21-game schedule.

Donovan Defends Rupp

A few days later president Donovan told UK alumni that he had ordered an investigation of Rupp after the basketball scandals and "from all we could learn, coach Rupp is an honorable man who did not knowingly violate the athletic rules."

Donovan said the investigation proved that Rupp committed no breach of ethics. "If I thought otherwise, I would have dismissed him," Donovan said.

Donovan said Rupp knew of money given to basketball players after Sugar Bowl games, but did not know of monthly payments made by alumni to other players.

"I and other university officials knew about and approved the $50 given to basketball players after two appearances in the Sugar Bowl," Donovan said. "When we first appeared in football bowls we learned that it was customary among all schools going to bowls to give their players extraordinary expense money.

"When we went to the Orange Bowl, we asked the Southeastern Conference about the expense money and were told we could award each player $200. When we went to the Sugar Bowl, we received permission to give the players $250.

"From that we reasoned it also would be within the rules to award basketball players $50 expense money after the Sugar Bowl basketball tournaments."

So Adolph Rupp was in virtual exile. Like another old campaigner, Napoleon Bonaparte, he would not stay there.

There were rumors that Rupp would retire, that he had had all the adversity he could take. He quickly put such rumors to rest.

"I'll not retire until the man who said Kentucky can't play in the NCAA hands me the national championship trophy," he said.

He set about that winter getting his team ready for the 1953-54 season. UK didn't practice as hard or as often as it would have had it been playing a schedule. However, Rupp and assistant coach Harry Lancaster now had time to polish up the team's offense and defense without the pressure of preparing for a particular game.

Four public scrimmages were held, three of them varsity intrasquad games, one a varsity-freshman game. One of the games drew 6,500 spectators on a cold night over icy streets.

It was a long, cold winter for UK fans. They had one consolation, though. They knew that next season, with Cliff Hagan, Frank Ramsey and Lou Tsioropoulos, UK surely would be able to contend for the national championship.

Adolph Rupp (left) and assistant coach Harry Lancaster continued to conduct practices during Kentucky's season of suspension.

'Big three' brings UK no. 1 rating after year in exile

There was a carnival atmosphere in Memorial Coliseum. About 13,000 spectators—1,500 of them standing—roared in delight as they watched the University of Kentucky basketball team drub Temple.

This wasn't just a routine game. This was the return of UK to basketball after a year's suspension. And if the night of Dec. 5, 1953, hadn't already been something special, Cliff Hagan would have made it so.

The satin-smooth senior center was popping in baskets from all over the court. He'd hook one in with that effortless action of his right arm, he'd go down court on the fast break and tip in a teammate's missed shot, he'd fake and drive around his defensive man for a layup.

No one was thinking about a record, though; not the fans watching or the players on the court. But early in the last period Adolph Rupp sent student manager Mike Dolan to the official scorer to find out Hagan's total.

"Thirty-nine," gasped Dolan after running back to the bench.

Rupp immediately yelled to guard Frank Ramsey to start feeding Hagan. Before Ramsey could pass the word along to the other players, forward Billy Evans started to shoot. Ramsey yelled for the ball. Evans hesitated, then threw the ball to Ramsey, who flipped it to Hagan near the corner. Hagan hooked it in, an incredible shot.

Now everyone in the Coliseum realized that Hagan must be near some sort of record. The UK players concentrated completely on getting the ball to him. A couple of players missed free throws on purpose, hoping Hagan could tip it in.

Finally he reached 49, with less than a minute to play. Temple didn't attempt to stall out the clock. One of the Temple players shot, and UK sophomore guard Linville Puckett grabbed the rebound and fired the ball the length of the court. Hagan took the long pass all alone and laid it in with 31 seconds to play.

Jerry Bird was a two-year starter after reserve duty in '53-54.

His 51 points broke the Southeastern Conference record of 50 set by Louisiana State's Bob Pettit against Georgia in 1952; broke his own school mark of 42, set in the 1952 SEC tourney against Tennessee; and erased the Coliseum record of 40, set by Bill Spivey against Georgia two years before.

Most important, those 51 points brought UK back to college basketball in spectacular fashion. The exile was over. When sports writers made out their ballots in the weekly ratings, surely they'd have to take notice of UK's smashing return, an 86-59 victory over Temple.

UK's players were hungry for recognition; so were the fans, and so was Adolph Rupp. Rupp knew it was just a matter of time until the entire nation would know that he had three of the finest players in the country on his team.

Celtics Drafted Big Three

The Big Three they would be called before the season ended. Cliff Hagan, Frank Ramsey, Lou Tsioropoulos. All three had been drafted by the pro Boston Celtics the previous season because under normal conditions that would have been the players' final year.

But after UK was suspended, the three decided to stay in school for their final year of eligibility. Their reason was simple: they wanted to win the national championship.

They weren't bitter about sitting out a season, although Ramsey pointed out that they had been punished for things that happened while they were still in high school. From the standpoint of playing their final season on a strong team, Ramsey was convinced the suspension helped them.

"If we had played that season we were suspended, we couldn't have beaten anybody," Ramsey would say in later years. "We only had six players. We practiced all season long with a bunch of freshmen."

Winning has always been important to Ramsey, from the time he made the junior high team as a fourth grader in Madisonville, Ky., to his years as an All-American at UK and even later as a pro with the Boston Celtics.

Hagan Vs. Ramsey

Ramsey began playing varsity basketball at Madisonville High as a sophomore, and by his junior year had blossomed into one of the area's best players. While this was happening, nearby Owensboro had a rising young star, Cliff Hagan.

A rivalry soon developed; not between the boys but between basketball fans in their home towns as to which was the better player. Curiously, they never played against each other in a regular-season game. Only once, when they were juniors, did their teams play. That was in the first round of the 1948 state tournament, Owensboro winning 68-34.

Ramsey played forward in high school until his senior year when he shifted to center. The regular center, Tom Harper (a high school football coach at Louisville Manual until moving into the college ranks and becoming head coach at Wake Forest University), became ineligible.

Ramsey and Hagan both were back in the state tournament as seniors. This time Madisonville lost in the quarter-finals on a last-second shot by Paris. Owensboro went all the way to the championship, Cliff Hagan thrilled the crowd with a record-setting 41 points in a 65-47 victory over Lexington Lafayette in the final.

Hagan still had half a year of school, but Ramsey was ready to think about college.

"I think Kentucky was the main one all along," he said. "The only other place I considered was Western Kentucky."

Kentucky was playing in the NCAA tournament in New York in March of that year, on its way too a second straight national championship. Ramsey went to the tournament as UK's guest, and after the final game of the state tournament, Hagan joined Ramsey.

Ramsey Still Growing

When Ramsey enrolled at UK in the fall of 1949, Rupp's office was in old Alumni Gym. The doorway was 6 feet 2 in height. Ramsey, wanting to make a good impression, tried to bump his head

Continued

Continued

on the top of the doorway as he went through. By bouncing a little, he barely made it.

He was still growing, though, and was listed as 6-3 all through UK. Actually, he was closer to 6-4.

Rupp knew from the start that the big blond freshman would be a great player and would be able to step right into the varsity starting lineup as a sophomore. Ramsey was the best rebounding guard Rupp had ever coached, although the player always said modestly it was because "I was usually bigger than the other guards."

Ramsey wasn't a great long shooter, but he was good enough to set up his defensiveman for quick, slashing drives to the basket. The picture Ramsey evoked was this: if UK absolutely had to have a basket, he would run over someone and get it.

Hagan was a player who seemed to have rehearsed every move he made on the court, he did things with such ease.

Rupp said Hagan had the "best touch of any player I ever coached." The 6-4 Hagan knew precisely how hard to put the ball on the backboard, whether on a rebound or a normal shot. With that touch, he had good timing and exceptional jumping abilty.

Hagan's hook shot was a thing of beauty. He had started learning it as a sophomore at Owensboro after going to a Western Kentucky College game and seeing Western's Bob Lavoy use it. By his junior year, Hagan had developed considerable skill with the shot. It was his trademark all through college and even into professional basketball.

Hagan's finest moment in high school was when Owensboro won the state championship. He would always say that was his greatest thrill, greater even than playing on a national championship team at UK or playing with the St. Louis Hawks when they won the pro championship.

Scoring a record 41 points in the state final game was important, too, but what few persons know is that Hagan wasn't sure he'd even play. After Owensboro defeated Louisville St. Xavier in the semifinals on the final day, Hagan and his teammates went back to the hotel to rest. After a few hours in bed, Hagan found he couldn't get up without getting severe cramps in his legs. Finally two teammates got him to his feet so he could leave for the championship game.

He wasn't sure his legs would hold up

Guard Gayle Rose was one of the best dribblers ever to play at UK.

for an entire game. Imagine his surprise when he gave one of the most unforgetable performances in the history of the tournament. After the game, timer William (Big Six) Henderson got the game ball to give to the young athlete. That was the start of a long friendship. Hagan would wear No. 6 at UK in honor of Big Six.

Lou Tsioropoulos had been better known for football, as a high school All-America, in his home town of Lynn, Mass. He wanted to stick to basketball in college, however, and concentrating on one sport had much to do with his steady improvement.

He was a starter on the 1951-52 UK team which was upset by St. John's in the

NCAA. Like Hagan and Ramsey, he wanted another crack at the national title. Tsioropoulos wasn't a super player on offense, but he supplied two vital segments to UK's 1953-54 team: rebounding and defense. Lou usually guarded the best scorer the other teams had at forward or center.

The Big Three, of course, started every game their final season. Rupp shuffled the starters at the other two positions. In the beginning, he had junior Gayle Rose, from Paris, Ky., in the backcourt with Ramsey, and another junior, Billy Evans of Berea, Ky., at a forward

Later, sophomore Phil Grawemeyer, a 6-7 forward-center from Louisville Manual (he had played for Dale Barnstable) moved into a forward spot, and Evans shifted out to guard in place of Rose. Rupp's final change put Evans back at forward in Grawemeyer's place and brought Linville Puckett of Winchester's Clark County High in at guard. The latter group started the last seven games.

UK Defeats LaSalle

UK's season was remarkably easy, although there were some good individual performances against Rupp's team. Dick Hemric of Wake Forest scored 28 against UK; Dick Garmaker of Minnesota got 23; Carl Widseth of Tennessee hit for 32; Clarence (Babe) Taylor, the Frankfort boy playing at Vanderbilt, scored 22; Denver Brackeen of Mississippi found the range for 26; DePaul's Ron Sobieszczyk hit 28, and Tom Gola, the graceful Mr. Everything from LaSalle, scored 16.

Kentucky whipped LaSalle 73-60 to win the UK Invitational Tournament. The UK players considered LaSalle the best team they met.

One of the tensest games was at St. Louis just before the UKIT. Tsioropoulos held St. Louis star Dick Boushka to 10 points as UK won 71-59. Ramsey scored 21 points, Hagan 18 and Tsioropoulos 15.

St. Louis' Kiel Auditorium wasn't the best place in the world for a Kentuckian to be that night. Several fights broke out near the UK bench, one of which started when Pat Hickey, the timer, fired a pistol ending a quarter close to UK assistant coach Harry Lancaster's leg. Lancaster promptly punched Hickey, who was the son of St. Louis coach Ed Hickey.

The only close call UK had on its regular schedule was against Xavier of Cincinnati, which lost 77-71 in Lexington. Two of the easiest games were against Georgia Tech—105-53 and 99-48. Among the Georgia Tech players were Bobby Kimmel, Lenny Cohen and Dick Lenholt, who would be burning for revenge the next season.

Among the reserves Rupp used were Willie Rouse, Pete Grigsby, Jerry Bird, Clay Evans, Hugh Coy, Jess Curry, Harold Hurst, Bill Bibb and Dan Chandler. All were sophomores except Rouse, a junior.

As the victories mounted, UK fans were talking more and more of UK's chances of sweeping through the big post-season NCAA tournament. Suddenly, late in February the news broke: The Big Three would not be eligible for the NCAA because they would be graduate students. Tsioropoulos already had re-

ceived his bachelor's degree and was working on his master's. Hagan and Ramsey would be graduated at the semester break.

'The Studious Three'

Now people called them "the studious three." If they had dropped out for a semester during their suspended year, they could have been eligible. Right to the end UK officials held out hope that due to the peculiar circumstances, the NCAA would permit the boys to play. But the NCAA refused to waive the rule.

Meanwhile, UK hadn't won the SEC

Linville Puckett became a starting guard on UK's undefeated team late in the season.

championship. UK had finished in a tie with Louisiana State, each with 14 victories. The teams didn't play during the regular season because of a hassle over the schedule.

Under the schedule setup at that time, UK and LSU played only once a season. Every other year the teams visited each other's court. UK's turn to go to LSU came during the suspension year. The question was: where would the game be played in the 1953-54 season? At UK, said UK. At LSU, said LSU.

The conference schools voted in favor of UK, on the theory one might suppose that it was not UK's fault it hadn't been able to keep its commitment. LSU then simply refused to go to Lexington. SEC officials backed down, then, saying it had no authority to force LSU to play.

After the teams finished in a tie, a playoff was arranged in Nashville. Although it was not mandatory to play for the title itself, it was necessary to choose a NCAA tournament representative. At this point UK had not decided whether it would go without the studious three.

Hagan and LSU's Bob Pettit each scored 17 points, but Ramsey played brilliantly, scoring 30 points, as UK won the playoff 63-56. LSU coach Harry Rabenhorse said, "Ramsey is the best guard in the country."

During the struggle, in which UK trailed 40-36 with six minutes left, Rupp suffered heart spasms. Many of the persons in Vanderbilt's gym that night wondered if he'd ever coach again. Perhaps that fourth NCAA title he wanted so badly was out of reach.

Immediately after the game, UK announced that it would not play in the NCAA. The tourney berth went to LSU, which lost to Penn State in the NCAA regional, then lost to Indiana University in a consolation game. LaSalle, the 13-point loser to UK in December, took the NCAA title. UK followers couldn't help but think, "That could have been Kentucky." The Helms Foundation gave UK the final No. 1 national ranking.

Both Hagan and Ramsey were named to All-America teams for the second time.

Revolt, 500th win spice Rupp's 25th year

The night of Jan. 8, 1955, in University of Kentucky basketball history could be called, "The Night the Mouse Ate the Cat."

Or maybe, "The Time It Rained in Death Valley." A tribute to a coach named John (Whack) Hyder wouldn't be bad, either: "The Night Kentucky got Whacked."

It's safe to say that no one took seriously Georgia Tech's visit to Memorial Coliseum. Only 8,500 spectators showed up, about 3,000 short of filling all the seats.

Several Tech players were familiar to UK's regular fans. Bobby Kimmel, the guard from Valley High near Louisville, was one. So were Lenny Cohen and Dick Lenholt. They had played the season before in two lop-sided losses to UK.

UK coaches hadn't bothered to scout coach Hyder's team, which had a 2-4 record. UK was sailing along with a 7-0 mark and was rated No. 1 in the nation.

It didn't take long, though, to see that Tech meant business. UK kept trying to get its high-powered offense into gear, but nothing worked well. With 15 minutes left, Tech was leading 38-30. UK went to a full-court pressing defense and Tech began to crumble. UK outscored the now desperate visitors 16-8 to tie the score at 46-46.

Hyder managed to steady his young team, and with a minute, 30 seconds to go UK led only 58-55..Kimmell coolly sank two free throws with 1:12 left. UK lost the ball taking it down court, giving Tech a chance to go ahead. But the shot was missed, with UK getting the rebound.

Only 15 seconds were left as UK started up court. Now Kimmel was pressuring UK guard Bill Evans. Suddenly 5-foot-9 Joe Helms slipped in behind Evans, stole the ball, angled to the right side and hit a 12-foot jump shot. Tech was leading 59-58.

UK had one last chance, but Linville Puckett missed a driving shot with only seven seconds to play. Phil Grawemeyer missed a bat-in attempt, and it was over.

The spectators sat for several minutes in disbelief. It was as if they expected some special ruling to nullify those last horrifying 15 seconds.

The defeat ended a home winning streak of 129, going all the way back to Jan. 4, 1943, when UK beat Ft. Knox, two nights after losing to Ohio State. Tech did it with just five players.

"Strategy?" Hyder pondered the question. "Naw, these kids just played their hearts out." Then he added, "They'll never believe this score in Atlanta."

Helms with 23 points and Kimmel with 18 did most of the Tech scoring. Phil Grawemeyer scored 19 and Bob Burrow 16 for UK.

The size of Tech's accomplishment cannot be overstated. This was an excellent Kentucky team, powerful in rebounding with a big front line, experienced guards in Evans and Puckett, and a center, Bob Burrow, who was showing All-American potential in his first year on the team.

Burrow was one of the most satisfying recruiting coups of Rupp's career. Cliff Hagan had graduated and Rupp needed a center to replace him. Burrow had been a 30-point-plus scorer for Lon Morris Junior College in Jacksonville, Tex. In two years, he had scored more than 2,000 points and led his team to the semifinals of the National Junior College Tournament in the spring of 1954.

Burrow was born in Malvern, Ark., played his first basketball at Poyen, Ark., about seven miles away, and became a good basketball player after his family had moved to Wells, Tex., before his junior year.

After his eye-catching scoring and rebounding at Lon Morris (35 miles from his home in Wells), Rupp recruited him through the efforts of two Owensboro, Ky., men—Don (Quack) Butler and Bill Thompson.

"I wasn't sure I could play for Kentucky," Burrow said later. "I had heard of UK as a big basketball school. However, I wanted the opportunity. I felt that if I wasn't good enough, I could always go down."

UKIT Field Is Strong

Rupp and Burrow both must have wondered if the 6-7 center was good enough after UK's first game of the 1954-55 season. He got just one field goal and wouldn't have had that if Linville Puckett hadn't passed up a layup to give the ball to Burrow. Phil Grawemeyer, a junior from Louisville, was the big scorer with

Bob Burrow came from a junior college to replace Cliff Hagan.

28 points as Louisiana State was beaten 74-58.

UK's starting forwards were 6-6 Jerry Bird, from Corbin, and the 6-7 Grawemeyer. At guards Rupp had Bill Evans of Berea and Linville Puckett of Winchester (Clark County High).

The UK team, particularly sophomore guard Gerry Calvert of Maysville, gave Rupp a scare in the next game. UK was leading at Cincinnati 71-69. Calvert went in late, after guards Puckett and Gayle Rose fouled out. With 21 seconds left, Calvert was fouled. He missed both free throws, but grabbed the rebound and popped in a five-foot shot with seven seconds left.

In the locker room, Louisville Times reporter Marvin Gay asked Calvert how it felt to be a hero. Rupp overheard.

"We won doing the wrong thing," he told Calvert. "What in the world made you take that shot when all you had to do was hold the ball?"

Replied Calvert: "After missing those

free throws, I knew I had to do something."

Burrow, who was nervous in the opener, loosened up and scored 12 points against Xavier. By the next game, against Temple, Burrow was hitting his 15 to 20-foot jumper as he did in junior college. He swished in 27 points as UK won 79-61.

A strong field was entered in the UK Invitational. Utah had a 7-0 record, La-Salle was 5-1, Southern California 5-1 and UK 3-0.

Gipe Leaves UK

UK, already ranked No. 1 by the Associated Press, had a terrific struggle to beat Utah in the tourney opener. UK held a 67-65 lead with 45 seconds to play and had possession of the ball at mid-court. Rupp called an out-of-bounds play which worked perfectly. Jerry Bird went under the basket for an easy layup to put the game out of reach.

The next night was a milestone in Rupp's career—his 500th college victory —as LaSalle was beaten 63-54. Tom Gola, 6-7 and as mobile as a 6-3 player, ranged all over the court to score 20 points and he pulled down 15 rebounds. Burrow was close to him with 18 points and 14 rebounds, and had 20-point support from Evans and 14 from Grawemeyer.

Burrow scored 25 points against St. Louis and 25 in a rematch with Temple, both UK victories. Then came the shocking loss to Georgia Tech.

UK won its next five games, although LSU was beaten by only 64-62 and Vanderbilt 75-71. A pair of Kentuckians, Babe Taylor of Frankfort with 25 points and Al Rochelle of Guthrie with 18, almost won for Vandy.

Now, a rematch with Georgia Tech. Surely UK would make Tech pay for that big upset at Lexington. Whack Hyder repeated his formula of the earlier upset, using only five men. This time the margin was even bigger, 65-59, as Tech controlled the game all the way. There was one change in the lineup which beat UK at Lexington: Gary Phillips replaced Lennie Cohen.

Bobby Kimmel scored 20 points for Tech and Joe Helms 24. Burrow with 20 was the only UK player with a good offensive game.

The day after the defeat the news broke that Logan Gipe, a sophomore from Owensboro, was leaving UK to play for Kentucky Wesleyan. "I wasn't satisfied at Kentucky," he said.

Then came the closest thing to a full-scale rebellion Rupp ever had at UK. It was more of a misunderstanding than anything. although it involved the breaking of one of Rupp's rules.

After the UK team returned to Lexington, from Georgia Tech (this was during the semester break), the players got together and decided they would go home overnight.

There should be no problem because Rupp hadn't scheduled a practice the next day. This wasn't the first time the UK players had gone home without permisson. Each time they agreed among themselves that everyone would go. If one got caught, they'd all get caught. Sort of a safety-in-numbers theory.

This time things went wrong. A student manager got word of the plan and squealed to Rupp. The coach sent someone to check the players' rooms. When no one was there, the coach called a practice for the next afternoon.

But the players got word of the practice and were back in time. They met at a service station near the Coliseum and made an agreement: "If he kicks one of us off, we'll all quit."

Rupp called a meeting of the squad. He went down the row of players sitting on benches, asking each boy: "Where were you last night?"

Each time the answer was, "At home."

Finally he got to a player who lived several hundred miles away. When he replied, "At home," Rupp scoffed, "You couldn't have gone home and got back."

Then Rupp told the players he was taking away their movie passes and some other privileges.

Linville Puckett, who had been receiving what he considered some unjust

Billy Evans, UK's floor leader, later made the Olympic team.

criticism for his play in the losses to Georgia Tech, stood up. "If you're going to take anything of mine, you can take everything," he said, and walked out.

Billy Bibb followed. Then Jerry Bird. Then the rest, all except Bob Burrow, who was in the school infirmary with a sinus infection, and Billy Evans.

This is where the misunderstanding begins. Evans, a married athlete, was never in on the plan the players hatched to go home. When he saw Puckett leave, he assumed that Puckett was leading a revolt. The players themselves were confused. Was Puckett quitting, or was he being kicked off? If it was the latter, the players felt honor bound to stick with him.

Evans followed the players out of the Coliseum and confronted Puckett. A fight almost ensued. Finally the players decided to go back inside and hold their own meeting. They explained to Evans, the

team captain, what had happened. Evans' main objective at this stage was to keep the team together.

Rupp and assistant coach Harry Lancaster were called in.

"Do you want to play?" asked Rupp. "If you do, be on the floor at 3:15."

Everyone practiced that day. But the next day Puckett didn't show up. He announced he was leaving UK. He said basketball at UK "isn't regarded as a game, but as a matter of life or death, with the resemblance of one going to war."

Two days later Puckett and Billy Bibb announced they both were applying for admission at Kentucky Wesleyan.

Puckett's phrase about "going to war" achieved a certain immortality at UK. The highest compliment that can be paid a player at Kentucky is, "He goes to war."

UK's next player loss came at DePaul as UK was winning 76-72 for the Wildcats' sixth straight victory. Phil Grawemeyer fell driving to the basket and suffered a broken leg. He was lost for the year, taking with him 13-point and 13-rebound averages.

UK didn't have an easy time winning the Southeastern Conference. The victory which put Rupp's team into a one-game lead over Alabama and just about wrapped up the title came late in February when UK beat Johnny Dee's Alabama team 66-52.

A UK reserve, Dan Chandler, and Alabama's Jim Bogan provided some excitement before the game when they began punching each other at midcourt during warmups. Chandler said that several of the Alabama players had cursed the UK players, and that Bogan had called him a "yellow so-and-so because I wouldn't step across the center line."

Now for the NCAA tournament. Rupp couldn't be too hopeful. He had only two starters left out of the five that opened the season. Puckett had quit, Grawemeyer had suffered the broken leg and Evans wasn't eligible because he had graduated.

Rupp picked John Brewer, a fine jump shooter from Anchorage, for Grawemeyer's forward spot. Gayle Rose had moved in at guard when Puckett left the team. Now Rupp needed to replace Evans, the brain behind UK's offense.

He chose Gerry Calvert, the 5-11 sophomore from Maysville. Calvert hadn't played much all season. He had been handicapped early with a broken finger and wore a cast on it for the first few games.

UK's first opponent in the NCAA regional tournament at Evanston, Ill., was tall and poised Marquette. The game was even until the last six minutes, then Marquette pulled away to win 79-71 behind center Terry Rand's 19 points. Rose scored 20 points, Burrow 19 and Brewer 16 for UK.

The next night Burrow scored 22 points, and Calvert—held to eight by Marquette—broke out with 19 points as UK buried Penn State 84-59 in the third-place game.

Burrow, who with Billy Evans had made the All-SEC team, was voted to the NCAA All-Regional team. After leaving UK, Evans would play with the Bartlesville (Okla.) Oilers and earn a place on the U. S. Olympic squad in 1956. He was one of UK's most underrated players.

'Slot machine' five was puzzle

"This team is like a slot machine. Something is set in there that makes it click or not click. It's played the worst basketball I've seen and some of the best."

Adolph Rupp was about to send his University of Kentucky team into action in the 1956 NCAA regional tournament at Iowa City, Iowa, and it was clear from his statement that he had no idea what to expect.

Everything came up roses the first night as UK center Bob Burrow scored 33 points in an 84-64 victory over Wayne University, only the second loss of the season in 20 games for the Detroit team.

The next night UK played Iowa.

Iowa was an excellent team, no doubt about it. It had won 17 and lost 5 in winning the Big Ten championship and had defeated Morehead State 97-83 in the NCAA regional. Still, the UK players were confident. Morehead had stayed close to Iowa until Steve Hamilton (a future major league pitcher) and Dan Swartz fouled out.

Rupp did his part in setting the mechanism of his slot machine. He assigned 6-foot-7 senior Phil (Cookie) Grawemeyer to guard 6-3 Carl (Sugar) Cain.

For the first 15 minutes of the opening half, Kentucky had slightly the better of it. Grawemeyer, playing the finest defensive game of his three years at UK, held Cain scoreless.

Then Rupp made a mistake. He pulled Grawemeyer out.

"I just want to give you a rest," Rupp told the senior.

"I don't need a rest," an exasperated Grawemeyer replied.

Meanwhile, Cain was hitting two quick baskets, so Rupp rushed Grawemeler back into the game. Too late. Sugar had broken out of his doldrums. Now he was confident and loose, pouring in the points. Sugar Cain at his best was a sweet player, indeed.

In those last five minutes of the half, Iowa took command and went on to win 89-77. Cain finished with 34 points, three more than Burrow.

So ended a year in which a Kentucky team had not fulfilled its promise; so ended a dream for Phil Grawemeyer.

The dream stretched back aways, back to when Grawemeyer was playing center

Phil Grawemeyer of Louisville made the switch successfully from a high school center to a first-string forward at Kentucky.

on good Manual teams coached by former UK player Dale Barnstable and Jack Burmaster. The slender 6-7 Grawemeyer helped Manual get to the state tournament two straight years, 1951 and '52, both times making the all-tournament squad. He was a Courier-Journal All-Stater in 1952.

Few could forget the game Grawemeyer played in the final of the state tournament in '52, against Cuba. Manual lost 58-52, but Grawemeyer scored 19 points and had seven of his team's 19 field goals.

There never was much question about where Grawemeyer would go to college. He greatly admired Barnstable and longed to follow in his coach's footsteps.

UK was on suspension in the 1952-53 season, Grawemeyer's freshman year, so he didn't play a game. It was an important year for him, though, because he got started making the change from center to forward.

"When I went to UK I couldn't handle

the ball and I wasn't an outside shooter," he said later, "so it was a tough change for me."

He also found out one of the reasons for UK's success in basketball. "Being thrown in against great players, you're gonna learn some things," he said.

There were some great ones there his freshman year—Cliff Hagan, Frank Ramsey, Lou Tsioropoulos, Billy Evans—as well as a fine freshman crop which included Jerry Bird, Linville Puckett and Pete Grigsby.

As a sophomore, Grawemeyer started about a third of the games as UK won 25 without a loss. One play that season stood out in Grawemeyer's mind. It was in the playoff for the Southeastern Conference title and a berth in the NCAA tournament at Nashville.

"Cliff Hagan drove in for a layup, missed it, then tipped it in from the other side," marveled Grawemeyer. "I had never seen anything like that."

Grawemeyer expected to have a fine

junior season. He was shooting and rebounding well in practice, and his confidence was high. But three weeks before the first game he suffered a fractured skull above an eye when he collided with another player in practice; Grawemeyer's head hit the floor.

That didn't keep him out of the starting lineup for the opener, though. He scored 28 points against Louisiana State, the most he would ever score in his college career. He went on to become one of the team's scoring and rebounding leaders. Then he suffered a broken leg near the end of the season and had to sit out UK's trip to the NCAA, including the loss to Marquette.

So there it was: two seasons, two disappointing finishes. The first came when UK skipped the NCAA because Hagan, Ramsey and Tsioropoulos were ineligible. And now a broken leg.

Front Line Returns

Grawemeyer had one last season to see his dream of playing on a national championship team come true.

On paper, it seemed that UK would be strong in the '55-56 campaign. The big front line was back; Grawemeyer, 6-6 Jerry Bird and 6-7 Bob Burrow.

At guard Rupp had 5-11 junior Gerry Calvert and 6-3 junior John Brewer with a 6-3 sophomore, Vernon Hatton, waiting for a chance. UK fans were optimistic. So were the voters in the pre-season Associated Press poll. They picked UK second to defending NCAA champion San Francisco.

It didn't take Rupp long to find out he was going to have his ups and downs. In the second game, Temple came in with a pair of classy guards, Hal Lear and Guy Rodgers, and beat UK 73-61. Rodgers scored 24 points, Lear 19. Rupp tried to hold Burrow, who had a sprained ankle, out of the game, but the big center was rushed into action when Temple took a 17-4 lead. He rallied UK, but not enough.

That also was Vernon Hatton's first start for UK. He scored 10 points.

UK had to overcome a seven-point DePaul lead to win its next game. Guard Ron Sobieszczyk with 24 points and center Ken Jaksy with 23 made it tough on UK.

UK then went to College Park, Md., to beat Maryland 62-61. Hatton scored Kentucky's last five points while Maryland was getting just one.

After beating Idaho easily, Kentucky was ready for the UK Invitational Tournament. Burrow scored 27 points as Minnesota lost 72-65. But with only 2:20 left in the game, Burrow went down with a badly sprained ankle.

Rupp Springs Double Pivot

He couldn't play the next night in the finals against Dayton, which had a 7-foot center, Bill Uhl. Rupp moved Jerry Bird to the pivot and the Corbin, Ky., senior scored 34 points. But Uhl pulled down the key rebounds and scored 20 points. Dayton also got 25 points from Ray Dieringer, 17 from Arlon Bockhorn and

rapped Kentucky 89-74. Gerry Calvert scored 18 for UK.

Rupp pulled a surprise the next game, putting Bird and Burrow into a double pivot at St. Louis. Burrow scored 40 points and Bird 17 as Kentucky romped 101-80. That was one of those nights Rupp was talking about when he said that "something is set in there which makes them click." Calvert dropped in 22 points.

UK won its next five games, all handily. One was 107-65 over LSU, in which Burrow scored 50 points. Burrow left the game with 46 points with 2:35 to play. With the crowd yelling, "We want Burrow," someone told Rupp of Burrow's total. Rupp quickly put him back in.

He got two more baskets, one field goal short of breaking Cliff Hagan's one-game UK mark of 51.

UK was up to fourth in the United Press poll when it went to Vanderbilt. Vandy had a 12-1 record and was 5-0 in the SEC. With two Kentuckians, Babe Taylor of Frankfort and Al Rochelle of Guthrie, getting 52 points between them, Vandy beat Kentucky 81-73.

Reserves used by Rupp throughout the season were Ray Mills, Ed Beck, John Crigler, John Brewer, Phil Johnson, Bill Smith, Bill Cassady, Lincoln Collinsworth and Harold Ross. Earl Adkins had scholastic difficulties and had to sit out the first half of the schedule so Rupp held him out for the entire season.

UK won its next six games before losing a rematch with DePaul at Chicago 81-79. Rupp was looking beyond this Saturday night game to a Monday battle with Vandy. UK beat Vandy 76-55, and five nights later met Alabama at Montgomery in a game which Kentucky had to have to even tie for the SEC title.

Alabama, whose first five players were in their fourth year as starters for coach Johnny Dee, had a 17-3 record and was 10-0 in the conference. UK was 17-4, 10-1 in the SEC.

UK's players felt the tension as early as noon on the day of the game. It built up more and more until by gametime some of them appeared to be in a daze. Hatton with 24 points and Burrow with 26 scored well, but Kentucky's defense was disorganized and confused. With former Louisville Flaget center Jerry Harper scoring 37 points, Alabama won 101-77. It was the first time any team had ever hit 100 against UK.

Alabama won the SEC championship. However, none of the Alabama starters was eligible for the NCAA tournament because they had played four years of varsity basketball. The SEC presidents voted to allow Kentucky to represent the conference in the NCAA.

Why had UK fallen short of great expectations? Grawemeyer believed it was partly because injuries—his own broken leg, the ankle problems of Bird and Burrow—took some of the movement out of UK's big players. UK also lacked an experienced guard in the backcourt, as Billy Evans had been the year before.

Burrow made the All-SEC team for the second straight year and also was named All-America by the U.S. Basketball Writers.

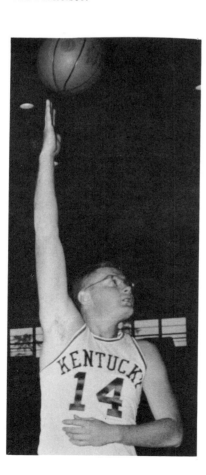

Rebounding was a strong point for center-forward Ray Mills of Manchester, Ky.

Phil Johnson of Lexington was a sophomore on the '55-56 team.

Hustling Gerry Calvert of Maysville had a good outside shot to go with his speed at guard.

Maysville's Calvert puts the go into UK's fast break

Adolph Rupp stood in the middle of the Memorial Coliseum basketball court, his team seated around him in a circle.

He held a basketball in his hands as he talked to his squad. He said he needed another starting guard and couldn't quite make up his mind whom to choose.

He called off the names of four certain starters to take their places on the court for some offensive work. Just then the ball rolled out of his hands and bounced down the court. One of the players jumped up from the circle, dashed after the ball and threw it back to Rupp.

"Well, here's a boy who wants to play. Get out there with the other four," Rupp said.

That's how red-haired Gerry Calvert got his chance to play at the University of Kentucky, stepping into the lineup for crippled UK in the 1955 NCAA regional tournament at Evanston, Ill.

Now, two seasons later, there was no doubt where Calvert fitted into Rupp's scheme. Calvert was UK's go-go guard. He made the team run. A 5-foot-11 bundle of energy, he buzzed up and down the court relentlessly.

The rest of the players had to run

their hearts out or they would've looked rather silly chasing him up and down the court. Calvert was the main reason Rupp had one of the finest fast-break teams in UK history in the 1956-57 season.

U of L Signs Calvert

The story has been widely told that Calvert went to UK without a scholarship. That's not true, but UK almost missed him and the University of Louisville had him and let him get away.

Calvert was a Courier-Journal All-State player for Earle Jones as a senior at Maysville, Ky., in 1953. A good long shooter, with the quick burst of speed needed to get in for layups, Calvert drew the attention of chief U of L recruiter John Dromo.

Calvert had always wanted to attend UK. His ambition was to "be another Ralph Beard." But UK didn't offer him a scholarship; U of L did. He signed with U of L.

Calvert made the Kentucky High School All-Stars in '53 for a second game that summer against Indiana's best. He hadn't played in an earlier game when

the Kentucky Stars, coached by Western Kentucky's Ed Diddle, lost at Indianapolis. Bruce Hale of Indianapolis got the idea of staging a second game—in Louisville.

Calvert was one of five new players chosen. U of L head coach Bernard (Peck) Hickman and his assistant, John Dromo, were picked as the new all-star coaches. But the Kentucky Stars lost again and Calvert didn't play enough to break a good sweat.

Calvert was disappointed and a little mad when he went home. About three weeks before school started, UK offered him a scholarship. He accepted.

"If they (Hickman and Dromo) had played me more in the all-star game, I would've gone to U of L," he said later. "I would've felt obligated."

As a sophomore in 1954-55, Calvert was handicapped by a broken finger and wore a cast for several games. He played in about two-thirds of UK's games as a reserve until Rupp game him a chance in the NCAA. He scored eight points the first night of the NCAA regional against Marquette, and came back with 19 the

next night against Penn State. Rupp knew he had found a player.

He's a Confident Senior

As a junior Calvert started all of UK's 26 games and averaged 11.2 points.

So he was confident that his senior year would be his best, and he was equally convinced that Kentucky has a team good enough to win the national championship.

Calvert was the only senior in the line-up with which UK opened the 1956-57 season. At the other guard was a 6-3 junior, Vernon Hatton, of Lexington. At the forwards were 6-4 sophomore Johnny Cox, Hazard, Ky., and 6-3 John Crigler, Hebron, Ky. The center was 6-7 junior Ed Beck, from Ft. Valley, Ga.

From the start Cox, Hatton and Calvert carried the scoring load. UK won its first three games, the biggest of which was 73-58 at Temple with Cox looping in 23 points. But the next game, despite 20 points by Cox, 21 by Hatton and 18 by Calvert St. Louis edged UK 71-70 on the Kentucky court.

St. Louis coach Ed Hickey called Cox "the greatest sophomore in the country," but Kentucky couldn't handle St. Louis' Jack Mimlitz (25 points) and Harold Alcorn (24).

The next game, as if to prove Hickey's point, Cox scored 34 points in a 76-55 victory over Maryland. Still using the old two-handed dip shot on free throws, Cox dropped in 12 of 12.

The next time out, UK lost another one-pointer 85-84 at Duke University. Duke's Bucky Allen stole the ball from Hatton with 20 seconds to play to score the winning basket. "He almost knocked Vernon down taking the ball," Calvert insisted.

First Defeat for Illinois

UK returned home for its own invitational tournament. Using its fast break to perfection, UK defeated Southern Methodist 73-67, although hook-shooting All-American center Jim Krebs scored 25 points for SMU. The next night UK beat Illinois, which had speedy Don Ohl at guard, 91-70. It was Illinois' first defeat in six games.

From there UK went to New Orleans to try for the Sugar Bowl title. UK appeared beaten by Virginia Tech, but John Brewer stole the ball on a throw-in after a Kentucky basket to get the winning goal with seven seconds left.

After squeaking past Virginia Tech 56-55, nationally third-ranked UK had an easy time beating Houston 111-76 for the title the next night. The Most Valuable Player Trophy went to Kentucky center Ed Beck, who scored 16 points the first night and 10 in the title game, and who had two good defensive and re-bounding contests.

Hatton was troubled with a sore appendix during the Sugar Bowl games. A few days before UK's first Southeastern Conference game with Georgia Tech, he underwent an appendectomy and John Brewer took his place.

John Crigler had his first big scoring game, 24 points, as Kentucky whacked Tech 95-72. Calvert hit for 29 in an 81-62 triumph over Chicago Loyola. Louisiana State tried a slowdown and gave UK trouble before falling 51-46.

Then UK ran into a cold-shooting night at Tulane and lost 68-60 as Auburn, Ind., product Cal Grosscup scored 23 points for the winners.

The next game was at Tennessee. Adrian Smith went in as a substitute guard for UK and scored 16 points in a 97-72 victory. That earned the Farmington, Ky., player a spot in the lineup in place of John Brewer. Two games later Smith hit for 24 points as Georgia Tech fell again 76-65. Then he scored 20 points against Georgia, and 18 against Florida. Hatton played for a few minutes in the

Center Ed Beck was Most Valuable Player in the Sugar Bowl tourney.

Georgia and Florida games, but appeared far from top form.

Hatton Gets the Call

When UK was behind Mississippi in a game played at Memphis, Hatton's adrenalin started flowing. With 13 minutes to play, UK trailed 53-42. Rupp sent in Hatton.

He hit from 30 feet. He stole the ball for a layup. After Cox dropped in a one-hander, Hatton hit another long shot. Before he was through Hatton scored 14 points and UK won 75-69. Kentucky never did figure out what to do about Ole Miss forward Joe Gibbon, though. He scored 29 points. After graduation, Gibbon would find a career in pro baseball as a pitcher with the Pittsburgh Pirates and Cincinnati Reds.

Defense was a problem for UK at Starkville, Miss., too. A 6-7 sophomore, Bailey Howell, who was definitely headed for stardom, scored 37 points for Mississippi State and UK lost 89-81.

Howell, who would have a great future in pro basketball, had 25-point help from a guard, Jimmy Ashmore.

Ed Beck, whose wife Billie, was dying of lung cancer, missed the next game at Chicago Loyola. But UK was hot from start to finish, and with Rupp speaking into the television cameras for the Chicago-originated "Tonight" show during the game, UK romped 115-65. Cox impressed Chicago sports writers with 32 points.

Rupp's most important reserves during the season were the 6-4 Ray Mills, a springy-legged forward who started at times in place of Crigler; John Brewer, also a starter at times at guard; Adrian Smith, who filled in so admirably when Hatton was ailing, and Earl Adkins, a good outside-shooting guard.

Other reserves were Lincoln Collinsworth, Harold Ross, Dick Howe, Billy Cassady, Bill Smith, Jay Bayless, John Hardwick, Lewis McManus and Charles Webb.

UK won its next four games, all in the SEC, to wrap up its 17th conference title and gain a berth in the NCAA tourney. With the tournament being played on its own court, UK was heavily favored to win the regional and advance to the final four.

The first night of the NCAA Kentucky ran out of gas in the second half and had a tough time getting by Pittsburgh 98-92. Brewer went in as a sub and hit eight of eight free throws or an apparently tired Kentucky team might have lost.

In the regional final, UK led Michigan State by 12 points 47-35 at halftime. But with guard Jack Quiggle scoring 22 points and 6-5 leaper John Green dominating the rebounding until he fouled out, MSU won 80-68. UK was behind 69-66, but faded badly near the end.

Johnny Cox was named to the All-SEC team and Gerry Calvert was chosen to play in the college East-West All-Star game.

Calvert, Ray Mills and Johnny Brewer were the only seniors, so Rupp would have plenty of experience to work with next season.

Vernon Hatton: clutch player of the fiddlin' five

Kentucky guard Vernon Hatton drapes one of the nets over his head after the victory over Seattle for the 1958 NCAA title.

"We've got fiddlers, that's all. They're pretty good fiddlers; be right entertaining at a barn dance. But I'll tell you, you need violinists to play in Carnegie Hall. We don't have any violinists."

Fiddlers. Not exactly a vote of confidence Adolph Rupp was giving his basketball team. Yet, it was exactly the way he felt after nearly a month of practice before the opening game of the 1957-58 season.

After three straight years of losing in the NCAA regional tournaments, Rupp was convinced that good players weren't enough. He wanted a super player or two, as Cliff Hagan and Frank Ramsey had been in UK's unbeaten season four years before and as Bill Spivey had been on the 1951 national champions.

Not that Rupp expected a poor season. With four starters back from a team that had won 23 games and lost 5, he knew he had a winner. He had 6-foot-4 Johnny Cox and 6-3 John Crigler to play forward, 6-7 Ed Beck at center, and 6-3 Vernon Hatton at guard. Gone was Gerry Calvert at guard, but 6-foot Adrian (Odie) Smith should be an adequate replacement.

Every starter was a senior except Cox, a junior from Hazard, Ky., who had led UK in scoring the year before with a 19.4 average. If anyone was capable of developing into a superstar, Rupp calculated, it was Cox. Not only was Cox an excellent one-hand jump shooter from the top of the circle, he could hit sweeping hook shots in close and was an exceptional rebounder.

Crigler, Beck Good Rebounders

Crigler, from Hebron, Ky., at the other forward was one of those unselfish players Rupp always seemed to find a place for. He, too, was a strong rebounder for his height and was capable of coming through with an occasional high-scoring game.

Beck had been a consistent scorer as a high school player at Ft. Valley, Ga., However, Rupp never encouraged him as a shooter for UK, so Beck began to

Don Mills (54) blocks the path of Seattle All-America Elgin Baylor in UK's 84-72 victory in the 1958 NCAA tournament. In the background are Johnny Cox (24), John Crigler (behind Baylor) and Vernon Hatton (52).

concentrate on rebounding and defense. He did both very well. As a junior he led UK in rebounding with 14 a game.

Smith had been a high school star at Farmington, Ky., but at 5-10, 150 pounds drew no notice from UK. He went to Northeast Mississippi Junior College for two years. In his second season there he was the fifth highest junior college scorer in the nation with a 27.2 average.

As a junior, his first year at UK, Smith was primarily a reserve. But when Vernon Hatton was out for a month after an appendectomy, Smith was one of UK's best scorers.

Hatton was a fascinating player. Confident, almost cocky, this product of Lexington (Ky.) Lafayette High had an uncanny knack of coming through in the tough spots. It would be difficult to select the best clutch player Rupp ever had, but Hatton would have to rate high on the list.

"My coach in high school, Ralph Carlisle (Rupp's All-Conference forward of 1936 and '37), always told me never to hide from the ball," Hatton said. "When the game got tough, I always tried to get the ball. This carried through into college."

Hatton was born in Owingsville, Ky., and didn't start playing basketball until his family had moved to Lexington and he was in Bryan Station Junior High School. He recalled seeing a notation his junior high coach made: "Hatton—very, very clumsy."

Hatton came under the tutorage of Carlisle as a 10th grader at Lafayette. Hatton played forward on the "B" team most of the season. He was moved up to the varsity of the last few games and Carlisle switched him to guard. Hatton was ready to quit.

"Try it for two weeks," Carlisle told him. "If you don't like it by then, I'll move you back to forward."

At first Hatton had problems dribbling and handling the ball. Soon, though, he began to get the hang of it and he stayed there. He also grew three inches and gained 25 pounds between his sophomore and junior years.

He was an All-State guard as Lafayette won the state championship his junior year. He was All-State and All-America his last season although injuries—Hatton had a bad ankle — prevented Lafayette from repeating as state champ.

At first Hatton agreed to attend UK. During the summer he changed his mind and signed at Eastern Kentucky. When the news broke that Hatton would go to Eastern, UK assistant coach Harry Lancaster pursued him to Huntington, W. Va., where the big guard was playing in an all-star game. Hoping to avoid Lancaster, Hatton stayed in the shower for an hour after the game. When he finally came out, there was the persistent Lancaster.

"Boy, you sure like to get clean, don't you?" Lancaster said wearily.

Not long afterward, Hatton agreed to attend UK.

He became a starter in the second game of his sophomore year. Two games after that he showed Rupp for the first time that phenomenal ability to produce under pressure. He scored UK's last five points in a 62-61 victory at Maryland.

Hatton was up to his old tricks as soon as the 1957-58 season started. In the opener against Duke, he scored 26 points, five of them in the last two minutes, as UK squeezed by 78-74.

Hatton scored 20 points and Crigler 22 at Ohio State as UK won 61-54 in the then new St. John Arena. UK played

Continued

UK's Johnny Cox (24), John Crigler (32) and Don Mills (54) surround a Seattle player after a rebound in the NCAA championship game in Louisville. No. 50 is Adrian Smith. The victory gave UK its fourth NCAA title.

Continued

marvelous team defense. Ohio State didn't get a single layup as UK's veteran players timed their defensive switches perfectly.

Ed Beck held Ohio State's massive 6-7 center, Frank Howard, to seven points. Howard made it big as a baseball slugger in the major leagues.

Next came the game Hatton will always be remembered for, against Temple in UK's Memorial Coliseum. First, Hatton sank a free throw with 49 seconds to go to tie the game 65-65 and send it into overtime.

UK seemed beaten when Temple's flashy guard, Guy Rodgers, hit a 15-foot shot with three seconds to play in the extra period. By the time UK got time out, only one second showed on the clock.

Rupp turned to Adrian Smith, who had fired an unsuccessful 60-foot shot near the end of the regulation time. "Well, Smitty, I guess we'll have to let you shoot another."

Assistant coach Harry Lancaster offered a suggestion: "Let's let Vernon try this one." Rupp agreed.

Temple's defense backed up, trying to protect against the long pass under the basket and the quick tip. Hatton took the throw near the sideline at midcourt, wheeled toward the basket and let fly with both hands. The ball nicked the metal rim, bounced back and forth several times, then dropped through. The Coliseum exploded with sound.

Near the end of the next overtime, Temple tied the score 75-75. The third overtime, though, was almost all Hatton's. He scored six of UK's eight points and Temple was defeated 83-81.

Maryland handed UK its first loss, 71-62. After St. Louis was defeated 73-60, Southern Methodist won its 38th straight regular-season home court victory, 65-64 over UK.

Next came the UK Invitational Tournament. The field was impressive: North Carolina, 4-0 and ranked No. 1 nationally;

UK, 4-2, rated fifth; West Virginia, 6-0, rated eighth, and Minnesota, 3-0 and 10th in the nation.

West Virginia, showing speed and an amazing streak of shooting accuracy late in the first half, downed UK 77-70 the first night. Then West Virginia beat North Carolina the next night 75-64 for the title.

West Virginia, which had a promising sophomore named Jerry West, vaulted to the No. 1 rating the following week.

UK won its next eight games. Vanderbilt almost upset Kentucky but reserve guard Earl Adkins of Ashland, Ky., went in after Adrian Smith had drawn four fouls and scored 25 points.

The streak was broken at Georgia Tech, 71-52. Terry Randall, a little guard from Columbia, Ky., scored 26 points for Tech.

After four more victories, UK went to Chicago and lost 57-56. Hatton was almost the hero in this one, but Loyola's Art

McZier stole his show. Hatton hit a 15-foot jumper with only a few seconds to play. Loyola got time out with a second left.

The ball was thrown to McZier, who hooked from 30 feet out and banked in the winning basket. UK lost one of its last four regular-season games, 64-63 to Auburn at Birmingham. It was the first time Auburn had ever beaten UK.

Phil Johnson was the No. 1 reserve forward throughout the year although he started several games. Sophomore Don Mills was Beck's understudy in the pivot, and Earl Adkins usually was the first substitute at guard. Other reserves were Bill Cassady, Lincoln Collinsworth, Lowell Hughes, Dick Howe, Harold Ross and Bill Smith.

Despite its worst regular-season record since 1940-41, UK was Southeastern Conference champion and would play in the NCAA regional. UK had one big advantage—the regional was scheduled in Memorial Coliseum.

The first night of the regional, UK eliminated Miami of Ohio 94-70. Notre Dame, which had a 23-4 record, defeated Indiana 94-87. Notre Dame coach Johnny Jordan was confident his Irish, led by high-jumping Tom Hawkins, would whip UK.

UK played its finest game of the year to hand Notre Dame the worst defeat in its history, 89-56.

On to Louisville's Freedom Hall for the NCAA finals. The Fiddlers had made it to Carnegie Hall.

Temple had a 26-2 record. One of the losses was to UK and the other to Oscar Robertson and the Cincinnati Bearcats. Now it had a chance to get even with UK in the Friday night round of the NCAA finals.

But that man Hatton was still around. UK, behind 60-59 with 23 seconds left, called time out. The plan was for Hatton to drive for the basket. Hatton dribbled down the right side, curved underneath the basket along the baseline, came out under the left side of the basket and laid the ball in with his right hand. There were 16 seconds left.

Temple had one last chance but sophomore guard Bill Kennedy bobbled the ball out of bounds to give UK the ball. That did it. UK was in the championship game against Elgin Baylor and Seattle, which had blistered Kansas State 73-51 to gain the finale.

Seattle coach John Castellani made a tactical mistake against UK. Rupp recognized it instantly: Baylor was guarding Crigler. Crigler began to drive for the basket. He quickly put three fouls on Baylor.

Now Baylor was taken off Crigler and put on the UK centers, Ed Beck and Don Mills. Hatton started driving down the middle, forcing Baylor to pick him up on the defensive switch. Baylor drew foul No. 4 trying to block a Mills hook shot, then could play only token defense against Hatton's slashing drives.

Hatton finished with 30 points and long-shooting Johnny Cox with 24. UK won 84-72. Rupp had his fourth NCAA crown.

Was it a fluke, this championship by the "Fiddlin' Five?"

Two things must be considered. Three of the Fiddlers' six losses had been by a point. Had those three games gone the other way, UK would have been one of the favorites for the national title, not a longshot.

Second, UK played the toughest schedule in the school's history up to that time. Almost every non-conference opponent was a veteran team, on the way to winning a conference championship or finishing high in the race.

The Fiddlers paid their dues. They deserved everything they got.

Vernon Hatton was named to the Helms Foundation All-America team. Hatton and Cox made the All-NCAA Tournament team and both were chosen All-Southeastern Conference by SEC coaches. Adrian Smith was headed into the Army, where he made the All-Army team and the 1960 U.S. Olympic team. Afterwards he would enjoy a long pro career.

Perhaps Rupp had a few violinists after all.

His eyes are closed but UK's Johnny Cox has the ball in a rebound battle against Seattle. Looking for a chance to help are Don Mills (54), Adrian Smith (50) and John Crigler (32).

Adolph lifted his eyes to the hills, and there stood Cox

The game was over. Hazard, a team with one of the poorest records in the state tournament, was the 1955 Kentucky high school basketball champion.

The tall, stoop-shouldered player who had done most to make Hazard's impossible dream come true stood on the University of Kentucky's Memorial Coliseum court and gazed solemnly at the crowd.

UK basketball coach Adolph Rupp, who had watched Johnny Cox score a record-breaking 127 points in the four state tourney games—32 of them in the 74-66 championship victory over Adair County—walked onto the court. He shook hands with the 6-foot-4 senior.

"How would you like to run up and down this court for the next four years?" Rupp asked.

"I guess that would be all right," Cox replied.

It's doubtful if even Rupp realized how important Cox would be to UK's basketball fortunes. In a few years, though, Rupp would look back and realize that without Cox UK could not have had one of the nation's finest teams in 1956-57; could not have won the NCAA championship in '58, and could not have earned the No. 2 national ranking in the '58-59 season.

In Cox's three years as a regular, UK won 70 games and lost 14.

Where does it all begin for a young basketball player in the hills of Kentucky? For Cox, it started in his own backyard at Fleming, Ky. He had a goal mounted on his house. But that didn't last long because the constant banging of the ball kept his father, a night-shift railroad worker, awake.

So Johnny had to move the goal to another small building in the yard. That's where he developed the hook shot with which he scored so often in high school and at UK. He'd spend hour after hour practicing the shot.

He started playing organized basketball in grade school. His mother didn't know he was playing until he was stricken with appendicitis. His coach, one of the women teachers, came to see Johnny in the hospital. "Johnny, you gotta get out of this hospital," she pleaded, "or I'm gonna lose all my games."

When he was in the ninth grade, Cox played mostly on the B-team, but occasionally got in a varsity game for Fleming-Neon High School. The next season he was a starter on the varsity.

Shortly after his junior year had started—basketball practice had begun—the Cox family moved about 50 miles to Hazard.

Immediately rumors of "undue influence" started. Afraid that the school might be suspended if they used Cox, Hazard officials held him out of basketball that season. As a senior, though, Cox was ready to go. He scored 1,026 for coach Goebel Ritter in regular-season play and followed with his record state tournament performance.

Although there were a number of colleges seeking his services (Ed Diddle of Western Kentucky was particularly high on him), there still was some doubt about Cox as a college prospect. The reason: he had played center in high school, getting a good many of his points on hook shots and rebounds. Could he move to forward and still score?

He answered that quickly at UK. He averaged 32.2 points in eight games as a freshman and set a one-game UK freshman scoring record with 44 points.

By the time he was a sophomore he had developed an accurate jump shot. "Number ten," Rupp would yell out the play, and Cox would go to the top of the circle to shoot behind a screen. Cox averaged 19.4 points, best on the team, as a sophomore. He fell off to 14.9, behind Vernon Hatton's 17.1, on the 1957-58 Fiddlin' Five.

There wasn't much doubt about the size of Cox's responsibility when practice for the 1958-59 campaign got under way. He was the lone starter back from the Fiddlers. The scoring and rebounding burdens would fall squarely on him.

Only two returning players other than Cox figured to be much help to Rupp. They were 6-6 senior forward-center Phil Johnson of Lexington and 6-7 junior Don Mills of Berea.

Rupp had two junior college guards, Sid Cohen of Kilgore (Tex.) Junior College and Bennie Coffman of Lindsey Wilson (Ky.). In addition, Rupp had a good crop of sophomores, including Bill Lickert, who had led Lexington Lafay-

ette to the 1957 Kentucky high school title; Dick Parsons, a long-shooting guard from Harlan; Bobby Slusher, a good shooter and rebounder from Four Mile, Ky., and 6-9 center Ned Jennings, who had played for coach Charlie Finnell at Nicholas County (Carlisle).

So it was not a team which had been together and acquired any sense of togetherness or teamwork. It was a team which had to be assembled. There never was a time throughout the entire season that Rupp felt certain he had the five best players on the first team. Indeed, this may have been impossible. It seemed that the five best one game were not necessarily the five best the next.

Rupp changed his lineup several times. No one could argue much with the results, however. UK won 23 and lost only two of its scheduled games. The team was rated No. 1 in the nation most of the season and was nosed out by Kansas State in the final polls before the NCAA tournament.

There is evidence, though, that this was not one of Rupp's great teams.

First, many of the big-name teams which had put strong, veteran players against the Fiddlin' Five the season before had been hit heavily by graduation and had not been as fortunate in rebuilding as Rupp. Second, UK did not win the Southeastern Conference title. Third, the team made a quick—and for UK fans, embarrassing—departure from the NCAA tournament.

The closest thing to a regular lineup Rupp had was 6-3 Lickert and 6-4 Cox at forwards, 6-7 Mills at center, with 5-9 Parsons and 6-0 Coffman at guards. However, Slusher got some starts at forward, with Lickert playing guard. Cohen moved into the first five at guard several times and Jennings got three starts in the pivot.

Others who played were Phil Johnson (son of UK's all-time best power football runner, Man o' War Bert Johnson, who played in 1934, '35, '36), Howard Dardeen, Lowell Hughes and Al Robinson.

Cox scored 26 points and Mills 20 as UK beat Florida State 91-68 in the opener. Hugh Durham, a 5-11 guard who had played for Louisville Eastern High, scored 30 for Florida State.

Rupp began to suspect he might have

"We won this thing last season," Johnny Cox seems to be reminding several Kentucky teammates as he points to the NCAA letters painted in the center of Louisville's Freedom Hall.

UK was practicing in the big arena for a game with Illinois. To Cox's left, in order, are Bill Lickert, Don Mills, Sid Cohen and Bennie Coffman.

a good season when UK defeated Temple 76-71. Temple led 41-34 at halftime at Philadelphia, but Cox scored 15 points and Parsons 10 in the second half to pull it out.

Cohen, a Brooklyn, N.Y., player recruited by Rupp at a coaching clinic for the U.S. Army in Europe, had his first big night with 19 points in a 78-64 victory over Duke.

After Southern Methodist and St. Louis were beaten, Maryland came to Lexington. UK was hopelessly behind, 54-51, with 10 seconds to play. UK called time-out and Coffman was told to drive for the basket.

Maryland coach Bud Milliken was doing some instructing of his own during the timeout. "Let them have the basket. Don't try to guard because we'll still be ahead by one," he said.

When Coffman drove under the basket, Maryland's Al Bunge couldn't resist. He tried to block the layup. Coffman's shot went in and he was fouled with three seconds to play. Coffman sank the free throw to put the game into overtime. Cox hit a 15-foot shot and Parsons dropped in two free throws in the extra period. UK won 58-56.

Slusher Comes Through

UK beat Ohio State 95-76 on the first night of the UK Invitational although Lickert and Mills were hospitalized with intestinal virus and didn't play. Slusher took Lickert's place and scored 23 points

and had 13 rebounds. Jennings started at center but Phil Johnson went in midway of the first half and played most of the game.

Mills was back in action the next night, scoring 17 points as a reserve as West Virginia was outgunned 97-91. Slusher scored 19 points in Lickert's place. Jerry West, now a junior, pumped in 36 points for the losers. "West is the best I've ever seen," Rupp said.

UK made it 11 victories in a row by downing Navy, Illinois and Georgia Tech. The win over Illinois was by 76-75 in Louisville's Freedom Hall. It drew 18,274 spectators over slick streets. UK almost blew the game when Illinois put on a full-court press in the last minute.

Vanderbilt ended UK's streak 75-66 at Nashville. Vandy was coached by young Roy Skinner, filling in for ailing head coach Bob Polk. Jim Henry of New Albany was Vandy's big scorer with 29 points.

After that SEC loss, UK won its next seven conference games before going into Starkville, Miss., to tangle with Mississippi State and its great Bailey Howell. Each team had an 18-1 record and each had lost once in the SEC. UK was ranked No. 1 nationally, State was 13th. Howell was third in the nation in scoring with a 28-point average.

He scored 27 points for James (Babe) McCarthy's State team as it whipped UK 66-58.

UK won its final five games, including

a 71-52 margin over Notre Dame in Chicago when Lickert scored 24 points and held Tom Hawkins to 13. Lickert also outrebounded the Irish All-America 17-13.

UK also got revenge on Vandy, 83-71, in Lexington. Cox hit a career-high 36 points with 17 rebounds as Tennessee was defeated 69-56 in the regular-season finale.

Mississippi State, which had a final 24-1 record, won the SEC title but passed up the NCAA tournament because of school officials' stand on racial integration. The SEC chose UK to represent it in the NCAA regional at Evanston, Ill.

UK's opening opponent: Peck Hickman's University of Louisville team which had a 17-10 record but which had won 12 of its last 15.

UK took a 29-14 lead before U of L started clicking. U of L's half-court pressing defense disrupted UK's offense more and more as the game progressed. Only Lickert with 16 points had a good shooting game for UK. Cox hit only 3 of 15 shots as UK lost 76-61.

The next night U of L scored another upset—88-81 over Michigan State to advance to the NCAA finals to be held in Louisville. UK, with Bennie Coffman hitting 28 points, lashed Marquette 98-69 for third place.

Cox and Lickert were selected to the All-Southeastern Conference team, and Cox was chosen All-America. Johnny had come a long way since those backyard hook shots.

Lickert helps UK jolt Lucas and company

Adolph Rupp, his face an expressionless mask, walked off the Memorial Coliseum court behind his University of Kentucky basketball team.

UK trailed Ohio State 59-49 at halftime and if there was anything that burned Rupp up, it was a loss at home. As soon as he and assistant coach Harry Lancaster reached the locker room, they began to outline changes in the game plan.

"We'll sacrifice our fast break to get more defensive rebounding," Rupp said. "When Ohio State shoots, everyone goes to the boards. We've got to keep them from getting those second shots."

Then Rupp ordered his team to the double-post offense made popular throughout Kentucky and Tennessee by Vanderbilt coach Bob Polk. If a team wasn't prepared for it, the offense usually was good for a number of layups and close-in shots.

Rupp had one last message for his players: "PLAY SOME DEFENSE! GET ON THOSE GUYS TIGHTER!"

When the second half started, UK started to break through the Ohio State defense. UK guards Bill Lickert and Bennie Coffman began to drive under for layups. Now Rupp was getting that tight defense he wanted. Ohio State had hit 25 of 39 shots in the first half for 64 per cent, but now Jerry Lucas, John Havlicek and Mel Nowell were missing a few more.

When it was over UK had won 96-93 in probably the greatest offensive display to that time in the Coliseum. Lucas scored 34 points and Havlicek 16 for Ohio State, but Lickert hit 29 and Coffman 26 for UK. UK shot 55.4 per cent for the game, Ohio State 49.4.

That victory was the high spot in a disappointing UK season. It was one of the most satisfying of many fine games Lickert would have in three years as an All-Southeastern player. He had that rare ability of playing his best games against the best teams.

Lickert had been twice an All-State player for coach Ralph Carlisle at Lexington Lafayette High — once as a center, then as a 6-3 guard his final season. He was chosen All-America as a senior.

In three high school seasons Lickert scored 1,745 points, an average of 22.2 a game. He averaged 24.4 his last season. His most memorable games were:

Adolph Rupp with his versatile star, Bill Lickert. Lickert, who usually played forward, was All-Southeastern Conference three times.

✔ Scoring 43 points against Madison Central, a Lafayette record.

✔ Leading Lafayette to the 1957 state high school championship with 26 points against Roy (Doc) Adams' Louisville Eastern team.

✔ And scoring 32 points in a beautiful all-round exhibition of basketball for the Kentucky All-Stars in a victory over Indiana's All-Stars at Louisville. In a game at Indianapolis, Lickert (he wore No. 1 as the state's Mr. Basketball) scored 18 points as Carlisle's Kentucky All-Stars won again.

As a sophomore at UK, Lickert's greatest performance was in a head-to-head duel with Notre Dame's Tom Hawkins. Lickert outscored the 6-5 Hawkins 24-13 and outrebounded him 17-13. That night

in Chicago Stadium, Frank McGuire moved his North Carolina team from seats at one end of the court to the other so that his players could watch Lickert's defense on Hawkins.

UK Loses Two Players

Lickert played forward mostly his sophomore year. He was back at that position again when his junior season, 1959-60, started. Rupp's No. 1 job was to find someone to replace Johnny Cox at the other forward.

This was a crucial question because Rupp had lost two players who figured high in UK plans at forward, Bobby Slusher and Howard Dardeen, for disciplinary reasons. Rupp realized the ab-

sence of Slusher, brilliant at times as a sophomore, could turn the whole season the wrong way.

Rupp opened the season with Lickert and 6-5 sophomore Allen (The Horse) Feldhaus, from Burlington, Ky., at forwards; 6-9 junior Ned Jennings, Nicholas County, at center, with 5-9 junior Dick Parsons, Harlan, and 6-1 Sid Cohen, Brooklyn, N.Y., at guards.

After a couple of games, Rupp moved 6-7 senior Don Mills of Berea into Feldhaus' place. Mills also started at center at times and 6-4 Carroll Burchett of Fuget, Ky., got a dozen starts at forward.

Coffman, the 6-foot senior from Huntington, W. Va., shared the starting guard positions with Parsons and Cohen. In the Ohio State game, Lickert was shifted to guard in place of Parsons to get more height in the lineup.

With the experience on his squad, Rupp figured to have another good season. But something went wrong—the schedule killed UK. After an opening victory over Colorado State, UK hit the road for four straight tough games.

The Wildcats beat Johnny Wooden's UCLA team 68-66 as Lickert scored 25 points and Cohen got five points right at the end. The next night Southern California trimmed UK 87-73. A week later at St. Louis, UK lost 73-61. UK ran its record to 3-2 by winning at Kansas 77-72 in overtime. Wayne Hightower hit 33 points for Kansas. Jennings came through with 27 for UK.

Lickert Impresses West

Next: the UK Invitational. As usual it was a strong field. North Carolina, UK's first opponent, was 3-0 and had defeated Kansas 60-49. West Virginia, with the incomparable Jerry West, was 6-0, and tall St. Louis had a 5-1 record.

UK got by North Carolina the first night 76-70. Jerry West was simply too good in the final. He scored 33 points despite suffering a broken nose, putting West Virginia well on the way to a 79-70 decision. Lickert, a good defensive man, guarded West, but got in foul trouble quickly. Even so, West said Lickert was "one of the best I've played against."

After outgunning Temple 97-92 in Louisville, UK returned home for the exciting offensive battle with Ohio State.

Beating the big Ohio State team reassured Rupp a bit as to the potential of the UK team. "If we'd played like this every game, we'd be undefeated," he said. To his players he said, "See what you can do if you put your mind to it."

Rupp's spirits plummeted in the next game. John (Whack) Hyder brought Georgia Tech to Memorial Coliseum and defeated UK 62-54.

Over the years Hyder had learned to disrupt UK's patterns by putting extreme defensive pressure on Rupp's forwards. It was difficult for UK to run plays when it couldn't get the ball to a forward at the proper place and the proper time. A Kentuckian, Dave Denton of Bowling Green, scored 18 points for Tech.

UK went to Nashville and beat Vanderbilt 76-59 as Carroll Burchett played his first good game. Burchett, a red-shirt the previous season, was slowed in the earlier

games while recovering from hepatitis. He hit 10 of 14 shots at Vandy and finished with 24 points.

After beating SEC opponents Louisiana State and Tulane, UK went to Tennessee without Lickert. Lickert had been experiencing pain in a thigh as far back as the Ohio State game. It steadily got worse, so bad that he had difficulty driving his car to the games. After hitting only three of 13 shots against LSU and three of 16 against Tulane, he had to reveal his trouble.

At first doctors feared he might have a tumor, but surgery revealed it to be calcification of a muscle.

UK overcame a 10-point deficit to defeat Tennessee 78-68. Next was a rematch at Georgia Tech, now leading the SEC

Strong Allen Feldhaus was a reserve forward as a UK sophomore.

with a 4-0 record. This time Tech's margin was even more decisive, 65-44.

Rupp had hoped to spring a surprise on Tech. He had planned to start Roger Newman, a 6-3 forward from Greenville, Ky., in Lickert's position. Newman had averaged 16 points a game as a freshman in 1956-57, had left UK, but now was back practicing with the team.

However, SEC commissioner Bernie Moore ruled that Newman was not eligible against Tech or for the rest of the season because he had played YMCA basketball during the academic year. UK's interpretation was that Newman was eligible because he was not a member of the UK team when he played YMCA basketball.

With Lickert still on the sidelines, UK downed Georgia, Florida and Mississippi. He got back into action for 11 minutes as a substitute in a 90-59 victory over Mississippi State. The long shooting of Parsons and Cohen wrecked State's zone.

After defeating Notre Dame and Vanderbilt (Lickert was back as a starter), UK was ready for the game which would decide whether Kentucky would fail to win the SEC championship for the second straight year. Auburn and UK each had two conference defeats.

UK trailed 61-60 with four seconds left and had possession on side court. Rupp wanted Lickert or sophomore Larry Pursiful to take the final shot. Cohen was to put the ball in play. He wanted to get the ball to Lickert but three Auburn players ganged up on the UK forward.

The quick-thinking Cohen thrust the ball back to the official.

"What are you giving the ball to me for?" asked the official.

"I didn't think you had asked if the captains were ready," Cohen replied.

"Yes, I did. Here's the ball. Let's go," the official snapped.

Then Cohen looped the ball to Allen Feldhaus under the basket. But 6-10 Auburn sophomore John Helmlinger swung an arm wildly to tip away what would have been the winning basket.

UK had to play the last 28 minutes without Dick Parsons, who went out with a sprained ankle. Auburn's winning margin was provided by a former Frankfort (Ky.) Good Shepherd High School player, Jimmy Fibbe, on two free throws just before UK's last desperate play.

Auburn went on to win the SEC with a 12-2 record, but was ineligible for the NCAA tournament because the school was on probation. The tourney berth went to second-place Georgia Tech, which finished with three SEC losses. UK, with four conference defeats, finished third after losing its final league game to Tennessee, 65-63.

A season-ending win over Pittsburgh gave UK an 18-7 record, the worst since the 17-8 mark of 1940-41. Yet, Rupp could look back and see how the outcome could have been a lot different. Slusher and Dardeen could have made a big difference at forward, a thin position all season.

The player losses made the early trip west even more difficult. "We just bit off more than we could chew," Harry Lancaster said.

Lickert's ailment, plus various other minor injuries, prevented Rupp from ever settling on a lineup. He used 16 different starting combinations.

Lickert, Mills, Cohen, Coffman, Parsons, Jennings and Burchett drew the most starting assignments. But Jim McDonald, a sophomore from Louisville St. Xavier, started eight games. Feldhaus and Pursiful started twice.

Others who played were Eddie Mason, Herky Rupp (Adolph's son), Harry Hurd, Roy Roberts and Al Robinson.

Fred Taylor's Ohio State team recovered well enough from its early loss to UK to win the Big Ten Conference and the NCAA championship.

In a crisis, Rupp turns to Dick Parsons

Carroll Burchett turned in his best games as a relief man for UK.

Adolph Rupp was desperate.

For the first time in his 31 years at the University of Kentucky, one of his basketball teams had lost three straight Southeastern Conference games.

Within six days UK had lost at Vanderbilt, Louisiana State and Tulane. With a record of 7-6, UK was well along the road to an utterly disastrous season. Rupp knew he had to do something.

He did. He turned to the smallest man ever to start for him at UK—5-foot-9 Dick Parsons. The coach never made a wiser decision.

Parsons had been a starter for most of his first two years at UK, years in which Rupp's guards had been on the small side. But as a senior this 1960-61 season Parsons had been pushed into a reserve role when Rupp decided to go with 6-4 Roger Newman as a running mate for 5-11 sharpshooter Larry Pursiful.

Now, after 13 games, Rupp strongly suspected he had made a wrong move. First, Newman wasn't a good ball handler and his shooting range was limited. Second, without Parsons UK didn't have as much speed and defensive quickness. Third, it didn't have as much leadership on the court.

Of course, this was all hindsight on Rupp's part. If he had realized at the start that playing Newman at guard wouldn't work, he wouldn't have tried it.

Rupp changed his lineup for a game with old rival Tennessee. Newman moved up to forward to team with 6-3 senior Bill Lickert. Parsons took over the guard position alongside junior Pursiful. Rupp stayed with 6-9 senior Ned Jennings at center.

The box score showed only modest contributions by Parsons. He scored eight points, and Newman didn't get a point at forward. But UK beat Tennessee 83-54.

Georgia Tech edged UK 62-60 at Atlanta in the next game on Roger

Kaiser's shot with two seconds to play. But Kentucky won its next 10 games to earn a berth in the NCAA regional tournament at Louisville. Parsons started every game in the winning streak.

He didn't score much, but with Parsons in the lineup UK cut down on the errors that has lost earlier games. In one game, against Auburn, Kentucky lost the ball only four times without getting a shot.

Parsons had been an all-round athlete at Harlan High School. He was all-conference in football as a quarterback and halfback, three times all-conference as a guard in basketball and a shortstop with professional possibilities on the baseball team. He also squeezed in some time with the track team, running the half-mile.

His senior year he made second-team All-State in basketball and his coach, Joe Gilly, urged him to think about attending UK.

Parsons, an intelligent guy who was third in his class academically, had some doubts. After all, he was small even by high school standards. Gilly convinced his clever guard that he had a future at Kentucky.

"If you think I can make it, I'd like to go," Parsons said.

One of Parsons' greatest assets was his defensive ability, thanks to some solid training by Gilly. Gilly insisted that his teams play man-to-man defense.

"Some of you may have a chance to play college basketball, and I don't want to hurt your chances by having you get used to standing around in a zone," Gilly said.

Parsons was one of UK's finest defensive players in his three years on the varsity. Rupp usually assigned him the best offensive guard and Parsons rarely let his coach down.

"If I could hold my man, it was like getting points myself," Parsons once said.

Parsons was one of seven lettermen

back for the 1960-61 season. Rupp had two junior college transfers, 6-5 Vince Del Negro of Northeast Mississippi and Doug Pendygraft of Lindsey Wilson.

Rupp was torn with indecision throughout preseason practice. In the opening game, a 72-56 victory over Virginia Military Institute, Rupp started 6-3 senior Bill Lickert and 6-5 junior Allen Feldhaus at forwards, Del Negro in the pivot and 6-foot junior Larry Pursiful and 6-4 senior Roger Newman at guards.

Newman, playing his first game for UK, made his debut a good one with 20 points. He had played freshman basketball at UK after making All-State at Greenville, Ky., but left his sophomore year, after some scholastic difficulties, to attend Furman. He was back at UK as a junior, only to be ruled ineligible (after joining the Kentucky team at midyear) because he had played a couple of YMCA games.

So his first year on the varsity would be his last. Newman had a world of potential, but he was lacking in some of the polish a player normally would acquire by his senior year.

The next game, against Florida State, was Parsons' undoing. He started at guard, Newman moving to forward in place of Feldhaus. Kentucky lost 63-58.

Rupp made some changes for the Notre Dame game in Louisville. He put 6-9 senior Ned Jennings in at center for Del

Adolph Rupp with the seniors of his 1960-61 team. From left are Roger Newman, Ned Jennings, Bill Lickert and Dick Parsons.

Negro, who hadn't scored a point in the Florida State loss. And he shifted Newman back to guard in Parsons' place. UK downed Notre Dame 68-62 before 12,000 fans in Louisville's Freedom Hall.

Rupp was elated when UK went to Greensboro, N.C., and defeated a North Carolina team rated third and fifth in two polls 70-65. UK hit 22 of 24 free throws in the second half (Pursiful was 11 for 11).

Then Kentucky went to Philadelphia where a 5-10 guard, Bruce Drysdale, popped in 25 points for Temple, a 66-58 victor.

Newman scored 24 points and Pursiful 21 as Kentucky bounced back to whip Illinois 83-78 in the opening round of the UK Invitational Tournament. UK led by only 78-76 with 47 seconds left when Jim McDonald intercepted a pass under the basket and scored a layup to put the game out of reach.

McDonald made a costly mistake the next night. With Kentucky leading St. Louis 60-58 in the championship game with 15 seconds to play, McDonald took a 15-foot shot. He missed, St. Louis rebounded and scored to send the game into overtime. St. Louis won it 74-72 on Tom Kieffer's jump shot with five seconds left. Lickert played superbly in the defeat, hitting 11 of 17 shots, scoring 29 points and leading both teams in rebounding with 12.

UK got back on the right track with three straight victories—over Missouri, Miami (Ohio) and Georgia Tech. Rupp couldn't find anyone who could handle Tech's Roger Kaiser, the All-America guard from Dale, Ind. Kaiser scored 38 points, the most anyone ever totaled against Kentucky. His total broke the old mark of 37 by Alabama's Jerry Harper, set in 1956 and equaled by Mississippi State's Bailey Howell in '57.

Then UK hit the skids with the three

losses to Vanderbilt, Louisiana State and Tulane. Enter Dick Parsons. After the victory over Tennessee and the loss at Georgia Tech, UK settled down to play its steadiest basketball of the season, even though center Del Negro had left school.

Part of the credit for Kentucky's success in the stretch must go to the relief work of Carroll Burchett. The 6-4 junior from Fuget, Ky., had a knack of playing his best as a substitute. Rupp put Burchett in the starting lineup for a couple of games when Newman was in a shooting slump. But Burchett didn't play as well as a starter, and Newman came off the bench against Georgia to score 24 points. Rupp put Newman back in the regular lineup.

Reserves available all season besides Burchett, Feldhaus, Pendygraft and Mc-

Jim McDonald made a timely interception and layup against Illinois.

Donald were Herky Rupp, the coach's son, Scotty Baesler and Bernie Butts. Harry Hurd, George Atkins, Roy Roberts and Pat Doyle were held out of action.

After winning three games in a row, UK went to Starkville, Miss., to play Mississippi State. Babe McCarthy's team was first in the Southeastern Conference with an 8-0 record and was 16-3 overall. Newman, by now beginning to feel at home at forward, scored 24 points as UK surprised State 68-62. Every time UK started to bog down, Newman came through with a basket.

Newman came back with 26 points as UK knocked off Johnny Wooden's UCLA team 77-76. Pursiful scored 21.

UK avenged its earlier loss to Vanderbilt, winning 60-59 in Lexington, then defeated Alabama, Auburn and Tennessee to complete the regular SEC schedule. Mississippi State won the SEC title with an 11-3 record, UK and Vandy finishing in a tie for second at 10-4. A playoff was arranged in Knoxville to decide the NCAA representative after Mississippi State decided not to go because of the integration issue.

Headed by Pursiful's 21 points, all five UK starters scored in double figures as Kentucky beat Vandy 88-67.

Rupp wondered afterwards if he had another Fiddlin' Five.

"But I won't say my club now is as good unless it can do what the '58 bunch did—win the NCAA," Rupp said.

It was no great surprise that after the playoff UK went to Chicago and lost 88-72 to Marquette in the last game of the regular season. It was the worst defeat of the season for Kentucky, which apparently suffered a letdown.

UK won its first game of the NCAA regional in Louisville, defeating Morehead 71-64 behind Lickert's 28 points and 16 rebounds. The University of Louisville lost by only 56-55 to No. 1-ranked Ohio State in the other first-round game in Freedom Hall before a record crowd of 18,883.

UK vs. Ohio State. There was little doubt that UK's chances were wrapped up in big Ned Jennings. He had to keep Ohio State center Jerry Lucas in check. But Jennings quickly got into foul trouble and had to turn the job over to the 6-4 Burchett. Burchett just wasn't big enough to handle the 6-8 Lucas.

Lucas, getting in close all the time, hit 14 of 18 shots and scored 33 points as Ohio State won 87-74. UK had one satisfaction: Newman scored 31 points and Lickert 17, a total of 48. Ohio State forwards John Havlicek (8) and Richie Hoyt (2) totaled 10. Lickert and Havlicek guarded each other.

It was UK's ninth loss, the most Rupp had endured in one season.

Lickert was named to the NCAA all-regional team, made All-Southeastern Conference for the third straight year and was chosen second team All-America by the Helms Athletic Foundation. Parsons joined the UK baseball team and made All-America shortstop that spring.

Lickert, Newman, Parsons and Jennings would not return next season, but Rupp was counting heavily on a 6-5 blond smoothie coming up from the freshman team, Charles (Cotton) Nash.

Nash and Pursiful put UK back into national picture

The theory is simple. It's like making war. You pose a threat over a wide area, spreading the defense. Then you hit the enemy. First one place, then another. Suddenly there's confusion and panic. Then total collapse.

Adolph Rupp had something like that in mind at the start of the 1961-62 basketball season. He could put strong, mobile 6-foot-5 sophomore Charles (Cotton) Nash at center. Nash would give Kentucky the inside scoring punch it had lacked for several years.

Out at guard Rupp would station a couple of 5-11 players, Scotty Baesler and Larry Pursiful. If one of them could blossom into an 18- to 20-point scorer, UK would have a Mr. Outside to go with Mr. Inside Cotton Nash.

Pursiful seemed the most likely to develop into a big point producer. The quiet senior from Four Mile, Ky., had been a regular the season before, averaging 13.4 points as the team's No. 3 scorer behind forwards Bill Lickert and Roger Newman. Rupp believed that with a little more confidence Pursiful could become the finest medium-range shooter in UK history.

Actually, Pursiful didn't lack confidence. He simply needed time to adjust to shooting behind the screens that UK set. Basically, it meant that he had to shoot a little quicker than he had in high school. A player has only a split second to decide whether or not to shoot. Frequently, Pursiful said, "No," and passed that ball to a teammate, while Rupp and assistant coach Harry Lancaster were yelling, "Yes."

Bill Lickert had the same trouble all through his career at UK. "I didn't have the shots," he'd say. Then the coaches would show him game films and say, "Yes you did. Here, here and here."

Pursiful came to UK with a background as a deadeye shooter. He played three years for Lone Jack High, near Four Mile. One of his teammates was Bobby Slusher, who also attended UK. Lone Jack lost only two games during Pursiful's junior year under coach G. H. Hendrickson, one to eventual 1957 state champion Lexington Lafayette and the other to Clay County in the semifinals of the regional tourney.

Pursiful's family moved a few miles to East Pineville his senior year, so he played his final high school season at Bell County for Willie Hendrickson (not G. H. Hendrickson's brother). Pursiful averaged 27 points a game and led

Bell County to the district tournament championship. Again Pursiful's team lost to Clay County in the regional.

Pursiful made The Courier-Journal all-state team after his senior season and signed with UK, which had started recruiting him as a junior. Curiously, no other school offered him a scholarship.

"I'd always wanted to go to Kentucky and I guess I had indicated that," said Pursiful, who also played for Ralph Carlisle's Kentucky High School All-Stars against Indiana's All-Stars in the summer of 1958.

Baesler Gets Good Start

Pursiful had an excellent freshman season at UK, averaging 19 points and hitting a high of 35 in one game. That was enough to convince Rupp the burr-haired youth could shoot.

Rupp kept after Pursiful to shoot more often all through the guard's sophomore year. On one trip when the UK players were about to leave for some shooting practice at the game site, Rupp told him: "You might as well stay here. You won't shoot anyway."

Pursiful started a couple of games near the end of his first season, and was in the

Scotty Baesler, stretching for a rebound, was a starting UK guard.

opening lineup for every game as a junior.

"I think everything you shoot is going in," Rupp, the psychologist, told him many times that season. So Pursiful put the ball in the air. He scored 21 points four times that season and he became more adept at slowing down to take the jump shot, then turning on the speed to drive under for the layup.

Rupp still wasn't absolutely sure that Pursiful would score high enough to be the threat UK needed to go with Nash for the 1961-62 campaign. There was a time early in the season when Baesler seemed to be the best bet to be the top long-range gun.

UK opened against Miami (Ohio) and won 93-61. Nash led the way with 25 points and 17 rebounds. Pursiful with 17 points and Baesler with 15 played well, but the competition wasn't the strongest.

The next game was against nationally third-ranked Southern California. Baesler, who had played at Lexington Bryan Station High, hit 12 of 18 shots and finished with 26 points. Nash didn't have a good game. Harassed by 6-5 Ken Stanley, Southern Cal's defensive ace, Cotton hit only 4 of 11 shots and scored 12 points as UK lost 79-77. After Cotton made three straight bad passes, Rupp pulled the big blond out to stay with 12 minutes left.

"Those two Kentucky guards are the best I've seen," Southern Cal coach Forrest Twogood said. "With a little more experience Kentucky is going to have a terrific basketball team."

Baesler popped in 20 points as visiting St. Louis was beaten 86-77. Rupp praised forwards Roy Roberts and Jim McDonald for "a wonderful defensive job" in holding Tom Kieffer to 13 points. Roberts started on Kieffer and, after tiring, turned the task over to McDonald with four minutes left in the first half. McDonald started the second half and stayed in until Roberts returned with seven minutes to play.

Roberts, 6-4, was from Atlanta, Ga., where he was a high scorer and an all-state performer. Held out of action during what would have been his junior season, Roberts had gradually developed into a defensive expert. A senior academically, he still had two years of eligibility.

"I learned a lot from Bill Lickert my year as a red-shirt," Roberts once said. "I guarded him most of the time during scrimmages, and he was great."

Cotton Nash (44) and Larry Pursiful (24) were UK's "Mr. Inside and Mr. Outside" in '61-62. Here they're helping beat Notre Dame 100-53.

Guarding Lickert paid off in another way, too. Lickert told Rupp that Roberts was the toughest defensive man he played against. Since Lickert usually drew the best defensive player on the other team, Rupp was impressed.

After easy UK victories over Baylor and Temple, Pursiful still hadn't had that explosive scoring game Rupp was looking for. It came in the UK Invitational Tournament. Pursiful took 27 shots and hit 17 of them for 34 points in the UKIT opener, a 96-69 triumph over Tennessee. The next night, in an 80-67 victory over Kansas State for the title, Pursiful scored 26 points. Mr. Outside had arrived.

UK had arrived back in national prominence, too, because Tex Winter's Kansas State team had won seven straight games and was rated third and fourth in two wire service polls. UK wasn't in the top 10.

Kentucky Wins 16 in Row

UK won its next 11 games, giving it a 16-game winning streak before it was broken by Mississippi State. One of the games in the streak was a 100-53 romp over Notre Dame in Louisville. Nash scored 31 points, hitting 12 of 21 shots. He thrilled a crowd of 16,925 with several high, arching 30-foot shots.

Pursiful, Baesler, Nash and Roberts started as they had every game, and Rupp had 6-4 senior Carroll Burchett in the lineup at forward for the third straight game in place of Allen Feldhaus.

Also playing against Notre Dame were Jim McDonald, Feldhaus, Ted Deeken, Charlie Ishmael, George Atkins, Herky Rupp, Pat Doyle, Tommy Harper, Doug Pendygraft and George Critz.

The next game, against Virginia, Rupp was able to use 15 players again. This time Harry Hurd played instead of Critz.

The game which most clearly showed the efficiency of UK's inside-outside attack was at Tennessee. Pursiful scored 30 points and Nash 30 as UK won 95-82. Burchett helped up front with 21.

Now that Burchett was starting at forward, Feldhaus became the ace fireman. He thrived in the role. The broad-shouldered 6-5, 225-pound senior came off the bench in three straight road games—at Georgia Tech, Georgia and Florida—to give UK a needed lift. In those three games he hit 14 of 21 shots and grabbed 24 rebounds. His best game was against Florida when he scored 16 points.

Throughout UK's winning streak, it became more apparent that the Southeastern Conference showdown game would be played on Feb. 12 in Lexington, against Mississippi State. When the date arrived UK had a 17-1 record, was leading the SEC at 8-0 and was ranked second in the nation behind Ohio State. Mississippi State was 18-1 and 7-1 (it had lost to Vanderbilt) and was rated ninth in the U.S.

Mississippi State took an early lead, then coach Babe McCarthy spread his players and ordered them into his stall offense. A little cat-and-mouse dribbling and passing, then a quick drive for a layup. State hit 11 of 18 shots in the first half, taking a 28-22 lead, and most of them were layups.

"Dribble for 15 minutes and play defense for five," McCarthy told his players at halftime. They did exactly that, dribbling away the time and hitting seven of their eight shots as State won 49-44. One factor in UK's loss was that Pursiful hit only one of 10 shots.

Only Cotton Nash's scoring inside kept UK close.

"I was hoping one of you fellows would ask me how we handled Nash," a jubilant McCarthy said afterwards to reporters. "I was going to tell you my daddy used to have a cotton gin and I was always good at handling cotton."

"He scored 23 points," a reporter reminded Babe.

"But that wasn't enough," McCarthy shot back.

Pursiful, who had scored only five points against State, got only five again in an 87-80 victory over Vanderbilt. Again Nash carried the load with 38 points. By now Nash was well on his way to winning the SEC scoring championship.

UK didn't lose another SEC game, finishing with a 13-1 record to tie Mississippi State. Since State had defeated UK, McCarthy could have had the NCAA regional berth which goes to the SEC champ. But for the third time State officials turned down the tourney bid because of their stand on integrated sports.

UK's first regional opponent at Iowa City, Iowa, was little Butler University. Rupp had campaigned to get Tony Hinkle's Butler team into the NCAA. "Who in the devil is Butler," a member of the NCAA tournament committee had asked Rupp. Rupp had carefully explained that although Butler was a small school, it had compiled a good record against a tough schedule. In an NCAA first-round game at Lexington, Butler had justified Rupp's faith by beating Bowling Green, Ohio, 56-55.

Bowling Green had a couple of future pro stars in the lineup — Nate Thurmond and Butch Komives.

That victory advanced Butler to Iowa City against UK. For a half, Butler's well-drilled team was all UK could handle. At the intermission, Kentucky led by only a point. Rupp switched from his usual single pivot attack to the double post offense that had baffled Ohio State two years before. With Nash scoring 23 points and Pursiful 26, Kentucky won 81-60.

Ohio State, meanwhile, gained the regional final against UK by whipping Western Kentucky 93-73 despite 26 points by Western's Bobby Rascoe.

Rupp knew he would have to hold down Jerry Lucas to beat Ohio State. UK's plan was for Carroll Burchett to play in front of the 6-8 Lucas with Nash slipping in behind him. However, Nash often failed to get there quickly enough. Lucas scored 33 points and State's defensive whiz, John Havlicek, held Nash to 14. Ohio State won 74-64. Pursiful was best for Kentucky with 21 points.

Despite the final loss, Rupp had much to be pleased about.

UK had bounced back into national prominence, and with Nash on hand figured to stay there for two more years. Nash became the first SEC sophomore scoring champ in 10 years (since Bob Pettit in 1952) with his 23.8 average. Pursiful set two UK shooting records, hitting 51 per cent from the field and 80.4 on free throws.

Nash and Pursiful both were named All-SEC and Nash was placed on the U.S. Basketball Writers' All-America team.

Cotton Nash not enough to keep Kentucky near top

Cotton Nash turned down a baseball bonus to play basketball for UK.

Pressure. Every athlete knows what it means. The heart beats a little faster, the hands sweat and concentration comes terribly, terribly hard.

No player ever arrived on the University of Kentucky varsity basketball team under more mental stress than Charles (Cotton) Nash. The pressure was there even before he played his first game, it was there the first time he stepped onto the Memorial Coliseum court before packed stands and it was there until the final second of his senior year.

Nash joined the UK team under a set of circumstances that never had been duplicated. When he was a freshman averaging 26 points a game, UK was struggling through the worst record in Adolph Rupp's career.

Who was going to lead UK out of the wilderness of losing basketball? Nash, of course. Rupp talked about the 6-foot-5 blond as "the finest sophomore in the nation."

UK fans waited confidently for him to turn his magic loose on the teams that had kept Kentucky out of the Southeastern Conference throne room for three straight years and out of the NCAA championship since the Fiddlin' Five of 1958.

Nash knew from the start what was expected of him, which must have taken a little of the fun out of playing. He never talked about it, though; never complained, probably because he had been intent on being the best for so long that this seemed just another step in the world of athletics.

If there is one sentence which described Nash, it is this: He hated to be second best. Perhaps it was because he had so much natural athletic ability that he somehow realized from the start that he would compete on a high level.

Or perhaps it was his father, Frank Nash, who started tossing a football and baseball at Cotton when he was only 5 years old, who cultivated the urge to succeed. No one really knows.

Cotton was born in Jersey City, N.J., in 1942 when his family lived in nearby Kearney, N.J. Basketball was the last sport he took up. He got interested in basketball when he was 11 after his family moved to Charlestown, Ind.

Cotton plays for Barker

Frank Nash worked for a chemical company, and the Nashes lived within the confines of the Indiana Arsenal. There were 10 or 12 boys about Cotton's age who played constantly on an outdoor court.

Cotton played grammar school and junior high basketball at Jeffersonville. When he was a 6-3 sophomore he started playing for Cliff Barker on the Jeff High School team. Barker, a member of Rupp's Fabulous Five of 1948, knew at once that Cotton was a star in the making. Cotton averaged 15.6 points a game that season.

Then Frank Nash got traveling orders —to Orange, Tex. Cotton enrolled in Orange High that spring of his sophomore year in time to earn a letter in baseball.

Meanwhile, Frank had discovered that a Texas transfer rule which applied only to football and basketball would cost his son a year of eligibility in those two sports.

Louisiana had no such rule, so the Nashes moved to Lake Charles, La., 40 miles away.

Cotton went out for football and became a fine pass-catching end on a state championship team. He made all-state in football, basketball and track. When he went out for track, as a discus thrower, he didn't make the traveling squad for the first meet.

He borrowed a discus and called up a former coach for some extra instruction. He worked on weekends as well as during his team's regular practices. In the fifth meet of the season he broke the state discus record. Even then Cotton had to be the best.

Lake Charles didn't have a baseball team but Cotton played summer baseball as a long-ball hitting third baseman and pitcher. He was offered a sizable bonus to play pro baseball after his last year in high school. The lure of college basketball was too strong.

He Breaks Freshman Records

He had averaged 27.2 points as a junior and 33.2 as a senior for coach Carrell Dowies. After approaches by many schools, Cotton narrowed the field to Maryland, UCLA, Michigan State, Texas A & M, Tulane, Kentucky and St. Louis. He chose UK, his dad said, because "when we saw the Coliseum, Cotton just seemed to belong there."

He broke seven freshman scoring records at UK. His sophomore season wasn't easy. Perhaps it was a tribute to Nash's ability, but Rupp showed little patience with the sophomore. A perfect

example was the Southern Cal game, when Rupp pulled Cotton out with 12 minutes to play and kept him out.

For the most part, though, there was little to fault about Nash's first season. He led the SEC in scoring with a 23.4 average, teamed with outside shooter Larry Pursiful to give UK its best one-two punch in several years and did more than his share in helping UK to a 23-3 record and third-place in the national polls.

There was one catch to all this: UK fans expected Nash to keep Kentucky near the top in '62-'63. He couldn't do it simply because he didn't have enough help. Pursiful was gone. Without Mr. Outside's long-range sniping, Mr. Inside suddenly drew a crowd every place he went on the court.

Concentrating on Nash didn't always work, but it succeeded often enough to drop UK all the way to fifth in the SEC and far down in the national ratings with a 16-9 record.

Even when Nash wasn't stopped, UK was beaten at times because the team didn't have enough scoring balance. That's what happened in the opening game. Nash scored 34 points but only one other starter, sophomore guard Sam Harper of Clinton, Ky., with 12, got into double figures as UK lost 80-77 to Virginia Tech.

A pair of Kentuckians helped Tech hand Rupp the only opening loss of his career. Leland Melear, a product of Louisville Manual High, scored 24 points for Tech. Guy Strong, from Irvine and

a member of UK's '50 and '51 teams, did the scouting on UK. Strong was assistant to head coach Bill Mathews.

Rupp's lineup for that game was Nash and 6-4 senior Roy Roberts of Atlanta at forwards, 6-6 sophomore Don Rolfes of Harrison, Ohio, at center, with the 6-2 Harper and 5-11 senior Scotty Baesler at guards.

Nash scored 15 points and Baesler 14 as UK went to Philadelphia and beat Temple 56-52. Back home Rolfes had his first good game with 13 points and 18 rebounds as Florida State was defeated 83-54. Nash had 19 points and 19 rebounds. Charlie (Chili) Ishmael, a 6-5 junior from Mt. Sterling, started at guard in place of Sam Harper and was No. 3 scorer with 13.

Nash's 27 points and 20 rebounds carried UK by Northwestern 71-60. Bill Rohr, coach of the Big Ten team, said Nash was the difference.

Next was North Carolina, which was the first team to go all out to hold down Nash's scoring. Dean Smith assigned a small player, 6-1 Yogi Poteet, to guard the UK All-America with the other four Carolina players in a zone. After 12 minutes Carolina went to a pressing man-to-man and stayed in it until near the end when Smith ordered his team back to the zone. When Nash tried to get in close, he was double-teamed. He scored only 12 points and UK lost 68-66.

"He's the best I've played against," Poteet said. "I put him in a class with Art Heyman and Jeff Mullins of Duke. I didn't realize Nash was so big and strong."

Kentucky bounced back to win the UK Invitational Tournament, downing Iowa and West Virginia. Nash scored 27 points against Iowa, then gave a fantastic display of 30-foot shooting to hit 30 points in a 79-75 triumph over West Virginia. West Virginia All-America Rod Thorn also scored 30. One of West Virginia's forwards was Gale Catlett, who would join Rupp as an assistant coach in 1971.

John Adams, a 6-6 sophomore from Rising Sun, Ind., had replaced Rolfes as starting center against West Virginia. He also started against Dartmouth and Notre Dame. However, Rolfes won the job back when he came off the bench to score 20 points (Nash had 26)) to help UK down Notre Dame 78-70 before 17,101 fans at Louisville.

Only Nash with 16 and Rolfes with 13 scored in double figures in an 87-63 upset loss at St. Louis.

UK lost 86-85 in double overtime to Georgia Tech at Lexington. Rupp pulled Nash and Rolfes both out of the game after 12 minutes of the first half and UK behind by 10 points. They didn't get back in until only eight minutes were left in the game. Mike Tomasovich won it for coach John (Whack) Hyder on two free throws with seven seconds left in the second overtime. Nash got three shots for the entire game, hitting two of them.

Nash was pouring in the points again, however, with 27, 24 and 27 in victories over Vanderbilt, Louisiana State and Tulane. Ted Deeken, the sophomore from Louisville Flaget, also was seeing considerable action at forward. He scored 18 points against Tulane.

Among the other players used by Rupp in various games were Pat Doyle, Randy Embry, Tom Harper, Ron Kennett, Terry Mobley, Denny Radabaugh and George Critz.

Tennessee jolted UK's conference title hopes by defeating Kentucky 78-69. Tennessee was coached by Bill Gibbs, filling in for Ray Mears. Mears was out that season with a nervous breakdown.

Two games later UK went to Atlanta and lost to Georgia Tech again, this time by 66-62. After that UK had eight SEC games left. Three of them were losses to Vanderbilt, Mississippi State and Tennessee. Deeken started the last seven games.

Nash passed the 1,000-point mark in career scoring with 14 against Florida, the 19th game on UK's schedule. He had reached 1,000 quicker than any player in UK history.

Nash finished the season with a 20.6 average, third in the Southeastern Conference behind Tulane's Jim Kerwin (23.0) and Mississippi's Don Kessinger (21.8). Nash was named All-SEC and was picked on the All-America first team for the second year by the U.S. Basketball Writers Association.

Rupp started a pair of sophomore guards, 5-10 Embry of Owensboro and 6-2 Mobley of Harrodsburg, the last few games. Of his experienced players, Rupp would lose only Baesler and Roberts. A crop of talented players was winning 14 of 17 games for coach Harry Lancaster. Perhaps Nash would get that supporting cast he needed.

Forward Roy Roberts of Atlanta was a defensive specialist and a starter for two seasons at Kentucky.

Zone helps keep up-and-down UK up (mostly) in '64

Selecting high school basketball players for college teams isn't an exact science. It isn't even an art, so unpredictable are the results. It's more like a gamble in which a coach can only hope he wins more than 50 per cent of the time.

The difficulty involved, as Notre Dame football coach Ara Parseghian once said, is that no one can be sure how a young man will mature.

There is, of course, considerable skill involved in choosing talent on the hoof. An experienced, knowledgeable talent scout will come up with a higher percentage of winning players than the novice. But no matter how many years a coach puts in the job, he always will be confronted with tough decisions.

Do I take Johnny Jones, who's tall but not a good jumper? Or how about Joe Smith, the good shooter who's slow afoot?

Harry Lancaster made decisions like that for Adolph Rupp for more than 20 years. As Rupp's chief assistant until named athletic director in 1968, Lancaster was Rupp's No. 1 recruiter. Like all recruiters, Lancaster won some and lost some, but UK's records from the mid 1940s until the late 1960s indicate that he succeeded far more often than he failed.

One of Lancaster's right decisions was made in the summer of 1960 when he signed Ted Deeken.

Deeken Was Flaget Center

There were many who thought the coach was making a mistake. Deeken was 6 feet 4, but he had been a center on 1960 Kentucky high school champion Flaget. UK didn't need any more 6-4 centers.

That meant Deeken would have to switch to forward. A good many players had made that change after going to UK, but at 6-4 Deeken would have to be a mobile forward.

Deeken had averaged 18 points a game for Flaget as a senior. He made the Courier-Journal All-State team that season.

There were several things Lancaster liked about Deeken. First, Ted was a terrific competitor. Second, he was a jumper who could rebound with the 6-6 and 6-8 players. Third, he had played forward as a junior and would not be completely new to the position.

As a freshman at UK, Deeken averaged 17 points a game. He impressed Rupp many times in practice during his sophomore year, but he wasn't consistent. After a bad day, he'd get depressed and have worse days.

Deeken began his junior season as a substitute and finished as a regular. He averaged 9.8 points, but that wasn't a true indication of his ability since he had only seven starts.

Deeken was determined to make his final season at UK a good one. He practiced all summer.

Rupp called Deeken "the most improved player on the squad" before the 1963-64 season's first game. The sight of Deeken operating so efficiently and confidently boosted Rupp's hopes for a great season.

Rupp Springs a Zone

The coach had seniors Cotton Nash and Deeken to play forward, 6-6 John Adams at center, and a flock of players to pick from at guard. Rupp had juniors Terry Mobley, Randy Embry, Sam Harper and Ron Kennett; senior Charlie Ishmael, who had started 17 games as a junior, and a tall, poised sophomore, Tom Kron, who had been compared to Frank Ramsey as a freshman.

Rupp also had a pair of talented sophomores, Larry Conley and Lloyd (Mickey) Gibson, and three seniors: guard Tom Harper, center Larry Lentz and forward George Critz.

Rupp called Conley, Kron and Gibson "the Katzenjammer Kids, because they're always popping off like the kids in the comic strip."

These were the players, then, who would carry Kentucky back to the No. 1 position in the national polls for the first time in five years. Missing was center Don Rolfes, who had dropped out of school and would attend the University of Cincinnati.

It was an unusual season in some ways. Rupp would use a zone defense for the first time in his career, UK would win the Sugar Bowl tournament and the Southeastern Conference championship, but Kentucky's NCAA participation would end in utter disaster. At its peak, UK was a delight to watch, truly a perfectly-running basketball machine; at its worse, it wasn't even a good team.

It was apparent that UK's scoring would be concentrated at forward—in Nash and Deeken. Each of them hit 28 points in an opening victory over Virginia. The other three starters were Adams, Mobley and Embry.

Nash had 33 and Deeken 20 as Texas Tech was beaten. The significant aspect in that game was the play of sophomore Conley. The Ashland, Ky., All-Stater scored 17 points as a substitute and dazzled the fans with his clever feeds to Nash for easy baskets. Northwestern assistant coach Brad Snyder, scouting the game, predicted that Conley would be starting UK's next game—against Northwestern.

He was right. Conley took Nash's forward spot, and the senior All-America moved into the pivot in place of Adams. With Embry and Mobley at guards, that was Rupp's starting lineup for most games in the first half of the season.

UK showed some scoring balance in knocking off strong North Carolina in Lexington. Nash was outscored 32-23 by high-jumping Billy Cunningham, but Deeken scored 22, Mobley 21, Ishmael 17 and Conley 15. Ishmael was sent in to play defense because the 5-10 Embry was having trouble guarding a taller Carolina player. The 6-5 Ishmael did the defensive job, but he also hit eight of 12 shots.

After beating Baylor, unbeaten UK was up to second nationally behind defending national champion Chicago Loyola in the Associated Press poll.

UK was favored to win its own invitational tournament. Rupp's Wildcats breezed by Wisconsin 108-85 the first night and Wake Forest defeated Princeton 86-67. Nash was the high scorer of the night with 33 although Princeton's Bill Bradley had 30. This was the first game in which Mickey Gibson played. He was on disciplinary probation for the first five games.

Bradley Sets UKIT Records

The next night Nash scored 28 points as UK beat Wake Forest 98-75. Bradley scored 47 points and hit 18 field goals—both UKIT records—in Princeton's 90-87 triumph over Wisconsin in the consolation game. His two game total of 77 also was a tournament record.

After UK defeated Notre Dame 101-81 in Louisville, the undefeated Wildcats were ranked No. 1 in both wire service polls. It was the first time on top for UK since the 1958-59 season.

UK celebrated its No. 1 rating by defeating Loyola of New Orleans 86-64 in the Sugar Bowl tourney. Duke, with Jeff Mullins scoring 23 points, got to the finals by beating Auburn 84-67.

Terry Mobley, who had scored only one point against Loyola, was UK's man of the moment in the final. With a minute and a half to play, he hit a corner shot to tie the score 79-79.

With only 47 seconds left, and in possession of the ball, UK called time. UK dribbled the time away until, with three seconds left, Mobley banked in a shot from about 13 feet out. Nash was UK's leading scorer with 30 points and was named Most Valuable Player in the tournament. Mullins scored 26 and Hack Tison 27 for Duke.

UK took a 10-game winning streak to Georgia Tech, which had beaten UK twice the previous season. With R. D. Craddock, a Kentuckian from Hart Memorial High, scoring 24 points, Tech upset Kentucky 76-67. Nash got 20 points and Deeken 18, but then the scoring dropped all the way to Embry's 10.

Two nights later UK was stunned again, this time 85-83 at Vanderbilt. John Miller hit the winning shot with a second to play. Keith Thomas, who had played for Roy (Doc) Adams at Waggener High, hit several clutch shots for Vandy in what he called "my greatest thrill since I've been playing basketball."

After home victories over Louisiana State and Tulane, UK was ready to welcome strong Tennessee to Memorial Coliseum. Tennessee was coached by 37-year-old Ray Mears, who had gone to Tennessee from Wittenberg College of Springfield, Ohio. The previous season, supposed to be his first at Tennessee, he had sat out because of illness. But now his team had a 10-2 record and was 3-0 in the SEC.

Mears' top players were guard Danny Schultz, from Middlesboro, Ky., and 6-7 forward A. W. Davis. Schultz, who quarterbacked the Tennessee 1-3-1 offense, was averaging 17.3. Davis was right behind at 17.1. Rupp wasn't sure he could match up with Mears' players, so he didn't try.

Rupp surprised Tennessee with a 1-3-1

Ted Deeken is caught flat-footed on a drive-in shot by Georgia Tech's R. D. Craddock. Deeken made All-Southeastern Conference.

zone defense, the first zone he had used at UK. Lancaster had introduced the 1-3-1 at UK the previous season, teaching it to Conley, Kron and company on the freshman team. Lancaster had picked up the zone from Chuck Noe, head coach at Virginia Tech, at a coaching clinic.

Rupp changed his lineup to make the "trap" zone more effective, putting tall Tom Kron out on the point of the defense. The zone held Schultz to 11 points and, although Davis scored 20, UK won 66-57.

Afterward a lighthearted Rupp said, "We never have played a zone. That was a stratified transitional, hyperbolic paraboloid defense."

Most reporters were gone, running to meet deadlines, by the time Mears finally emerged from his locker room. Waiting was Russell Rice of the Lexington Leader. Mears told Rice that Kron's height was a factor in the success of UK's defense. "They were playing three of our men. They weren't worried about the other two . . . It's a good defense. That's all I can tell you," he said.

Rupp credited T. L. Plain, the former Kentucky Wesleyan coach, and Lexington Henry Clay High coach Elmer (Baldy)

Gilb with major contributions to the victory. They had done the scouting.

Next Georgia Tech came to Lexington. UK played an errorless second half to get revenge 79-62. Kron was still in the lineup. He had earned a starting spot with his play against Tennessee.

After a 77-72 victory at Florida, Rupp went to Georgia looking for his 700th career victory. He got it, too, 103-83 with Nash scoring 33 points and Deeken 29. No. 700 came in old Woodruff Hall, where Rupp had lost for the first time as a college coach back in 1931.

Lancaster kidded Georgia coach Harbin (Red) Lawson about the age of the old gym. "I believe Sherman's boys worked out here before they marched to the sea in the Civil War," Lancaster joked.

Rupp was serious when he asked, "Is our dressing room still a public toilet?"

He felt better when Lawson said, "No," because the UK coach knew that a Tennessee team had once been blocked in by a crowd of fans waiting to use the toilet facilities.

Embry to the Rescue

After beating Georgia, UK went home to down Mississippi and Missisippi State. UK tried a zone on State but it didn't work. So Randy Embry replaced Kron and Kentucky won 65-59 with a man-to-man. Embry hit three of four shots. More important, he shut off clever guard Doug Hutton in the second half. The victory put UK into the SEC lead with an 8-2 record, half a game ahead of Georgia Tech (7-2).

After Vanderbilt and Auburn were beaten, UK began to sag. First Alabama knocked off the Wildcats 65-59. After Tennessee was beaten 42-38 for the SEC title, St. Louis came to UK and won 67-60. It was plain that Kentucky was entering the NCAA regional at Minneapolis, Minn., far below the form it had displayed at mid-season in winning the Sugar Bowl. In addition, Gibson had an argument with UK trainer Joe Brown and was dropped from the squad by Rupp.

UK's first NCAA opponent was Jim Snyder's Ohio University team, which had beaten the University of Louisville in a first-round game. Candy Johnson and the other UK cheerleaders were there to give Kentucky some sideline support, but it didn't help. Nash had one of his worst games, scoring only 10 points and hitting four of 14 shots, as Kentucky lost 85-69. Mobley and Conley with 17 each were the only effective starters. Embry got 12 points as a reserve.

The next night Nash played much better, getting 23 points, but Chicago Loyola (loser to Michigan on the first night) defeated UK 100-91 for third place. It was UK's most dismal showing ever in the NCAA.

Nash and Deeken both made All-Southeastern Conference. Nash, who averaged 24 points a game to lead the SEC in scoring for the second time in three years, also was a consensus All-America. Nash also had become UK's all-time high career scorer with 1,770 points, moving ahead of Alex Groza's 1,744.

UK struggles, but Dampier and Riley show promise

It was halftime and Adolph Rupp stood at one end of the University of Kentucky locker room. His players sat on benches around the room listening to the coach give instructions for the second half.

As the players got to their feet to go back out on UK's Memorial Coliseum court, Rupp looked at Louie Dampier.

"If you get the shots, take 'em, but don't be a hog," Rupp said.

Dampier, who had scored 19 points in the first half, followed orders. He took his shots. When the game was over UK had defeated Iowa State 100-74, Dampier scoring 37 points.

Thirty-seven. More than Frank Ramsey, more than Ralph Beard, more than any UK guard had ever scored in one game. Making the performance all the more amazing, this was only Dampier's third college game.

Dampier came to UK from Southport, Ind., near Indianapolis. He was recruited as a senior by UK assistant coach Neil Reed.

"I'll never forget the first time I ever saw Louie," Reed once recalled. "I had gone to look at a player named Rick Jones of Muncie and I was with a bunch of Indianapolis coaches. They told me that without a doubt the boy to get was at Southport, Louie Dampier.

"I went out to watch him practice and no one would even tell me which one he was. They thought I was a scout from another high school. Finally I got down to a little guy wearing knee guards, looping the ball in on free throws. After practice, the coach (Blackie Braden) introduced me, and I told Louie he had a scholarship to UK."

Dampier didn't commit himself, but Reed continued to drop by occasionally to see the slender guard. At the end of the season Rupp saw the 160-pound senior hit nine straight field goals in a game. Dampier finally chose UK because "it played pattern basketball, about the same as I played at Southport."

Dampier, who had scored a school career-record 1,011 points in two years as a regular at Southport, averaged 26.7 points as a UK freshman. His 427 points were only 49 behind Cotton Nash's record, but Cotton had played two more games.

Rupp hardly knew what to do with Dampier as UK practiced for the start of the 1964-65 season. No one appreciates talent more than Rupp, and it was obvious that Louie was loaded with ability.

However, Rupp had several experienced guards. At forward, though, UK was thin and Rupp knew he would have to start sophomore Pat Riley there. Starting Dampier would mean two sophomores in the lineup.

"Dampier plays a lot like Vernon Hatton (UK All-America in 1958)," Rupp said at one practice. "Just medium fast but one of those guys who can solo on his own. They're the type who can go and get a basket when you need it."

Finally Rupp decided to go with the 6-foot Dampier in the opener against Iowa. If senior Terry Mobley hadn't missed two weeks of practice with an eye injury, he probably would have started instead of Dampier.

Other starters were 5-10 Randy Embry of Owensboro, Ky., at the other guard, 6-6 John Adams of Rising Sun, Ind., at center, with 6-3 Riley of Schenectady, N.Y., and 6-3 Larry Conley of Ashland, Ky., at forward.

Dampier got off to a good start, drop-

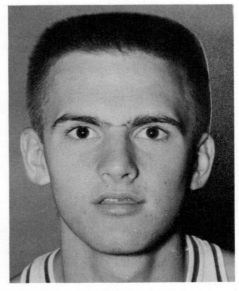

Guard Randy Embry's specialty was a long two-hand shot.

ping in 9 of 18 shots as UK beat Iowa 85-77. The Iowa players were not impressed.

Iowa guard Jimmy Rodgers said, "Kentucky isn't as good as two years ago when I played against them." And Iowa center George Peeples, who scored 21 points, commented, "Kentucky is going to have a hard time against any team with a big center."

Rupp moved 6-5 junior Tom Kron into Dampier's starting spot the next game—against North Carolina at Charlotte. The idea was to get more height into the line-up. UK lost 82-67 as a future pro star, Billy Cunningham, tallied 22 points for North Carolina.

Next was the Iowa State game when Dampier returned to the lineup to stay following his 37-point spree. Embry, the deadly little two-hand shooter, wasn't so fortunate. He came out of the game with a pulled side muscle and would miss UK's next outing, against Syracuse.

Kron, a versatile athlete who had played guard, center and forward against Iowa State and had hit all five of his shots, took over for Embry. He staked out a claim to a starting job by scoring 30 points, hitting 11 of 16 shots. Dampier scored 31 points, giving UK's starting guards a phenomenal 61 points.

At this point, although no one knew it, Rupp had put four players together in the lineup who a year later would be the nucleus of a great team. Still missing was a center. John Adams was a strong, rugged player but he was right in between on the assets an exceptional center must have. At 6-6 he wasn't quite tall enough to be a big man, yet he wasn't quite quick enough to be a consistent high scorer.

He was a tough competitor, though, and without his muscle under the basket it's doubtful if Kentucky could have had a winning season. And for one night Adams looked like some sort of secret weapon to Illinois coach Harry Combes.

When Combes brought Illinois to the UK Invitational Tournament, Rupp told him that he had been having trouble getting much scoring at center. The next night Adams hit 8 of 14 shots and 8 of 10 free throws for 24 points, all the while pulling down 17 rebounds as UK trimmed West Virginia 102-78.

"Wait until I see Adolph," complained Combes, whose team was to play UK the

Guard Terry Mobley played a major role in a victory over Auburn.

Sophomore Louie Dampier scored 37 points against Iowa State.

next night. Illinois advanced to the final by whipping Dayton 104-86.

Thoren Is Too Much

UK rarely had been the underdog in the UKIT. This was one of those times. Illinois had speed, scoring punch from all over and a center, 6-9 Skip Thoren, whom Combes called "the finest in the country."

Illinois, leading only 85-84 after Terry Mobley hit a jump shot with 50 seconds to go, won 91-86 on free throws. Thoren scored 27 points and had 22 rebounds. Dampier was top gun for Rupp with 16 points.

The victory was Illinois' sixth in seven games. UK's record slipped to 4-2 and there was much trouble on the horizon. At this point Dampier was leading the team in scoring with a 19.5 average, followed by Kron at 16.2 and Riley at 15.2.

UK's first game after the tournament was at St. Louis. Rupp knew exactly what his problem would be—St. Louis was too tall. Up to this game UK had used only one kind of zone defense—the same 1-3-1 Rupp had surprised Tennessee with the previous season. Rupp was sure it wouldn't do against St. Louis because St. Louis had too much height along the baseline.

So Rupp tried a 1-2-2 zone. It worked pretty well, too, but when Adams fouled out with 12 minutes to go UK didn't have the size to win. With substitute Bob Cole scoring 19 points, St. Louis won 80-75.

If there were any lingering doubts about UK's lack of prowess, Notre Dame erased them in Louisville's Freedom Hall after the Christmas break. The physically powerful Irish pulled down 81 rebounds to only 44 for UK in a smashing 111-97 victory before 17,000 fans. The shooting of Ron Reed (32 points), Jay Miller (23) and Larry Sheffield (21) tore up UK's zone defense.

Adolph Answers Fans

UK was hurt some by Conley's inability to go at top speed because of an ankle injury. He got only two points and two rebounds. If there was any consolation for Rupp, it was that sophomore Dampier finally had a good road game with 32 points. He had scored only two at St. Louis.

UK's 4-4 won-lost record was Rupp's worst start of his career, so a breather over Dartmouth was most welcome. At this time the fans were grumbling. They were saying that Rupp wasn't working hard enough to get players, that he was turning too much of his recruiting over to assistants.

"People who say that are just fools," he said. "The only reason we don't have big men on our team now is because boys who said they were coming didn't keep their word."

Rupp said he was sure he had landed 6-8 Gary Bradds, who went on to make All-America at Ohio State, as well as 6-8 Bill Hosket of Ohio State and 6-7 Ron Kozlicki of Northwestern.

Among the players visited personally by Rupp were the Van Arsdale twins of Greenwood, Ind., Dick and Tom, who at this stage of the season had led Indiana University to an unbeaten record.

Rupp could have used some of those recruiting near-misses in a game against Vanderbilt. With 6-9 Clyde Lee—surely Vandy's finest player of all time—scoring 41 points, Roy Skinner's Vanderbilt team crushed UK 97-79 in Lexington.

Conley, who didn't start the game for UK because of a shooting slump, came off the bench to score 23 points. That performance got him his job back from Kron, who had been shifted up to forward. Mobley had taken over the guard position.

UK didn't have much trouble getting by Southeastern Conference foes Louisiana State and Tulane. A trip to Knoxville brought a 77-58 loss to Tennessee. It was the worst beating Kentucky had taken from Tennessee since 1917. A. W. Davis, another one of the players Rupp had tried hard to recruit, scored 24 points.

Vandy Out of Reach

After the game Tennessee coach Ray Mears had a little joke to play on Rupp. He displayed a sheet of paper for newsmen to read. On it were the words: "Iconoclastic defense with disharmonious tendencies."

That was Mears' answer to Rupp, who after surprising Tennessee with a 1-3-1 zone the year before, said: "That was no zone. That was a stratified transitional, hyperbolic paraboloid."

A victory for UK over Auburn was senior guard Terry Mobley's shining hour. He had gotten back into the starting lineup two games before when Conley was benched again. Before the Auburn game, Mobley got his teammates together for a meeting. "Play as a team, not as individuals," he urged them.

Then he scored 18 points as UK won 73-67.

Watching was Jeff Mullins, the former Lexington Lafayette High and Duke University star who was with the pro St. Louis Hawks.

"Terry's a tough player," said Mullins, who remembered the winning basket Mobley had scored against Duke in the Sugar Bowl tournament the previous season. "He always comes up with the big play."

After a loss to Florida, UK braced itself to put together a five-game SEC winning streak. The streak was broken at Vanderbilt, but UK did itself proud in losing 91-90. That man, Lee, scored 33 points.

Among the reserves Rupp was using were Gene Stewart, Larry Lentz, Ron Kennett, Brad Bounds and Frank Tully.

By now it was clear that no team was going to catch Vandy in the SEC race. UK lost its next two games, to Auburn and Alabama, then finished with victories over Tennessee and Alabama.

Vandy won the SEC with a 15-1 record. UK was down in fifth place at 10-6. Kron, Dampier and Riley were named to various All-SEC teams.

Rupp's splendid sophomores, Dampier and Riley, already were thinking about next season.

"I'm not satisfied because we lost 10 games and I played about four real bad ones," Riley said. "I need to shoot better next season (he hit 43.2 from the field)."

Said Dampier:

"I was up and down at first, like getting 37 points in one game and two in another, but I settled down in the second half of the season. I need to improve on everything."

Sacrifices of Conley and Kron make UK team go

Every coach knows what it takes to make up a great basketball team. You need shooting first, and after that in no particular order, rebounding, defense, passing and teamwork.

Those are the basics. What the coaches don't know is just how much of each ingredient is necessary. They can only generalize. A tall team, for instance, can skimp a bit on speed. A small team needs all the speed it can muster, along with exceptional shooting and passing.

Adolph Rupp was sure he knew what his problem would be during the 1965-66 season—lack of a good, big center. The question was: did he have enough of everything else to overcome the weakness?

The answer was yes, but there still was a grave threat to UK's season. Ego. The players' ego. All of Rupp's top players had been scoring stars in high school. No basketball team has room for five high scorers. Would any of the players sacrifice for the sake of the team?

Two did. Tom Kron and Larry Conley talked it over and agreed that their most valuable contributions would be as passers and playmakers. Let the others have the headlines and the glory.

With that decision, Kentucky was assured of an exciting and colorful team.

Conley was the complete player before he ever stepped onto the court at Memorial Coliseum. He had been a regular forward on the Ashland team which won the state tournament his junior year, 1961.

Conley, Kron Were Leaders

The next year he averaged 20 points and 14 rebounds a game as a center to lead Ashland to the finals of the state tournament, where it lost to Louisville St. Xavier.

"His leadership qualities are tremendous," his coach, Bob Wright, said.

Conley, son of former Marshall College player and well known referee George Conley, could have taken his choice of more than 30 scholarships.

Kron averaged 16 points a game for Gunner Wyman at Tell City, Ind., as a senior. Like Conley, Kron was a playmaker, rebounder and leader. Kron was born in Owensboro, Ky., but moved to Tell City when he was five years old. He and Conley played against each other in the 1962 Indiana-Kentucky high school all-star series.

Both Conley and Kron were impressive as sophomores at UK. Conley started most of the games. Kron became a starter at mid-season after a fine defensive performance against Tennessee. Both were regulars as juniors, but they weren't happy being part of Rupp's worst record to that time.

Jaracz Wins Job

Rupp lost one starter, center John Adams, off the team which won 15 and lost 10 in '64-65. Two centers up from the freshman team fought for the vacancy and 6-5 Thad Jaracz beat out 6-8 Cliff Berger.

So Rupp would have 6-3 Pat Riley and 6-3 Conley at forwards, Jaracz in the pivot, with 6-foot Louie Dampier and 6-5 Kron at guards. Rupp knew his four returning starters had ability. If only they could put it together just right and if Jaracz could fit in. Rupp wasn't pessimistic, not after a few practices.

"I honestly believe that man-for-man we just might have in the making a better team than we had in 1958, when we won the national title," Rupp said.

Not many persons agreed. Some preseason polls didn't have UK in the top 20.

After UK defeated Hardin-Simmons 83-55 in the opener, losing coach Lou Hensen described Kentucky as "a good little team. When it runs into a big boy, it's going to have trouble."

Jaracz was the only UK player to score in double figures in the opener, a fact which may have influenced Hensen's thinking. Rupp paraded Jim LeMaster, Tommy Porter, Bob Tallent, Cliff Berger, Brad Bounds, Steve Clevenger, Gary Gamble, Gene Stewart and Larry Lentz into the game.

The next game, though, Jaracz scored 22 points and pulled down 13 rebounds as UK downed Virginia. Jaracz broke loose for 32 points at Illinois in his next start as UK won 86-68. From now on, Kentucky would be taken seriously in the polls.

Jaracz, a 230-pound product of Lafayette High in Lexington, seemed out of place at center. He simply looked too short to take care of himself against players 6-8 and 6-9. But he had a couple of things in his favor: speed and quickness.

"He looks like a big freight train barreling down the floor on the fast break," one coach said.

Jaracz was very quick at running and going to the basket after getting the ball in the pivot.

Northwestern was beaten, then UK scored easy victories over Air Force and Indiana to win the UK Invitational Tournament. After six games, UK hadn't been defeated or outrebounded.

Rupp had to find a replacement for Dampier in the second half at Texas Tech. After Dampier left with a sprained ankle, sophomore Bob Tallent, from Langley, Ky., went in and scored 13 points in Kentucky's 89-73 triumph. But UK lost the rebound battle by one.

Notre Dame was no match for Kentucky in Louisville, bowing 103-69 before 17,952 fans. Riley scored 36 points and held Notre Dame's scoring ace, Jim Monahan, to seven.

"The night I scouted Notre Dame, Monahan got 32 points," said John Lykins, then coach at Frankfort, Ky., High School and a part-time scout for UK. "Pat really did a fine job on him."

St. Louis held UK to an 80-70 victory in Lexington. Then Jaracz hit 11 of 15 shots and scored 26 points as Florida was defeated 78-64. A player Rupp had tried to recruit, Gary Keller, tallied 19 for the losers.

"We had no idea Jaracz was that outstanding," Florida coach Norman Sloan said. "He showed us some excellent moves off the post and he was quicker than we thought."

Cliff Berger, the sophomore from Centralia, Ill., went in for Jaracz near the end of the game at Georgia and hit four free throws in an overtime as UK squeezed out a 69-65 decision.

Vanderbilt still had 6-9 Clyde Lee and he still was the best center in the SEC. He scored 30 points against UK and Vandy guard Keith Thomas dropped in 24. But UK had Louie Dampier's 24 and five players scoring in double figures to defeat Vandy 96-83.

"Kentucky has teamwork," Vandy

Larry Conley, dwarfed by the leaping Oliver Darden of Michigan, grabs a rebound in the NCAA Regional game at Iowa City. Other UK players are Tom Kron (30) and Thad Jaracz (55). Cazzie Russell is visable behind Jaracz.

coach Roy Skinner said. "They have five men who can run and shoot."

Said Rupp: "This is the most unselfish team I've ever had."

After rolling by Louisiana State and Auburn, UK ran into a slowdown by Alabama and its coach, Hayden Riley. UK won the game 82-62 after a close first half. Dampier had to settle for 13 points as Alabama used a "box and chaser" on the UK guard. One man was assigned to guard Dampier while the other four played a zone.

After Dampier scored 42 points as Vandy was beaten again, the Associated Press and United Press International polls showed UK (16-0) second in the nation to Duke (15-1).

Ken Rosemond of Georgia tried a slowdown on UK and like Alabama made it a close game for a half. UK won 74-50.

As the season progressed, Rupp began to get more service out of Berger at center. When Rupp considered scoring

the prime consideration, Jaracz was in the game. When defense against a tall man was needed, in went Berger. However, Jaracz continued to start the games.

After Florida was defeated for the second time, running UK's record to 18-0, the wire services announced a new No. 1 team. Rupp's Runts, as Kentucky was being called, had made it to the top for the first time since January of 1964.

UK ran its unbeaten string to 23 with five more SEC victories. Joe Dan Gold's Mississippi State team gave Rupp a scare before losing 73-69. Victory No. 23 was over Tennessee 78-64 at Lexington, which clinched at least a tie for the SEC title for UK. But Tennessee was without its rugged rebounding star, Howard Bayne, who would play in a rematch a week later in Knoxville.

Tennessee broke UK's streak 69-62 as Ron Widby scored 22 points, Red Robbins 18 and Bayne 12 for the winners. Bayne helped Tennessee outrebound UK 43-31. Even with the loss, UK sewed up the SEC

crown as Vanderbilt lost to Mississippi State.

Vandy had a 13-3 SEC record. UK was 14-1 with a remaining game against Tulane. Four nights after a romp over Tulane, UK was at Iowa City, Iowa, to play Dayton in the NCAA regional tournament.

Dayton, with 6-11 Henry Finkel scoring 36 points and Don May 16, gave UK plenty of trouble before losing 86-79. UK had to go to its 1-3-1 zone defense in the second half to stop Finkel. Kentucky also switched to a 1-3-1 offense, with Jaracz moving out to the top of the free throw circle to set screens for Dampier. Louie scored 34 points and Pat Riley 29.

Michigan, a physically powerful team with Cazzie Russell and Oliver Darden, got by Western Kentucky 80-79.

UK vs. Michigan. "We'll 1-3-1 'em," said Lancaster, who scouted Michigan. "They're too strong to play one-on-one."

Pat Riley was at his best against Michigan, pumping in 29 points to match Russell's total as Kentucky won 84-77 in the most bruising battle of UK's season.

"This is the worst beating I ever took in a basketball game," said the slender Conley, who had 14 points and eight rebounds.

Now it was on to College Park, Maryland, where Kentucky would meet its rival for the No. 1 position in the polls, second-ranked Duke. Duke, 25-3, had a magnificent team with 6-7 Jack Marin, 6-7 Mike Lewis and 6-1 Bob Verga (all future pros).

However, Verga was sick and didn't play much against UK. Conley also was sick with a bad cold and played about half the game. With Dampier scoring 23 and Riley 19, UK won 83-79. Duke got 29 points from Marin and 21 from Lewis.

Texas Western gained the final against UK by downing Utah 85-78, and not many at courtside gave Don Haskins' Texas team much chance against Kentucky.

Kentucky shot its worst percentage of the season, 38.6, and lost to Texas Western 72-65. UK had five more field goals; Texas Western hit 28 of 34 free throws.

UK had plenty of good medium-range shots in the first five minutes of the game. However, when the shots didn't go in, Texas Western began playing more aggressive defense. Bobby Joe Hill stole the ball from Kron for an easy layup. Seconds later he took the ball away from Dampier for another layup.

"I'm not sure we could've beaten anybody, the physical shape we were in," Rupp's assistant, Harry Lancaster, said.

Conley was still ailing, Riley had an infected toe, and the entire team was all used up from the previous night's grueling game with Duke.

UK wasn't overlooked when individual honors were passed out. Dampier and Riley were named to the NCAA all-tournament team, all the UK starters were selected All-SEC, and Riley and Dampier both made All-America. Jaracz was on the third team on the Associated Press All-America.

Rupp wasn't overlooked, either. The United Press International named him Coach of the Year.

It was quite a year for Rupp and his Runts.

Lack of leadership, Riley's aching back put UK on the skids

For one season Pat Riley was the best forward ever to play at the University of Kentucky.

That was the year of "Rupp's Runts," when Kentucky came within one victory of capturing the NCAA championship.

Riley was a 6-foot-3 superman: leading scorer and rebounder on the team; a 51.5 per cent shooter from the field, many of his shots taken under the toughest defensive pressure; a streak on the fast break.

He did it all in a reckless style unmatched in the school's history.

But like the Superman, who wilts in the presence of kryptonite, Riley wasn't invincible. His weakness was in the small of his back. He suffered a slipped disc of the spine while water skiing in the summer of 1966.

Without telling coach Adolph Rupp about the injury, Riley went with the rest of the UK team to play in the International Universities Tournament in Israel late that summer. The problem gradually got worse.

No one can be certain how much a healthy Riley would have meant to Kentucky in the season of 1966-67. Surely he could have turned a few games around. As it was, Riley slipped in every phase of the game and UK skidded to Rupp's worst record by far—13-13.

A Season for Pills

If the season was painful for Rupp, it was sheer agony for Riley—physically and mentally. He played all season despite pain which extended into his left leg. There were times Rupp considered asking the hard-muscled senior to quit, but the coach never did.

Riley took pills all season. Pills for pain, pills for relaxing the muscles and pills for sleeping. Every night when he went to bed he pulled on a corset attached to weights and pulleys. All night long he would stay "in traction," easing the pain.

Pat Riley turned down football offers to play basketball at UK.

Making the injury even tougher to take, Riley had never been seriously hurt in his long athletic career. He had been an All-America football quarterback at Linton High in Schenectady, N.Y. Before that he had won a number of swimming and diving medals and ice skating trophies in his age groups before deciding to concentrate on football and basketball.

He had offers of football scholarships from many of the nation's best teams, including Alabama and Michigan State. He chose to accept a basketball scholarship at UK "because basketball requires less practice time than football and I thought I'd accomplish more in school."

Curiously, neither Rupp nor assistant coach Harry Lancaster saw Riley play in high school. They took someone else's word on Riley's ability. That, and they liked his statistics: 1,000 points for his high school career, only four fewer than Barry Kramer made at the same school. Kramer, a couple of years ahead of Riley, went on to become one of the nation's highest scorers and an All-America at New York University.

Even with his impressive high school scoring, Riley was no cinch to be a star at UK. He had been a center in high school and had to develop a better outside shot to play forward at Kentucky. He played both center and forward as a Kentucky freshman, averaging 20 points a game.

As a starting forward on the varsity his sophomore year, Riley's average slipped to 15 a game. He hit 43 per cent of his shots.

As a junior on the Runts, Riley bloomed. On a good night, he simply was impossible to stop. Even when closely covered, as he was in several tourney games, Riley would leap off the floor as if propelled by springs and shoot over his opponent.

Riley was no statistical cripple his senior season, 1966-67. His totals would

have made many players happy. But they weren't up to his junior season totals and they weren't a true indication of how far he had slipped from one season to the next.

His scoring fell off four points to 17.4. His rebounding went from 8.9 a game to 7.7. His shooting percentage dropped from 51.6 to 44.2. And he no longer played the game with the dash and fire which had made him Most Valuable Player of the Southeastern Conference, MVP of the NCAA regional at Iowa City and first-team All-America.

Riley's decline, plus the graduation of Larry Conley and Tom Kron, was too much for Kentucky to cope with.

No one suspected at the start that things would be so bad. The pre-season polls had UK No. 3. Riley didn't seem to be suffering in the opener as he scored 23 points and grabbed 11 rebounds in a 104-84 victory over Virginia. "We're a little better than we were in our first game last year," Riley said.

Then Came Illinois

Rupp had replaced Larry Conley with 6-4 Gary Gamble, a junior from Earlington, Ky. Bob Tallent, a 6-1 junior from Langley, Ky., had taken over Kron's place at guard. Thad Jaracz, 6-5, and 6-foot Louie Dampier were back at center and guard.

UK quickly found that Riley was far too optimistic. First Illinois beat UK 98-97, with Riley getting only four rebounds. Kentucky managed to outgun coach Larry Glass's Northwestern team 118-116 at Evanston, Ill. Both teams were red-hot. Riley scored 33 points, including the final two of the game on free throws. He was followed by Dampier with 32, Jaracz with 23 and Tallent with 20. Jim Burns, a 6-4 guard for Northwestern, got 34.

Kentucky returned home for two games and lost them both—to North Carolina 64-55 and to coach Tommy Bartlett's tall Florida Gators 78-75. With 6-9 Gary Keller and 6-10 Jeff Ramsey doing the heavy work, UK was badly beaten on the boards by Florida.

For the first time in Rupp's regime, UK had lost three straight times at home.

Rupp blamed UK's demise on two factors: lack of height, lack of leadership. "We could be sitting here unbeaten if we had either Conley or Kron—just one of them," Rupp said. "We have no leadership whatsoever."

Rupp also was dissatisfied with the play of Conley's and Kron's replacements. He felt that Tallent, who was a fine outside shooter with great range, made too many mistakes. Gamble was a good rebounder but lacked the passing skill and shooting ability of Conley.

Loss to Cornell Is Shocker

Rupp began experimenting at forward. First he tried Jaracz there briefly, with 6-8 junior Cliff Berger moving into the starting lineup at center. Then the coach tried guard Jim LeMaster at forward, and he played well there as Kentucky won the UK Invitational Tournament by beating Oregon State and Kansas State.

Cliff Berger rebounds as Gary Gamble (50) waits to help.

Any idea Rupp had that UK might be finding itself were rudely dispelled by Cornell. Courier-Journal writer Billy Reed said flatly before the game that Kentucky would beat Cornell. But the Ivy League school refused to cooperate, whipping UK 92-77. Rupp said the loss "came as a shock."

With Dampier and Tallent hitting like crazy from long range, UK bombed Notre Dame 96-85 in Louisville. Tallent scored 28, Dampier 24 and Gamble, now back in the lineup, came through with 17 points. He had scored only 19 in eight previous games. Notre Dame's sharp-shooting forward, Bob Arnzen, of Ft. Thomas, Ky., got 26.

Among UK's reserves as the season went along were guards Steve Clevenger and Phil Argento and forwards Tommy Porter, Brad Bounds and Gene Stewart.

Vanderbilt dealt Kentucky another home court loss 91-89 and the son of one of Rupp's old players helped do the Wildcats in. Joe Hagan's son, Tommy, who had played for Joe Reibel at Louisville St. Xavier, scored 17 points for Vandy.

This was the start of a three-game losing streak for UK. Florida won at Gainesville 89-72 as Riley, who always had trouble against Florida, went 0-for-8 from the field.

Georgia coach Ken Rosemond stalled his way to a 49-40 victory over UK at Athens, Ga. At the half, UK led 8-6. Georgia opened up a little in the second with Mayfield, Ky., junior Jim Youngblood scoring 16 points (he had 20 for the game).

Back home UK beat Auburn 60-58 on Tallent's driving basket with seven seconds left.

Tennessee came to Lexington and edged Kentucky 52-50 on two free throws by Tom Hendrix, who had played his high school basketball for Hardin McLane at Elizabethtown, Ky.

UK won its next four games, all in the SEC, before losing another home game — this time 77-72 to Mississippi State.

Tallent Gets the Ax

Next came a 76-57 loss at Tennessee and an incident with Tallent that led to the junior guard's dismissal from the squad. During the game, as he brought the ball upcourt, Tallent flipped the ball over to Dampier. Dampier, looking straight ahead, didn't see it. The ball went out of bounds and Tallent was jerked from the game.

Rupp and Tallent exchanged bitter words when the player reached the bench. Later, in the locker room, there was another exchange. When Tallent reported to practice after the team returned to Lexington, he was told by equipment manager George Hukle that no more equipment would be issued to him (Tallent).

Rupp didn't come out of the hassle without a few scars. He was reprimanded by John Oswald, then the UK president, and criticized by the UK student newspaper, The Kentucky Kernel. "Did Rupp Choke?" the Kernel asked, a reference to a statement by Rupp that Tallent couldn't play well under pressure.

After bouncing back to beat Mississippi State and Georgia, UK went on its second three-game losing streak of the season — at Alabama, Auburn and Vanderbilt.

Riley was just barely hanging in there as the season neared the end. He hit only 4 of 18 shots against Alabama and 3 of 14 against Auburn. He pulled himself together for one last great effort, in the final game against Alabama. UK had to win to gain a 13-13 split for the season. Riley scored 28 points as UK won 110-78.

Tennessee won the SEC championship with a 15-3 record. UK, 8-10, was tied for fifth place. Dampier was the only Kentucky player to make All-SEC.

A year of frustration was over and help was on the way. Harry Lancaster's freshman team, with Mike Casey, Dan Issel and Mike Pratt leading the way, had won 18 of 20 games.

Casey among best of UK sophs

Mike Casey had a knack of being in the right place on the court.

When the last basketball has bounced and someone walks up to Adolph Rupp in the Valhalla for old coaches and asks, "Who were your greatest sophomores at Kentucky?" his list will read like a roll call of All-Americas.

Ralph Beard . . . Alex Groza . . . Frank Ramsey . . . LeRoy Edwards . . . Johnny Cox . . . Cotton Nash.

There will be more, of course. One player Rupp surely will not overlook is Mike Casey. Not the Mike Casey who came back as a senior after a badly broken leg, maybe a step or two slower. But the Casey who stepped onto the court at UK in 1967.

Ah, there was a player; a sort of genius at making the right play and at being in the right place to do it. He had all the talent anyone could want: a shooter, rebounder, good moves inside and out and a special brand of poise that is as precious as pure gold.

No, he wasn't too sharp on defense, but not many players come to Rupp with much in the way of defensive skills

Casey was a natural athlete, good at everything he tried. He worked at basketball, though, from his first exposure to the game. He first started shooting baskets on his family's farm in Shelby County near Finchville, Ky. (the Caseys had moved there from Mike's birthplace of Henderson, Ky.). Later, after moving to Simpsonville, Ky., he spread straw on the frozen barnyard so he could shoot baskets in the winter.

Played for Harrell

He followed UK's games on the radio and by the time he reached the seventh grade at Simpsonville, he had decided he wanted to play for Adolph Rupp.

Later he came under the tutelage of Bill Harrell at Shelby County High. Harrell, now head coach at Morehead State University, put some polish on the raw talent of Mike Casey. He put a chair out on the court and made Mike dribble up to it and jump for a shot. If Mike floated instead of going straight up, he fell over the chair. He learned.

Casey played in 96 games for Shelby County and scored 2,088 points in four years there. He also earned four letters

in baseball and one in football until Harrell suggested that football was a poor risk for a young man with a basketball future.

As a senior he led Shelby County to the state basketball championship, scoring 20 points in each of the first two games against Knox Central and Harrison County, 31 against Thomas Jefferson and 23 in the final victory over Male. He averaged 28 points a game that season as Shelby County won 33 and lost one.

That summer he was Mr. Basketball for the Kentucky All-Stars against Indiana's stars.

Always he was the clutch player. Rupp recognized it in Casey from the start, even in scrimmages when Casey's team would have trouble. Suddenly Casey would start jumping a little higher, shooting a little straighter, finding something extra.

There was never a better example of Casey getting what Rupp called "that animal look in his eye" than the eighth game of Casey's sophomore year. UK trailed Notre Dame 58-50 in Louisville's Freedom Hall with eight minutes to go.

Casey went to work. He stole the ball and dribbled the length of the court for a layup. In the next few minutes he hit a jump shot, then another layup on a fast break, and finally another layup after stealing the ball. The ballots already were in naming Notre Dame center Bob Whitmore the game's Most Valuable Player. But they were chucked into the nearest waste basket and Casey was handed the first Bernie A. Shively award (in honor of the UK athletic director, who had died three weeks before).

He Led Freshman Scorers

But to return to the start of Casey's career at Kentucky. He enrolled as a freshman as part of what may have been UK's finest frosh team. Dan Issel, Mike Pratt and Casey were considered the top three, but the squad also had Jim Dinwiddie, Bill Busey (a teammate of Casey at Shelby County), Terry Mills and Randy Pool. The freshman team finished 18-2. Casey was the team's leading scorer with a 23.5 average, followed by Issel with 20.8 and Pratt at 20.1.

The step up to the varsity wasn't difficult for Casey, although Rupp and as-

sistant Harry Lancaster recognized those defensive flaws from the start. The 6-4 Casey was at forward for the first game of his sophomore year, at Michigan. The rest of the lineup had 6-5 senior Thad Jaracz (the only holdover from Rupp's Runts) at forward, 6-8 Issel at center and 6-1 senior Steve Clevenger and 6-3 senior Jim LeMaster at guard.

Casey got 14 rebounds, one less than Issel, and poured in 28 points as Michigan fell 96-79. Michigan's high-jumping forward, Rudy Tomjanovich, had 27 rebounds and 17 points.

UK beat Florida 99-76 and Xavier of Cincinnati 111-76. Phil Argento, a 6-2 junior from Cleveland, Ohio, started in place of Clevenger against Xavier and responded with 23 points.

Argento fell off to five points in a 64-49 victory over Pennsylvania, so Clevenger was back in the lineup against tough North Carolina. With 6-11 Rusty Clark outscoring Issel 23-13, and two future pros, Larry Miller (19 points) and Charlie Scott (15) playing well, North Carolina won 84-77.

Two aspects of the loss at Greensboro, N.C., disturbed Rupp: Casey got only seven shots, and Carolina's guards, Dick Grubar and Scott, outplayed UK's. Rupp pondered some changes.

For psychological reasons, the next game was ideal for one change. Rookie Mike Pratt, 6-4, from Dayton, Ohio, was moved into a starting forward job against the University of Dayton in the UK Invitational Tournament. Casey was shifted back to guard in place of Clevenger. Pratt scored 15 points, hitting 7 of 12 shots and grabbing 15 rebounds, as Kentucky won 88-85. Casey was high with 27 points.

Frank McGuire's South Carolina team, which had defeated Cincinnati 64-61 the first night, took a 21-15 lead over UK in the championship game. But a pair of UK subs, Tommy Porter and Gary Gamble, hit several baskets from the corners against McGuire's zone to start Kentucky to a 76-66 victory. Frank Standard scored 24 points for South Carolina.

UK had a good shooting night in overwhelming Vanderbilt 94-78 at Nashville. Casey and Argento (again a starter) with 25 points each and Pratt with 20 led the scorers. Tom Hagan tallied 21 for Vandy.

Held to one point in the first half, Argento scored 23 in the second to help UK squeeze by at Alabama 84-76. Rich Deppe of Louisville had 11 rebounds for Alabama, which matched UK on the boards 44-44.

UK's five-game winning streak was broken at Florida 96-78. Neal Walk, Florida's 6-11 center, outscored Issel 28-12 and outrebounded him 23-7.

UK went home to beat Georgia 104-73. Issel, driving for the basket with 15 minutes left in the game, went up over the back of Georgia's Ray Jeffords and landed on the floor. The UK soph left the game with a mild concussion.

Argento Hurt—Out for Season

Back on the road, UK lost two straight —74-73 at Auburn and 87-59 at Tennessee.

Issel had his best scoring game with 20 against Auburn. Tennessee, playing "as well as we'll ever play," according to coach Ray Mears, simply took Kentucky apart. Twenty points by reserve Bobby Croft, 18 by Bill Justus and 16 by Tom Boerwinkle sparked Tennessee's attack. Kentucky also lost the services for the season of Argento. He suffered torn ligaments in his right ankle when he fell near the end of the game. Steve Clevenger took over Argento's job.

Next were Louisiana State and Pistol Pete Maravich. Pistol Pete, a 6-5 sophomore, pumped in 53 points (with 52 shots) but UK's balanced attack—including 31 points by Casey—overpowered LSU 121-95.

Then Rupp took his team to Oxford, Miss., to get the victory he had wanted for a long time. It was the 772nd triumph of his 38 years at UK. The hotly-contested 85-76 decision made Rupp the winningest coach in college history, lifting him past his old college coach, Phog Allen, who had won 771 games in 46 seasons at Kansas.

Pistol Pete scored 44 points in LSU's rematch with UK in Lexington, but again Kentucky won. This time Casey hit for 29 in a 109-96 scoring duel. After Mississippi was beaten again and then Mississippi State, Tennessee came to Lexington.

Steve Clevenger replaced injured Phil Argento in the UK lineup.

UK had a chance to take over the Southeastern Conference lead by beating Tennessee and that's just what happened, 60-59. Thad Jaracz and Issel were the heroes. Jaracz scored six points in the last six minutes and hit Issel with a pass under the basket for what proved to be the winning field goal with 25 seconds to play.

UK now had a 10-3 SEC record to Tennessee's 9-3. UK won its remaining five games to finish with a 15-3 conference mark. Tennessee lost twice more and took second at 13-5.

Issel Gains Confidence

UK's starters in the stretch drive were Jaracz, Pratt, Issel, Casey and Clevenger. Rupp also used Jim LeMaster, Cliff Berger, Gary Gamble, Tommy Porter, Bill Busey, Randy Pool and Art Laib. Benny Spears, an early-season reserve, did not play later in the campaign. Rupp

Thad Jaracz moved to forward to make room for sophomore Dan Issel.

held three sophomores—Jim Dinwiddie, Terry Mills and Clint Wheeler—out of competition to preserve their year of eligibility.

Dan Issel emerged as a more confident, consistent player in the closing game. He scored 22 points against Mississippi State, 31 against Georgia's Bob Lienhard, 28 against Alabama and 23 against Vanderbilt.

With the advantage of playing on its home court, UK was favored to win the NCAA Mideast Regional and a trip to California for the finals. Kentucky rolled impressively by Maruqette 107-89 the first night. Marquette coach Al McGuire tried to psych his players up before the game by complaining about the uniforms they had to wear, the end of the court they warmed up on and the bench they had to occupy.

Issel turned in one of his finest games, hitting 14 of 18 shots and scoring 36 points. Marquette star George Thompson drew four fouls in the first half and was whistled out for good with 17:51 to play in the second half.

In the other half of the double-header, Fred Taylor's Ohio State team defeated East Tennessee 79-72.

Ohio State had been fortunate to get to the regional, finishing in a tie for the championship only because Iowa lost its final game to Michigan (the team UK had beaten badly in the opener at Ann Arbor, Mich.). Ohio State then won a playoff with Iowa for the NCAA berth.

The regional title game boiled down to the last five seconds and one play. Ohio State had possession of the ball under its own basket, but Kentucky led 81-80. During a timeout Taylor called the play. Dave Sorenson and Steve Howell would cross and one of them would take a close-in shot.

In the UK huddle, Steve Clevenger asked, "Should I foul?" It was a good question. UK, playing a zone, had committed only three fouls in the half. Another foul would have given Ohio State a chance to tie the game but almost no chance to win it in regulation because the bonus free throw would not have been in effect. If Ohio State had hit the free throw, UK probably would have had time for one final shot. If that missed—overtime. The decision was, don't foul.

The worst part about the situation was that Ohio State was almost certain to get an almost unmolested shot. Certainly UK wasn't going to play aggressive defense on any shot and take a chance on a two-shot foul.

On the throw-in, Sorenson took the ball and banked the ball in from about 10 feet out. It was an easy shot, one he probably could have hit 80 per cent of the time. UK lost 82-81 and a lot of "California, Here We Come" buttons were sailed off into bushes outside Memorial Coliseum.

Ohio went to Los Angeles for the NCAA finals and lost its first game, to North Carolina, but defeated Houston for third place. UCLA won the championship.

Casey's final 20.2 scoring average was the second best for a sophomore in UK history. Cotton Nash had averaged 23.8 six years before.

Mike Pratt was a blend of strength and finesse

If Mike Pratt had come along two years earlier, the University of Kentucky basketball team might not have taken its shocking nosedive the season after Rupp's Runts broke up.

A major reason for UK's decline when Pat Riley and Louie Dampier were seniors was that the unselfish pair of Larry Conley and Tom Kron was gone. Pratt was sort of a Conley-Kron wrapped up in one package.

Pratt was a senior at Meadowdale High School in Dayton, Ohio, when the Runts delighted UK followers and startled the world of college basketball in 1966. He made frequent trips to Lexington to see them play, and he loved to watch the clocklike teamwork which was a trademark of the smallish UK team.

Rupp and assistant coach Joe Hall didn't have to recruit as hard as they thought. Pratt was enchanted with the UK style: the fast break, the crisp passing, the all-round good shooting. He could see himself a part of all that.

He learned part of his basketball on outdoor courts around Dayton. Mostly he learned to take care of himself under the baskets, and he found that not all players are eager to pass the ball.

"In those games they don't pass you the ball," he once said, "so if you want to shoot, you have to go after it yourself."

Pratt was a starter for three and a half years in high school, and while he was a good team player, he also got his points. He scored 1,396 points in 76 games, a Dayton-area record.

Strength Impresses Rupp

Joe Hall knew as soon as he saw Pratt play that the husky youth would fit perfectly into UK's system. Pratt confirmed the soundness of Hall's judgment as a freshman when he averaged 20 points a game and led the team in assists (passes leading directly to a basket).

Adolph Rupp was impressed with Pratt's strength and ability as a sophomore. "I thought Pat Riley was strong," marveled Rupp, "but this Pratt kid is the strongest kid I've ever seen play basket-

ball. When he gets in position for a rebound, you have only two choices: let him have it or foul him. You can't move him."

Pratt was ill early in his sophomore year at UK and wasn't a starter for the first five games. Once he gained a place in the regular lineup, he quickly became one of the team's top players. He averaged 14 points a game that season, third behind Mike Casey and Dan Issel.

With Pratt, Issel and Casey back for their junior years, Rupp expected much of his team for the 1968-69 season. Two weeks before the opening game fate played a dirty trick on Pratt and Rupp. The muscular forward came out of a scrimmage with a broken finger on his left hand.

Rupp had to find a new combination. First he moved 6-4 Mike Casey from

Phil Argento was Most Valuable Player in the Notre Dame game.

guard to forward. Larry Steele, a 6-6 sophomore from Bainbridge, Ind., was holding down the other forward.

Issel, of course, was taking care of the center position in fine style.

At guard Rupp had Terry Mills and Phil Argento, both 6-2.

Mills was a sophomore in eligibility, having been red-shirted (held out of competition), the season before. It was a valuable year for Mills because he had an opportunity to make the switch to guard. He had been a forward at Knox Central High School, near Barbourville, Ky., where he had been one of the state's highest scorers with 1,622 points in three years.

Argento was back for his final season. He had been a terrific scorer on a freshman team on which most of the scholarship players had been wiped out by scholastic difficulties. He had scored 50 points in one game, 48 in two others, and once had hit 46.

As a sophomore he had been a valuable reserve and had started three games. He was a starter as a junior until a little past mid-season when he suffered a badly injured ankle. At the time he was averaging 13 points a game.

So this was Argento's last chance for a full season as a regular, and he meant to make the most of it.

Some of the pre-season ratings had UK picked second, behind UCLA. "I think we would rate in the top 10, but with Pratt out—no," Rupp said.

UK had no trouble whipping Xavier 115-77 in the opener at Lexington as Casey and Issel scored 29 points apiece and Steele pitched in 16. Xavier's 6-10 Luther Rackley hit only three of 15 shots and was called four times for goal tending.

UK had to fight for its life at Miami in the dedication game for the Oxford, Ohio, institution's new Millett Assembly Hall. Casey came through with three straight baskets near the end when UK was about to crack in the face of a pressing Miami defense. "Casey is the guy who put it to us when they had to have it down the stretch," Miami coach Tates Locke said after Kentucky's 86-77 victory. Miami's Frank Lukacs scored 20 points.

North Carolina, which had most of the players back who had defeated UK the year before, came to Lexington and downed Kentucky 87-77. This was Pratt's first game. Wearing a cast on his hand, he scored 14 points. Casey had 26 and Issel 19, but UK didn't have enough to go with them. Charlie Scott, an Olympic player the previous summer, hit 19 points over UK's 1-3-1 zone.

Pratt started the next game, against Pennsylvania at Philadelphia, and came through with 17 points. Issel had 26 and Casey 18 in a 102-78 UK victory. By now Kentucky was down to fourth in the Associated Press poll, behind ULCA, North Carolina and Davidson.

UK had a wild shootout with Michigan in the UK Invitational Tournament, finally winning 112-104 as Issel scored 24 points. Issel outplayed Michigan star Rudy Tomjanovich by a wide margin in the first half, but Rudy finished with 25 points.

The UKIT final pitted Kentucky against Army, which had edged Bradley 54-52. Kentucky broke open the game with four straight baskets in the first few minutes of the second half—the "killer period," Rupp calls it—to beat Bob Knight's slow-paced Army team 80-65. Issel, who had 22 points in the title game, was named the UKIT's Most Valuable Player.

Something Had to Give

"Kentucky has two good-shooting guards," Knight said, "and you can't defense the pivotman and the guards both. You have to give up something."

Issel turned in another sparkling performance, 31 points and 14 rebounds, as Notre Dame was defeated 110-90 before 18,000 fans in Louisville. Argento played his finest game as a Kentucky Wildcat, popping in 27 points. He hit 11 of 16 shots from the field and afterward was named the game's Most Valuable Player.

Then came one of those incomprehensible games which pop up every so often. UK went to Chicago Stadium and lost 69-65 to Wisconsin. UK hit just 38 per cent of its shots and Wisconsin 56 per cent. It was a big morale booster for Wisconsin coach John Powless, who had been a basketball and tennis player at Murray (Ky.) State University.

Rupp got a scare on a trip to Mississippi. Dan Issel got poked in the eye in the first half of a game against Ole Miss. After some medical attention from Dr. V. A. Jackson of Lexington, traveling with the UK team, Issel re-entered the game in the second half and hit four of six shots as UK won 69-59. A reserve forward, Randy Pool, who scored eight points in the last 11 minutes after relieving Larry Steele, and Casey, with 14 points in the second half, also played key roles in the Southeastern Conference victory.

Steele Plays Good Game

After defeating Mississippi State, UK returned home to defeat Florida 88-67. Issel and Neal Walk played each other even, but Steele had his first hot-shooting game. He hit nine of 14 shots, mostly from the corners against Florida's 1-3-1 zone for 18 points.

Mike Pratt, shooting over a screen set by Dan Issel, started his junior year with a broken finger.

UK had too much balance for Georgia, winning 88-68 although Bob Lienhard outscored Issel 27-18. Then Kentucky went to Tennessee to squeeze out a 69-66 triumph. The game was almost even in every respect except that UK shot a little better—54 per cent to 45.

Pistol Pete Maravich was up to his old tricks when UK went to Louisiana State. He hit 20 of 48 shots and scored 52 points but UK won 108-96. As usual UK played a zone defense against Pete.

After beating Alabama 83-70, UK went over 100 points its next three games in easy victories over Vanderbilt, Auburn and Mississippi. Auburn showed a marvelous sophomore guard, John Mengelt of Elwood, Ind., who dazzled Memorial Coliseum fans with 17-for-28 shooting and 42 points.

Kentucky won its 11th straight game by trimming Mississippi State 91-69, but the string was broken 82-81 at Florida. Issel outscored Walk 30-19, but Kentucky played poor defense in many one-on-one situations.

Afterwards Rupp complained about a couple of mistakes sophomore Bob McCowan made. Two nights later at Georgia, Rupp had nothing but praise for McCowan. The Dayton, Ohio, guard replaced Argento midway of the first half, and scored 16 points while playing the rest of the game. UK won 85-77, Rupp's 800th coaching victory, according to National Collegiate Athletic Association figures. UK had claimed 800 for Rupp back on Jan. 27, including in the total five games Rupp's Runts had played in the World Universities Tournament in Israel in the summer of 1966.

Back home, UK was pushed to beat Louisiana State 103-89. Pete Maravich scored 45 points against a zone defense and had 20-point help from Danny Hester. Issel gave an All-America performance with 36 points and 29 rebounds.

Alabama was beaten 108-76 in Lexington. Besides his starters, Rupp used McCowan, Pool, Art Laib, Jim Dinwiddie, Clint Wheeler, Terry Mills and Bill Busey. By now sophomore guard Greg Starrick, an excellent outside shooter, had grown tired of sitting on the bench and had left UK. He would enroll at Southern Illinois.

Vanderbilt upset UK 101-99 in Nashville despite a truly great game by Issel—41 points and 13 rebounds. Rudy Thacker scored 23 points for Vandy, followed by Tom Hagan and Perry Wallace with 22 apiece. Despite the loss, UK clinched at least a tie for the SEC title as Auburn upset Tennessee 71-60.

UK wrapped up the championship by defeating Auburn 90-86, with Issel scoring 34 points and Casey 23. After UK beat Tennessee in the regular-season finale, Rupp said he had a better team than the year before: "It's a better shooting team."

A rematch with Marquette awaited Kentucky in the NCAA Mideast Regional at Madison, Wis. Al McGuire had his players and the crowd in a vengeful mood. "Hey, Hitler," the Marquette fans yelled at Rupp, apparently a reference to the fact that he had no black players.

On the court, Marquette was aggressive, bumping into UK players even when the ball wasn't in play. Had one of the Kentucky players retaliated with any force, it's doubtful if anyone could have prevented a riot. It was a frightening situation which seemed to affect UK's play. "Someone could have got killed," one Kentucky player said.

UK was killed on the scoreboard, 81-74. Marquette ganged up on Issel inside, holding him to 13 points. That left Steele open but the sophomore could hit only one of six shots. The next night UK barely outlasted Miami of Ohio 72-71 for third place.

So it was all over; another case of "wait until next year."

Issel, Casey and Pratt made various All-SEC teams, and Issel was named All-America. What they all really wanted was to play on an NCAA championship team.

Dan Issel: UK's super scoring machine

Perhaps it was inevitable, this mating of the man and the moment. Or maybe there was something about Dan Issel — a perfect blend of strength and skill — that made it seem natural.

But there he was, running up and down the University of Mississippi basketball court and working a kind of magic that enthralled the 7,500 spectators.

With their team 28 points behind at halftime, the Ole Miss rooters could have started thinking about an early start for home. But they didn't leave. After Issel scored 29 points in the first 20 minutes, the fans knew they were witnessing something special. Issel wasn't as spectacular as Pistol Pete Maravich, but Kentucky's big blond was an awesomely efficient piece of basketball machinery.

Issel started the second half with a flurry of baskets. He hit a couple of layups, a hook shot, and two more layups. By now the UK student manager, Doug Billips, was yelling out Issel's total every time the UK center ran up the court.

Issel got his 50th and 51st points on a drive-in shot, knocking Mississippi's Tom Butler to the floor. That could have been Issel's fifth foul, but the officials didn't call it. Then with 5:47 left to play, UK's 6-foot-8 All-America center hit a 17-foot turnaround jump.

That shot gave Issel the one-game Kentucky scoring record of 53 points, breaking a mark of 51 set by Cliff Hagan on Dec. 5, 1953, against Temple.

Issel breaks Nash's record

Only a few minutes earlier Issel had shattered Cotton Nash's UK career record of 1,770 points.

With five minutes left and UK assured of the victory (120-85 was the final score), UK coach Adolph Rupp pulled Issel out. As the spectators cheered, a smiling Rupp shook hands warmly with Issel. And, although the coach didn't say it, he must have been thinking, "Well Dan, I kept my promise."

It was a promise made at the beginning of the season, several weeks before UK started practice. UK's players were engaged in the usual pre-season conditioning program, an agonizing experience which no Kentucky player ever learned to like. The players reached the point of rebellion. One afternoon they refused to run.

Rupp could've taken the get-tough approach to the situation and eventually have forced the players to fall into line. Instead, he talked to Issel. "Dan," Rupp said, "you've got a chance to be the highest scorer in Kentucky history. If you'll go out there and run, I'll do everything in my power to see that you make it."

Issel put on his sweat clothes and ran that afternoon with Jim Andrews, Larry Stamper and the rest of the freshman team. No other varsity player showed up to work out. But the next afternoon they were all back, and nothing more was said about the incident.

Rupp kept his word. It's doubtful if any UK player ever had as much opportunity to score as Issel did his senior year. Going into the NCAA regional tournament that season, No. 2 center Mark Soderberg had played only about half an hour. Issel finished with a 33.9 scoring average and a career total of 2,138 points.

All this from a player who was third choice on UK's shopping list in 1966.

Issel, who twice had been an All-State and All-America high school player at Batavia, Ill., got the message fast when he visited the UK campus. He picked up a copy of the school newspaper, the Kentucky Kernel. There was a story in it about the recruiting campaign being waged by UK assistant coach Joe Hall.

There were players mentioned at every position, including two centers. There were the names of Mike Casey, Jim Dinwiddie, Randy Pool and Terry Mills. Nowhere did Dan find his name.

"I couldn't help but feel I wasn't No. 1," Issel said later. He went home and signed with Wisconsin. After UK failed to sign the two other centers on its list, Hall renewed efforts to land Issel.

Dan's father paid the expenses for another trip to UK. They decided that's where Dan would play.

Issel could have had his pick of a hundred schools.

He had a good freshman year at UK with a 17.7 rebounds and 20.8 points a

Dan Issel had some assistance from coach Adolph Rupp in becoming UK's all-time leading scorer.

game. But he found the switch to varsity competition a tough hurdle.

Issel scored in double figures the first seven games his sophomore season, ranging from a high of 18 to a low of 13. Suddenly he hit a slump: six points against Notre Dame, seven against Vanderbilt, eight against Alabama, 12 against Florida, and not a point against Georgia. He missed the last 15 minutes of the Georgia game, however, after taking a hard fall.

After that Issel started to come on. He had to settle for nine points at Tennessee but that was the only one of the last 15 games he failed to score in double

figures. Probably his finest performance was against Marquette in the NCAA regional when he scored 36 points.

As a junior and an All-America Issel was a model of consistency in averaging 26.6 points and 13.6 rebounds. His high was 41 against Vanderbilt, and three times he reached 36 points. He hit 53.4 per cent of his shots.

Going into his final season Issel had scored 1,190 points for UK. He needed 581 to break Nash's career record.

Rupp Is Ailing

Rupp had some physical problems before the first game was played. Troubled with diabetes, Rupp had a foot infection that was slow to heal. The ulceration had been caused by a shoe rubbing his foot. His doctor ordered him to stay away from the office and to keep the foot elevated.

However, the coach refused to miss practices. And he refused to miss the games. He sat on the sidelines with his foot resting on a cushion and stool.

There was an element of uncertainty about UK's prospects because Mike Casey was sitting out the season with a broken leg. "Crushed, not broken," Rupp said. It had happened during the summer in an auto accident. The loss of Casey was no small matter to a man intent on winning an NCAA title.

Issel with 34 points and Mike Pratt with 28 led UK to a 106-87 romp in the opener. Larry Steele was at forward with Pratt. The starting guards were 6-4 Jim Dinwiddie of Leitchfield, Ky., and 6-2 Terry Mills of Barbourville, Ky. Rupp used reserves Bob McCowan, Kent Hollenbeck, Randy Noll, Tom Parker, Mark Soderberg, Bill Busey and Stan Key.

UK smashed a good Kansas team 115-85. This time Rupp used all the players who got in the opener, plus Art Laib and Clint Wheeler.

North Carolina, which had beaten UK five of six games since Dean Smith had been coaching the Chapel Hill, N.C., university, would be more difficult. Issel scored 41 points and Pratt 27 as UK won 94-87 before 11,666 at Greensboro, N.C. The victory came four hours after the Kentucky players learned they had been voted No. 1 in the Associated Press poll.

After Indiana was beaten 109-92, UK played Navy in the first round of the UK Invitational. Issel scored 40 points and had 18 rebounds in a 73-59 Kentucky victory. George Janky, a center from Chicago whom UK had tried to recruit ahead of Issel and now playing for Dayton, was held to 12 points by Duke in the other half of the UKIT doubleheader. Duke won 72-67.

Duke center Randy Denton gave Issel fits in the title game, grabbing 21 rebounds and scoring 28 points, but UK won 98-76. McCowan, who had scored 16 points the night before in relief against Navy, was hot again. He tallied 25 against Duke and was voted the UKIT Most Valuable Player.

Beating Notre Dame at Louisville was an offensive duel all the way. UK had Pratt, the game's Most Valuable Player with 42 points, and Issel with 35. The Fighting Irish had Austin Carr, who hit

20 of 27 shots in scoring 43 points. UK finally won 102-100.

After beating Miami of Ohio and Mississippi to run their win streak to nine, the UK players were disappointed by the Associated Press poll: UCLA, 8-0, had taken over first place.

After Mississippi State was defeated, UK prepared for a trip to Florida and Georgia. The day before UK left, Rupp announced that McCowan and Randy Pool had been dropped from the team for curfew violations.

Issel scored 37 points in an 88-69 margin over Florida, one point more than Florida's outside shooter, Andy Owens. Terry Mills, in the lineup for McCowan, hit 14 points.

Guards Jim Dinwiddie (right) and Terry Mills looks for a chance to double team Indiana's Jim Harris.

Issel outscored his old center rival, Bob Lienhard, 32-17, although UK barely squeezed by Georgia 72-71. UK couldn't have won, though, without 6-for-8 shooting by sophomore guard Kent Hollenbeck, who went in for Mills late in the first half.

By now Rupp had become keenly aware of the value of guard Jim Dinwiddie. Dinwiddie, who had waited two years for a chance to play (one as a red-shirt) was another one of those unselfish players who often are the difference between success and failure.

UK went home to beat Tennessee 68-52,

with McCowan back in action after being reinstated by Rupp. Pool had to wait awhile longer to get back in good graces.

The next game was against Louisiana State. For the first time in three years, UK played a man-to-man defense against Pete Maravich. Terry Mills started out guarding the 6-5 All-America, then McCowan tried it, and Larry Steele finished up. When it was over, Maravich had scored 55 points, a Coliseum record, but Kentucky won the game 109-96.

UK ran its unbeaten streak to 15 by defeating Alabama 86-71. Roy Skinner's Vanderbilt team snipped the string behind Tom Arnholt, a guard from Columbus, Ind. He scored 28 points as Vandy won 89-81.

Key Saves a Game

UK started another streak by edging Auburn 82-81. Reserve guard Stan Key hit six of nine shots to save UK in that road game. Rupp had Key and another sophomore, 6-7 Tom Parker, in the lineup at Mississippi as Issel scored the record-breaking 53 points. Parker replaced Steele, who had suffered a broken wrist in practice. Parker scored 22 points and shot so well for the rest of the season that Rupp never returned Steele to the regular lineup.

Issel would always consider the record at Mississippi his greatest thrill at UK, partly because his father was there to see it. His wife, the former Cheri Hughes of Lexington, was there, too.

A UK cheerleader in Dan's first two varsity seasons, the pretty blonde rates Dan's 53-point game the most exciting she saw, but remembers with special fondness a game Dan played at Georgia as a sophomore. After they returned to Lexington that night on separate planes, she and Dan had their first date.

UK had run its newest streak to five when it went to Baton Rouge to play LSU again. Maravich scored 64 points, but Issel wasn't far behind with 51 as Kentucky won 121-105.

Issel, now a super scoring machine, scored 47 at Alabama although UK had to struggle for a 98-89 victory. By now UK was back on top in the AP ratings.

UK finished its regular season by downing Vanderbilt 90-86, Auburn 102-81 and Tennessee 86-69. It was on to Columbus, Ohio, for an 18th appearance in the NCAA tournament.

UK outshot Notre Dame 109-99 although Austin Carr scored 52 points for the losers. Issel rang up 44. Now UK faced Jacksonville with 7-foot Artis Gilmore and an amusing and colorful coach Joe Williams.

Dan Issel scored 28 points in 30 minutes before going out on fouls. Jacksonville's Vaughn Wedeking deliberately ran in front of Issel to draw the fifth foul. Issel and Rupp both said the foul should have been called on Wedeking. Issel did not have the ball at the time.

UK also lost Pratt, Mills and Steele on fouls. The subs, including Mark Soderberg in place of Issel, played their hearts out, but Jacksonville won 106-100.

Issel made the All-NCAA Regional team for the third straight year. He and Pratt both were named to the All-Southeastern Conference team and Issel was chosen All-America again.

Larry Steele had hustle, speed with unselfish attitude

When Larry Steele ran onto the basketball court, he looked more like a skinny, bowlegged kid on roller skates than a player.

But as soon as the first ball was tossed up, he was all player: a good long shooter with a soft one-hand push shot, a slick passer on the fast break, and a forward with far above average speed.

He had one other asset which made him a valuable man for the University of Kentucky for three years and which helped him earn a place on the Portland Trail Blazers pro team after graduation: hustle. All-out hustle from the opening whistle to the last.

One of Steele's staunchest admirers was Vanderbilt coach Roy Skinner, who made the most of hustle himself when he played for Paducah (Ky.) Junior College and later at Presbyterian College.

"He makes Kentucky go," Skinner said many times in Steele's three years at UK.

And as long as Kentucky won, Steele was happy. Take his senior year, when he averaged 13 points a game. He was capable of averaging 17 or 18, but he quickly saw that with four other excellent shooters in the starting lineup, he could contribute more as a passer and rebounder. He was Larry Conley and Tom Kron, of the 1966 Rupp's Runts, all over again.

There were times, though, when Steele knew he had to put the ball through the hoop. One of those times was late in his final season in a game at Auburn. A victory would clinch Kentucky's fourth straight Southeastern Conference championship. Tom Parker, UK's other forward, wasn't getting many shots and when he did shoot, he didn't hit. Steele took over. He started popping in the baskets from long range. When it was over he had hit eight of 12 shots and all six of his free throws. UK won 102-83.

Afterwards Steele talked about his attitude toward scoring: "It's like that old saying, 'Too many chiefs and not enough Indians.' You can have too many shooters. I'm satisfied to give up the ball and let someone else put it in the basket."

Steele did have one weakness—a penchant for getting hurt. He missed stretches of both his last two years with

Larry Steele put winning ahead of his scoring average.

broken bones. Only his sophomore year, when he was a starter on UK's nationally seventh-ranked team, did he escape injury.

Steele was an All-State player at Bainbridge, Ind., High School. He chose UK over many scholarship offers after finishing with a career total of 1,550 points. He averaged 17.7 points as a freshman at UK.

When the 6-foot-6 Steele moved up to the varsity, coach Adolph Rupp was looking for a replacement for graduated Thad Jaracz. After watching Steele go after rebounds in several scrimmages, Rupp knew he had a starting forward. "His defense isn't the greatest and he's not scoring well, but his rebounding is fine," Rupp said. "He's just a little timid about shooting."

He was third in rebounding behind Dan Issel and fifth in scoring that first season.

He was rebounding and shooting well as a junior (15 points a game) when after 17 games he suffered a broken right wrist. Tom Parker, a brilliant shooting sophomore from Collinsville, Ill., replaced Steele. UK kept winning and Parker was averaging 17 points, so Steele never started another game all season.

Rupp counted heavily on Steele's maturity and experience for the 1970-71 season. Parker, 6-7, and Steele quickly nailed down the starting forward positions.

Tom Payne, a 7-foot sophomore from Louisville Shawnee High and Rupp's first black player, beat out junior Mark Soderberg at center. Payne's timing around the basket left much to be desired, but he was agile and he was a good 15-foot shooter. Payne, ineligible for the UK freshman team, had the potential to be All-America, Rupp believed.

Rupp was loaded with guards. He might have been better off with three good ones instead of the five he had: Mike Casey, Jim Dinwiddie, Kent Hollenbeck, Terry Mills and Stan Key. Rupp decided on Casey, back for his final season after sitting out a year with the badly broken leg, and 6-4 junior Hollenbeck, from Knoxville, Tenn., as starters.

There was dissension from the start. Dinwiddie felt that he had outplayed Casey in pre-season practice and deserved the starting job. Dinwiddie, who has been Issel's No. 1 feeder the previous season, put part of the blame on team trainer Claude Vaughan.

Vaughan, an economics teacher at UK, was close to Rupp, and Dinwiddie said that the trainer influenced Rupp in favor of Casey. Later in the season, a brief scuffle broke out on a plane flight between Dinwiddie and Vaughan.

UK had a close call in its opener, going to a 1-3-1 zone defense in the late stages to outscore Northwestern 115-100 at Evanston, Ill. Parker with 23 points and Steele with 20 carried the team's offense. When Casey scored just five points, fans wondered if the senior guard had regained the strength in his broken leg.

Casey, always the competitor, came through with 25 points as UK went home to defeat Michigan 104-93. Michigan coach Johnny Orr had a great player, Henry Wilmore, who went right over top of Steele for 17 field goals in 21 attempts and a final 40 points. Parker's shooting was off (nine points), but Steele hit 24.

Parker was back in form in West Virginia's beautiful new 14,000-seat arena (it was designed by Carl Staker, captain of Rupp's 1942 team). He scored 24 points, Hollenbeck got 23 and Casey 19 as UK won 106-100. Stan Key's clutch shooting was important, too. He scored nine points in seven minutes late in the second half.

Then that old injury jinx struck Steele again. He suffered a broken right thumb in practice four days before the game he wanted most to play—at Indiana University. IU had one of its top players, 6-7 sophomore center Steve Downing, out with an injury.

Larry Stamper, a 6-6 sophomore from Beattyville, Ky. (Lee County High), took Steele's place. He hit only two of 10 shots, but Parker scored 24 points and the other three starters were in double figures as UK won 95-93 in overtime. Mark Soderberg played part of the game at forward, scoring 13 points, leading Kentucky in rebounds with 13 and blocking several shots.

UK was too big for DePaul in the UK Invitational opener, winning 106-85. Casey was high scorer with 26 points.

Weatherford Jolts UK

Purdue appeared inept in beating Kansas State 87-68 in the other UKIT first-round game. There seemed no way George King's Purdue squad could stay close to UK in the title game. But with Larry Weatherford, a clever guard, dropping in 27 points—the same as Casey scored for UK—Purdue upset its host 89-83.

UK got fine play from 6-11 sophomore

An injury sidelined Kent Hollenbeck near the season's end.

Jim Andrews as Oregon State was beaten 84-78 in Lexington. Rupp played a double pivot in the second half with Andrews near the basket and Soderberg (in for Payne) playing a high post. Andrews hit seven of 12 shots and finished with 19 points.

Soderberg started at forward the next game, against Notre Dame in Louisville. But this time he didn't get much done and UK lost 99-92. Steele, his thumb taped, played as a reserve, picking off nine rebounds and scoring 15 points. Austin Carr scored an even 50 for the Irish on 21-for-32 shooting.

With Steele back in the lineup, UK started its Southeastern Conference season with a 103-95 victory at Mississippi. Johnny Neumann, who had been called "better than Pete Maravich," was 20-for-50 from the field in scoring 47 points for coach Bob Jarvis' Rebels.

After UK won 79-71 at Mississippi State, Mark Soderberg left the UK squad. He was obviously unhappy at not playing in either of the games in Mississippi.

Soderberg, who enrolled at the University of Utah, implied that he should have been playing instead of Payne. "Since Payne is the first Negro there, Rupp tried to bend over backwards to show he wasn't prejudiced," Soderberg said.

UK downed Florida 101-75 with 51 per cent shooting, then beat a slowdown by Georgia coach Ken Rosemond 79-66.

Payne took some heavy verbal abuse at Tennessee, where UK lost 75-71. "The players, the coaches on the bench, everybody, was trying to provoke us into a fight," Payne said afterwards. "One time, one of their guys told me, 'Don't get too close to me. I might punch you in the mouth.'"

A big problem for UK was that it couldn't stop the fallaway jump shots of Tennessee guard Jimmy England, who scored 25 points.

At Louisiana State, Jim Andrews blocked what would have been the winning shot by Al Sanders as UK won 82-79. After blocking Sanders' layup attempt with about three seconds left, Andrews hit two free throws.

At Alabama, UK had to struggle to win 86-73. Alabama coach C. M. Newton had lost his star forward, Wendell Hudson, two nights before with a broken wrist. Bad luck hit UK during the game with Alabama—Mike Casey left the game midway of the second half with a badly sprained right ankle.

Dinwiddie replaced the injured Casey in the starting lineup. Parker was at his best in the next game, scoring 30 points and grabbing 13 rebounds in a 102-92 victory over Vanderbilt.

Casey played as a reserve the next two games—victories over Mississippi and Mississippi State at Lexington. Neumann scored 46 again for Ole Miss. After the Mississippi State game, on a Monday night, Rupp announced he was checking into the UK Medical Center for treatment of the ulcerated right foot which had troubled him the previous season. He turned the team over to Hall for a trip to Florida and Georgia.

UK lost 74-65 at Florida, then won 107-

Seven-foot Tom Payne scored 39 points against LSU.

95 at Georgia as Casey went in as a sub and scored 21 points.

Back home UK defeated LSU 110-73 as Rupp watched from a seat near the bench, his right foot resting on a stool. He did no coaching. Hollenbeck, who had suffered a groin injury in practice, didn't play, so UK's starting guards were Casey and Dinwiddie. They would remain in the lineup the rest of the season.

Payne had his finest game in the romp over LSU, scoring 39 points and taking 19 rebounds while holding Sanders to five points.

By defeating Alabama and Vanderbilt again, UK clinched a tie for the SEC title. Then came the 102-83 victory at Auburn, in which Steele decided to become a scorer, when Kentucky wrapped up the championship.

A final victory over Tennessee (Rupp had returned to his coaching duties three days before) and UK was ready for a trip to Athens, Ga., to play in the NCAA Mideast Regional tournament. Well, ready isn't quite the word. Western Kentucky, champion of the Ohio Valley Conference, pressured UK right out of its offense into 26 turnovers in beating Rupp's team 107-83. Only Parker, with 23 points, played well for UK. Seven-foot Jim McDaniels scored 35 points for Western.

The next night Marquette, which had lost 60-59, to Ohio State, trimmed UK 91-74. Western went on to the NCAA finals by defeating Ohio State 81-78.

There have been many tales told of dissension on the UK team. Some of them are true. There was some side-taking by players in the Dinwiddie vs. Casey debate. But rumors about fights between players and Payne were false. The closest was when Payne and Larry Stamper squared off during a poker game. The argument was over a quarter, not basketball.

Three UK players—Steele, Payne and Parker—were named All-SEC by the conference coaches.

Rupp's Victory Record Seems Safe

In 26 years of college coaching—two at Indiana State and 24 at UCLA—Johnny Wooden has averaged 22 and a fraction victories a season for a 583-154 record.

If the 61-year-old native of Martinsville, Ind., coaches for 10 more years and wins 29 games a season, he still will come up one victory short of Adolph Rupp's 874.

So unless Wooden coaches for longer than anyone expects, Rupp's record has to be considered out of reach. It may well stand for all time unless the present limit of regular-season games (26) is drastically increased.

Rupp's winning percentage of 82.1, however, could be surpassed in the next five or six years if Wooden continues to coach and UCLA stays at or near the top. But even that will take some doing. For instance, if Wooden's teams win 88 of their next 90 games (which would cover at least three years), the UCLA coach's percentage would be 81.0, still a shade below Rupp's.

The NCAA title race is no contest. Wooden's teams have won eight, Rupp's four. However, that competition could have been a lot closer had Rupp been more fortunate a couple of years.

If 7-foot Bill Spivey had returned for his senior season in 1951-52, UK would have had probably its greatest team and would have been one of the strongest favorites in NCAA tournament history.

The 1953-54 team went unbeaten in 25 games but didn't play in the NCAA tourney after it was discovered that graduate students weren't eligible. Had Rupp or athletic director Bernie Shively been alert to the rule, Cliff Hagan, Frank Ramsey and Lou Tsioropoulos could have dropped out of school a semester the previous season when UK was on suspension. In effect, the players were penalized for wanting the extra education.

Wooden, Rupp at Top

There have been many fine coaches in college basketball. You wouldn't want much better than Frank McGuire (South Carolina), Al McGuire (Marquette), Ray Mears (Tennessee), Fred Taylor (Ohio State) or Bob Polk (St. Louis) on the current scene. Or if you go back a few years, Ed Hickey (St. Louis), John Benington (St. Louis and Michigan State before his death), Hank Iba (Oklahoma State), George Keogan (Notre Dame)

and Johnny Mauer (UK, Tennessee and others) rate high.

On the basis of accomplishment, Rupp and Wooden have to rank at the pinnacle.

Adolph Rupp doesn't know any more basketball than many other coaches. The contrary may be true. There may be coaches who are better technicians.

But he's a great fundamentalist who believes in work and leaving nothing to chance. Cliff Hagan, for one, believes that the No. 1 reason for UK's continued success has been "hard work. Kentucky coaches outwork other coaches."

Rupp, himself, doesn't disagree with Hagan. The coach simply put it another way when asked the most important factor in his career: "Attention to detail."

Rupp was a stickler for working out detailed game plans before most other coaches even knew what a game plan was.

Although he has been known to be profane in the heat of a game, Rupp likes to paraphrase the Bible in conversation. Once, when asked about the source of

Tom Parker, a fine outside shooter, was Player of the Year in the SEC.

some of his players, Rupp said, "I will lift up mine eyes unto the hills, from whence cometh my help."

Johnny Cox, for example.

Another time, when asked how he picked his players, Rupp pointed to his door, which is 6 feet, 2 inches high. "If they don't bump their heads, I don't even bother to shake hands."

In a more serious vein, Rupp once said, "The first thing I look for is reflex action. Next is size. A boy must be big enough to play the game. If he is over six feet, he must have speed to go with it. Next I look for good habits—shooting, passing, poise. Courage is next. Can a player keep battling when the going gets rough?"

Rupp hasn't always been right in his handling of athletes. Some players simply haven't responded to being jerked out of a game for a mistake. Boys who play better after a pat on the back didn't belong on a Rupp team. He believed in "taking them to the woodshed."

Over the long haul, who's to say he was wrong? Perhaps the player who can't take pressure from his coach shouldn't be handling the basketball in a crucial situation before 15,000 spectators.

Rupp's greatest thrill as a coach?

"I guess seeing our boys stand on the winners' platform in the Olympics in London would have to be one of my biggest," he said.

"Of course, my 1958 team, which couldn't beat anybody, winning the NCAA was a big one, too. So was my undefeated team of 1954. I guess those were my biggest thrills."

Rupp takes pride in having played a part in the South's rise in basketball. "At least they give us credit for it, so I guess we've had something to do with it," he noted.

Rupp has never named his No. 1 disappointment, but it might have been the failure of his 1966 "Rupp's Runts" to win the NCAA championship game.

Rupp's best coaching job? Almost impossible to determine. He has nearly always done well the season after losing a batch of star players. The 1949-50 season, after the departure of Ralph Beard, Wallace Jones and Alex Groza, was one of Rupp's finest performances.

Noll Could Have Helped

After the unbeaten 1954 team was riddled by graduation, Rupp fooled everyone the next season when only two losses to Georgia Tech marred his regular-sea-

Adolph Rupp and his coaching staff watch intently during a Kentucky game. From left are Dick Parsons, Gale Catlett and Joe Hall.

son record. And he got a lot of mileage out of the 1958-59 squad the year after losing four starters from his Fiddlin' Five.

It's doubtful, though, if Rupp ever got more out of his material than he got in 1971-72. UK won 21 games and lost 7 with a team which most persons close to the situation felt would have to struggle to win half its games.

This was not exactly the team which Rupp and assistant coach Joe Hall recruited. They didn't anticipate that three walkons would dress every game, including the NCAA tournament games against Marquette and Florida State.

The first defection had come two years before when 6-foot-7 sophomore forward Randy Noll of Covington had departed. Although he had talent, Noll was worried that he might not get a chance to play much basketball for UK. So he went to M a r s h a l l University in Huntington, W.Va., laid out a year and came back in 1971-72 with a brilliant season.

Oh, how Rupp could have used Noll, who averaged 16.8 points, 12.6 rebounds (best on his team) and shot 49 per cent from the field for a Marshall team which won an at-large berth in the NCAA tournament. Making his loss all the more painful to Rupp, forward was a thin position all season for UK.

Next came the loss of Tom Payne to the professional Atlanta Hawks. Payne, the first black ever to play for Rupp, was a 16.9 scorer and 10.1 rebounder in his only season for UK.

Then Kent Hollenback. He suffered a broken foot in a conditioning program before regular practice started and before a series of mishaps had ended, the

foot had been broken four times. He could have played forward or guard.

Rupp finally settled on a lineup of 6-7 junior Larry Stamper of Beattyville, Ky., and 6-7 senior Tom Parker of Collinsville, Ill., at forwards; 6-11 junior Jim Andrews, originally from Lima, Ohio, but now a resident of Huntington, W.Va., at center, with 6-3 senior Stan Key of Hazel, Ky., and 5-9 sophomore Ronnie Lyons of Maysville, Ky., at guards.

Rupp's key reserves were sophomore Rick Drewitz and senior Bob McCowan. He also played sophomore Ray Edelman and Dan Perry. The walkons were Kirk Chiles, Larry Miller and Greg Smith.

Rupp has always said that the winning tradition UK has built over the years has become a vital part of Kentucky's continuing success. Certainly that was true with this team. From the start, no matter how many persons said UK was in for a poor season, the players insisted they were going to have a good team.

Rupp's players surprised him by knocking off Northwestern, Kansas and Kansas State before losing in double overtime to Indiana in Freedom Hall when Parker sat out the last 15 minutes with a sprained ankle.

McCowan Stars in Relief

Parker didn't play at all in a loss to Michigan State, the low point of the UK season. Just before the UK Invitational, a pair of black players off the UK football team, Darryl Bishop and Elmore Stephens, joined Rupp's squad. They were walkons, but both had been fine high school players.

McCowan, back on the UK team after

sitting out the previous season for disciplinary reasons, was the difference in an 83-79 UKIT victory over Missouri, scoring 15 points as a substitute. The next night Andrews with 28 points, Parker with 23 and Ronnie Lyons with 21 led UK over Princeton 96-82 for the UKIT title.

Kentucky didn't play well but had little trouble with Digger Phelps' Notre Dame team in Freedom Hall.

UK got a good start in the Southeastern Conference by beating Mississippi and Mississippi State in Lexington. But Rupp's Wildcats lost road games to Florida and Georgia and the SEC race settled down to a duel between Kentucky and Ray Mears' Tennessee Volunteers.

Near the end, road losses to Louisiana State and Alabama left UK a half-game behind Tennessee. Rupp's answer, with Auburn and Tennessee left to play— hard work. Except for Dr. V. A. Jackson, the practices were closed. Rupp wanted no distractions by anyone going and coming. The practices lasted about 45 minutes longer than normal.

"They were the hardest practices, by far, in my three years at Kentucky," student manager John Ferguson said.

UK beat Auburn easily and edged Tennessee 67-66 at Knoxville to gain a tie with the Tennessee for the SEC title (14-4 records). But UK got the NCAA Mideast Regional berth at Dayton for having beaten Tennessee twice.

UK went into the regional without Bishop and Stephens, who had been dropped from the squad after missing the plane to LSU and Alabama. It's doubtful if any team in the final 16 of the NCAA was as thin in reserves as Kentucky.

UK played a fine game to beat Marquette 85-69 at Dayton. UK employed a 2-3 zone for the first time to keep Marquette at long range. Marquette didn't hit (35.9), UK did (54.9). And UK guards Lyons and Key were able to handle Marquette's full-court press.

Parker missed 13 minutes of the second half with a sprained ankle, but Drewitz filled in admirably for him.

Next was Florida State, which had beaten Minnesota 70-56 in the other first-round regional game. UK, obviously feeling the wear and tear of its victory over Marquette, was no match for the tough Florida State defense. Coached by Hugh Durham, the same fellow who had scored 30 points for Florida State against UK in December of 1958, Florida State won 73-54.

Andrews made the All-Regional team. He and Parker both were chosen on the All-SEC team selected by the conference coaches. Parker was named SEC Player of the Year by the Associated Press.

One question kept bobbing up all through the season: will this be Rupp's last season or will UK waive its mandatory retirement rule?

Nine days after UK's loss to Florida State, the UK Athletic board met and decided that the retirement rule would apply to the 70-year-old coach.

Coach Rupp, the "man in the brown suit," a member of basketball's national Hall of Fame, was now "Mister" Rupp. But he had left a mark of excellence on basketball which could never be erased.

RUPP'S RECORD, LEADING SCORERS

Losses Set in Bold Type
1930-31: Won 15, Lost 3
CAPTAIN—Carey Spicer

Date	Team	Site	UK	Opp.
Dec. 18—Georgetown		H	67	19
Dec. 27—Marshall		H	42	26
Dec. 31—Berea		H	41	25
Jan. 3—Clemson		H	33	21
Jan. 10—Tennessee		H	31	23
Jan. 16—Chattanooga		H	55	18
Jan. 21—Vanderbilt		A	42	37
Jan. 31—Tennessee		A	36	*32
Feb. 6—Wash. & Lee		H	23	18
Feb. 9—Georgia Tech		H	38	34
Feb. 13—Georgia		A	**16**	**25**
Feb. 14—Clemson		A	**26**	**29**
Feb. 16—Georgia Tech		A	35	16
Feb. 20—Vanderbilt		H	43	23

SOUTHERN CONFERENCE TOURNAMENT
(Atlanta, Ga.)

Feb. 27—N. Carolina State			33	28
Feb. 28—Duke			35	30
Mar. 2—Florida			56	36
Mar. 3—Maryland (final)			**27**	**29**
SEASON TOTALS			679	469

*Overtime.

LEADING SCORERS

Player	Pts.	Avg.
Louis McGinnis, Sr., F	175	10.3
Carey Spicer, Sr., F	188	10.4
George Yates, Jr., C	126	7.0
Forest Sale, So., C	62	7.0
Jake Bronston, Sr., G	76	4.2

1931-32: Won 15, Lost 2
CAPTAIN—Ellis Johnson

Date	Team	Site	UK	Opp.
Dec. 15—Georgetown		H	66	24
Dec. 18—Carnegie Tech		H	36	34
Dec. 23—Berea		H	52	27
Dec. 30—Marshall		H	46	16
Jan. 2—Clemson		H	43	24
Jan. 14—Clemson		A	30	17
Jan. 15—Sewanee		A	30	20
Jan. 16—Tennessee		A	29	28
Jan. 21—Chattanooga		H	51	17
Jan. 30—Wash. & Lee		H	48	28
Feb. 3—Vanderbilt		A	61	37
Feb. 6—Duke		H	37	30
Feb. 8—Alabama		H	50	22
Feb. 13—Tennessee		H	41	27
Feb. 20—Vanderbilt		H	**31**	**32**

SOUTHERN CONFERENCE TOURNAMENT
(Atlanta, Ga.)

Feb. 26—Tulane			50	30
Feb. 27—North Carolina			**42**	**43**
SEASON TOTALS			743	456

LEADING SCORERS

Player	Pts.	Avg.
Forest Sale, Jr., F	235	13.8
John DeMoisey, So., C	142	11.8
Darrell Darby, Jr., F	132	7.8
Ellis Johnson, Jr., G	61	3.6
Howard Kreuter, Jr., G	50	3.6
Charles Worthington, Sr., G	50	3.1

1932-33: Won 20, Lost 3
CAPTAIN—Forest Sale.

Date	Team	site	UK	Opp.
Dec. 12—Georgetown		H	62	21
Dec. 17—Marshall		N-1	57	23
Dec. 20—Tulane		H	53	17
Dec. 21—Tulane		H	42	11

Dec. 30—Chicago		A	58	26
Jan. 2—Ohio State		H	**30**	**46**
Jan. 6—Creighton		A	32	26
Jan. 7—Creighton		A	**22**	**34**
Jan. 10—South Carolina		H	44	36
Jan. 14—Tennessee		A	42	21
Jan. 16—Clemson		H	67	18
Jan. 28—Tennessee		H	44	23
Jan. 31—Vanderbilt		A	40	29
Feb. 1—Clemson		A	42	32
Feb. 2—South Carolina		A	**38**	**44**
Feb. 6—Mexico U.		H	81	22
Feb. 11—Georgia Tech		H	45	22
Feb. 13—Alabama		N-2	35	21
Feb. 18—Vanderbilt		H	45	28

SEC TOURNAMENT
(Atlanta, Ga.)

Feb. 25—Mississippi		49	31
Feb. 26—Florida		48	24
Feb. 27—Louisiana State		51	38
Feb. 28—Mississippi State		46	27
SEASON TOTALS		1,073	630

N-1, Ashland; N-2, Birmingham.

LEADING SCORERS

Player	Pts.	Avg.
Forest Sale, Sr., F	321	14.0
John DeMoisey, Jr., G	265	11.5
Billy Davis, So., G	149	6.5
Darrell Darby, Sr., F	93	4.0
Ellis Johnson, Sr., G	80	3.5

1933-34: Won 15, Lost 1
CAPTAIN—John DeMoisey

Date	Team	Site	UK	Opp.
Dec. 9—Georgetown		H	41	12
Dec. 14—Marshall		H	48	26
Dec. 16—Cincinnati		H	31	25
Dec. 21—Tulane		A	32	22
Dec. 22—Tulane		A	42	29
Jan. 12—Sewanee		A	55	16
Jan. 13—Tennessee		A	44	23
Jan. 20—Chattanooga		H	47	20
Jan. 27—Tennessee		H	53	26
Feb. 1—Alabama		N-1	33	28
Feb. 3—Vanderbilt		A	48	26
Feb. 8—Alabama		H	26	21
Feb. 10—Georgia Tech		H	49	25
Feb. 15—Sewanee		H	60	15
Feb. 17—Vanderbilt		H	47	27

SEC TOURNAMENT

Feb. 24—Florida			**32**	**38**
SEASON TOTALS			688	379

N-1, Birmingham.

LEADING SCORERS

Player	Pts.	Avg.
John DeMoisey, Sr., C	185	11.5
Bill Davis, Jr., G	135	8.4
Dave Lawrence, Jr., F	125	7.8
Jack Tucker, Jr., F	62	4.1

1934-35: Won 19, Lost 2
CAPTAINS—Dave Lawrence, Jack Tucker.

Date	Team	Site	UK	Opp.
Dec. 10—Alumni		H	61	10
Dec. 13—Oglethorpe		H	81	12
Dec. 20—Tulane		A	38	9
Dec. 21—Tulane		A	52	12
Jan. 2—Chicago		H	42	16
Jan. 5—New York U.		A	**22**	**23**
Jan. 14—Chattanooga		H	66	19
Jan. 18—Tulane		H	63	22
Jan. 19—Tulane		H	55	12
Jan. 26—Tennessee		H	48	21
Feb. 1—Alabama		N-1	33	26
Feb. 2—Vanderbilt		A	58	22
Feb. 5—Xavier		A	40	27
Feb. 9—Georgia Tech		H	57	30
Feb. 11—Alabama		H	25	16
Feb. 13—Michigan State		A	**26**	**32**
Feb. 16—Tennessee		A	38	36
Feb. 22—Creighton		H	63	42
Feb. 23—Creighton		H	24	13
Mar. 2—Vanderbilt		H	53	19
Mar. 7—Xavier		H	46	29
SEASON TOTALS			991	448

N-1, Birmingham.

LEADING SCORERS

Player	Pts.	Avg.
LeRoy Edwards, So., C	345	16.4
Dave Lawrence, Sr., F	192	9.1
Jack Tucker, Sr., F	68	4.5
Warfield Donohue, So., G	65	3.2

1935-36: Won 15, Lost 6
CAPTAIN—Andy Anderson

Date	Team	Site	UK	Opp.
Dec. 6—Georgetown		H	42	17
Dec. 17—Berea		H	58	30
Dec. 23—Pittsburgh		H	35	17
Jan. 8—New York U.		A	28	41

(1935-36 continued)

Date	Team	Site	UK	Opp.
Jan. 14—Xavier		A	36	32
Jan. 17—Tulane		H	49	24
Jan. 18—Tulane		H	39	21
Jan. 21—Michigan State		H	27	19
Jan. 25—Tennessee		H	40	31
Feb. 1—Vanderbilt		A	23	32
Feb. 3—Alabama		A	32	30
Feb. 7—Alabama		H	40	34
FEB. 10—Notre Dame		A	20	41
Feb. 11—Butler		A	39	28
Feb. 15—Tennessee		A	28	39
Feb. 18—Xavier		H	49	40
Feb. 21—Creighton		H	68	38
Feb. 22—Creighton		H	29	31
Feb. 24—Vanderbilt		H	61	41

SEC TOURNAMENT
(Knoxville, Tenn.)

			UK	Opp.
Feb. 28—Miss. State			41	39
Mar. 1—Tennessee			28	39
SEASON TOTALS			812	644

LEADING SCORERS

Player	Pts.	Avg.
Ralph Carlisle, Jr., F.	221	10.5
Joe Hagan, Sr., F	164	7.8
Garland Lewis, Sr., G	146	6.9
Warfield Donohue, Jr., G	62	3.0
Andy Anderson, Sr., G	41	2.0

1936-37: Won 17, Lost 5
CAPTAIN—Warfield Donohue.

Date	Team	Site	UK	Opp.
Dec. 9—Georgetown		H	46	21
Dec. 12—Berea		H	70	26
Dec. 15—Xavier		A	34	28
Dec. 21—Centenary		H	37	19
Jan. 2—Mich. State		H	28	21
Jan. 5—Notre Dame		N-1	28	41
Jan. 8—Creighton		H	59	36
Jan. 14—Mich. State		A	23	24
Jan. 16—Akron		N-2	32	22
Jan. 23—Tennessee		A	43	26
Jan. 30—Vanderbilt		A	41	26
Feb. 1—Alabama		N-3	38	27
Feb. 3—Tulane		A	28	35
Feb. 4—Tulane		A	28	25
Feb. 8—Mexico U.		H	60	30
Feb. 10—Alabama		H	31	34
Feb. 13—Tennessee		A	24	26
Feb. 20—Vanderbilt		H	51	19
Feb. 22—Xavier		H	23	15

SEC TOURNAMENT
(Knoxville, Tenn.)

			UK	Opp.
Feb. 26—Louisiana State			57	37
Feb. 28—Georgia Tech			40	30
Mar. 1—Tennessee			39	25
SEASON TOTALS			860	593

N-1, Louisville; N-2, Cincinnati; N-3, Birmingham.

LEADING SCORERS

Player	Pts.	Avg.
Ralph Carlisle, Sr., F	205	9.8
Joe Hagan, Jr., F	150	6.8
Homer Thompson, So., C	109	5.0
Warfield Donohue, Sr., G	81	3.7
Bernie Opper, So., G	74	3.4

1937-38: Won 13, Lost 5
CAPTAIN—J. Rice Walker

Date	Team	Site	UK	Opp.
Dec. 5—Berea		H	67	33
Dec. 18—Cincinnati		H	38	21
Dec. 22—Centenary		H	35	25

SUGAR BOWL TOURNEY

			UK	Opp.
Dec. 29—Pittsburgh			40	29
Jan. 8—Mich. State		A	37	42
Jan. 10—Detroit		A	26	34
Jan. 15—Notre Dame		A	37	47
Jan. 22—Tennessee		H	52	27
Jan. 29—Vanderbilt		A	42	19
Jan. 31—Alabama		N-1	57	31
Feb. 5—Xavier		A	32	39
Feb. 7—Mich. State		H	44	27
Feb. 12—Alabama		H	27	21
Feb. 14—Marquette		H	35	33
Feb. 17—Xavier		H	45	29
Feb. 21—Vanderbilt		H	48	24
Feb. 26—Tennessee		A	29	26

SEC TOURNAMENT
(Baton Rouge, La.)

			UK	Opp.
Mar. 3—Tulane			34	36
SEASON TOTALS			725	541

N-1, Birmingham.

LEADING SCORERS

Player	Pts.	Avg.
Joe Hagan, Sr., F	185	10.3
Fred Curtis, Jr., F	115	6.4
Bernie Opper, Jr., G	97	5.7
Homer Thompson, Jr., C	93	5.2
Mickey Rouse, So., G	76	4.5

1938-39: Won 16, Lost 4
CAPTAIN—Bernie Opper

Date	Team	Site	UK	Opp.
Dec. 2—Georgetown		H	39	19
Dec. 10—Ky. Wesleyan		H	57	18
Dec. 17—Cincinnati		H	44	27
Dec. 21—Wash. & Lee		H	67	47
Jan. 4—Long Island		A	34	52
Jan. 6—St. Joseph's		A	41	30
Jan. 14—Notre Dame		N-1	37	42
Jan. 21—Tennessee		H	29	30
Jan. 28—Alabama		N-2	38	41
Jan. 30—Vanderbilt		A	51	37
Feb. 4—Marquette		H	37	31
Feb. 8—Xavier		A	41	31
Feb. 11—Alabama		H	45	27
Feb. 13—Miss. State		H	39	28
Feb. 18—Tennessee		A	36	**34
Feb. 21—Xavier		H	43	23
Feb. 25—Vanderbilt		H	52	27

SEC TOURNAMENT
(Knoxville, Tenn.)

			UK	Opp.
Mar. 2—Mississippi			49	30
Mar. 3—Louisiana State			53	34
Mar. 4—Tennessee			46	38
SEASON TOTALS			878	646

**Two overtimes
N-1, Louisville; N-2, Birmingham.

LEADING SCORERS

Player	Pts.	Avg.
Fred Curtis, Sr., F	184	9.2
Homer Thompson, Sr., C	128	7.1
Keith Farnsley, So., F	127	6.4
Mickey Rouse, Jr., G	104	5.5
Marion Cluggish, Jr., C	106	5.3
Bernie Opper, Sr., G	92	4.1

1939-40: Won 15, Lost 6
CAPTAIN—Layton Rouse

Date	Team	Site	UK	Opp.
Dec. 9—Berea		H	74	24
Dec. 16—Cincinnati		H	30	39
Dec. 21—Clemson		A	55	31

SUGAR BOWL TOURNEY
(New Orleans, La.)

			UK	Opp.
Dec. 27—Ohio State			36	30
Jan. 1—Kansas State		H	53	26
Jan. 6—Xavier		A	42	41
Jan. 8—West Virginia		H	47	38
Jan. 13—Notre Dame		A	47	52
Jan. 20—Tennessee		H	35	26
Jan. 27—Alabama		N-1	32	36
Jan. 29—Vanderbilt		A	32	40
Feb. 3—Marquette		A	51	45
Feb. 10—Alabama		H	46	18
Feb. 12—Xavier		H	37	29
Feb. 13—Miss. State		H	45	37
Feb. 17—Tennessee		A	23	27
Feb. 19—Georgia Tech		A	39	44
Feb. 24—Vanderbilt		H	43	38

SEC TOURNAMENT
(Knoxville, Tenn.)

			UK	Opp.
Feb. 29—Vanderbilt			44	31
Mar. 1—Tennessee			30	29
Mar. 2—Georgia			51	43
SEASON TOTALS			892	724

N-1, Birmingham.

LEADING SCORERS

Player	Pts.	Avg.
Layton Rouse, Sr., G	175	8.3
Keith Farnsley, Jr., F	154	7.3
Marion Cluggish, Sr., C	151	7.2
Lee Huber, Jr. G	100	5.2
Jim King, So., C	60	3.5

1940-41: Won 17, Lost 8
CAPTAIN—Lee Huber

Date	Team	Site	UK	Opp.
Dec. 7—Alumni		H	62	25
Dec. 12—West Virginia			46	34
Dec. 13—Maryville		H	53	14
Dec. 18—Nebraska		H	39	40
Dec. 19—Creighton		A	45	54
Dec. 20—Kansas State		A	28	25
Dec. 27—Centenary		H	70	18

SUGAR BOWL TOURNEY
(New Orleans, La.)

			UK	Opp.
Dec. 30—Indiana			45	48
Jan. 4—Notre Dame		N-1	47	48
Jan. 9—Xavier		A	48	43
Jan. 11—West Virginia		A	43	56
Jan. 18—Tennessee		A	22	32
Jan. 20—Georgia Tech		A	47	37
Jan. 25—Xavier		H	44	49
Feb. 1—Vanderbilt		H	51	50
Feb. 3—Alabama		A	38	36
Feb. 8—Alabama		H	46	38
Feb. 10—Mississippi		H	60	40
Feb. 15—Tennessee		H	37	28
Feb. 17—Georgia Tech		H	60	41
Feb. 24—Vanderbilt		H	58	31

SEC TOURNAMENT
(Louisville)

			UK	Opp.
Feb. 27—Mississippi			62	52
Feb. 28—Tulane			59	30
Mar. 1—Alabama			39	37
Mar. 2—Tennessee			33	36
SEASON TOTALS			1,182	943

N-1, Louisville.

LEADING SCORERS

Player	Pts.	Avg.
Jim King Jr., C	149	6.0
Waller White, Jr., F	143	6.0
Lee Huber, Sr., G	143	5.6
Keith Farnsley, Sr., F	124	5.2
Marvin Akers, So., G	105	4.8
Milt Ticco, So., F	102	6.0
Carl Staker, Jr., G	91	4.0

1941-42: Won 19, Lost 6
CAPTAIN—Carl Staker

Date	Team	Site	UK	Opp.
Dec. 6—Miami, Ohio		H	35	21
Dec. 13—Ohio State		A	41	43
Dec. 16—Nebraska		H	42	27
Dec. 22—South Carolina		H	64	25
Dec. 30—Texas A & M		H	49	29
Jan. 2—Wash & Lee		H	62	32
Jan. 10—Xavier		A	40	39
Jan. 17—Tennessee		A	40	46
Jan. 19—Georgia		A	51	26
Jan. 20—Georgia Tech		A	63	53
Jan. 24—Mexico		H	56	26
Jan. 31—Georgia		H	55	38
Feb. 2—Alabama		A	35	41
Feb. 7—Notre Dame		A	43	46
Feb. 9—Alabama		H	50	34
Feb. 14—Tennessee		A	36	33
Feb. 16—Georgia Tech		H	57	51
Feb. 21—Xavier		H	44	36

SEC TOURNAMENT
(Louisville)

			UK	Opp.
Feb. 26—Florida			42	36
Feb. 27—Mississippi			59	32
Feb. 28—Auburn			40	31
Mar. 1—Alabama			36	34

POST-SEASON GAME
(Louisville)

			UK	Opp.
Mar. 14—Great Lakes			47	58

NCAA REGIONAL
(New Orleans, La.)

			UK	Opp.
Mar. 20—Illinois			46	44
Mar. 21—Dartmouth			28	47
SEASON TOTALS			1,161	928

LEADING SCORERS

Player	Pts.	Avg.
Marvin Akers, Jr., G	187	7.5
Mel Brewer, Jr., C.	177	7.0
Milt Ticco, Jr., F	124	6.0
Ermal Allen, Sr., F	120	4.8
Ken England, Jr., G	116	4.8
Carl Staker, Sr., G	113	4.5
Jim King, Sr., C	93	3.9
Waller White Sr., F	90	3.6

1942-43: Won 17, Lost 6
CAPTAIN—Mel Brewer

Date	Team	Site	UK	Opp.
Dec. 12—Cincinnati		H	61	39
Dec. 19—Wash. St. Louis		H	45	38
Dec. 23—Indiana		N-1	52	58
Jan. 2—Ohio State		H	40	45
Jan. 4—Ft. Knox		H	64	30
Jan. 9—Xavier		A	43	38
Jan. 16—Tennessee		A	30	28
Jan. 18—Georgia		A	60	28
Jan. 19—Georgia Tech		A	38	37
Jan. 23—Notre Dame		N-1	60	55
Jan. 26—Vanderbilt			39	38
Jan. 30—Alabama		A	32	41
Feb. 1—Vanderbilt		A	54	43
Feb. 6—Alabama		H	67	41
Feb. 8—Xavier		H	48	36
Feb. 13—Tennessee		H	53	29
Feb. 15—Georgia Tech		H	58	31
Feb. 20—DePaul		A	44	53

SEC TOURNAMENT
(Louisville)

Feb. 25—Tulane			48	31
Feb. 26—Georgia			59	30
Feb. 27—Miss. State			52	43
Feb. 28—Tennessee			30	33

POST-SEASON GAME

Mar. 6—Great Lakes		N-1	39	53
SEASON TOTALS			1,124	887

N-1, Louisville.

LEADING SCORERS

Player	Pts.	Avg.
Milt Ticco, Sr., F	233	10.1
Mel Brewer, Sr., G	193	8.4
Marvin Akers, Sr., G	162	7.0
Mulford Davis, So., F	154	7.0
Kenny Rollins, So., G	118	5.4
Clyde Parker, So., G	65	3.3

1943-44: Won 19, Lost 2
CAPTAIN—None

Date	Team	Site	UK	Opp.
Dec. 1—Ft. Knox		H	51	18
Dec. 4—Berea		H	54	40
Dec. 11—Indiana		N-1	66	41
Dec. 13—Ohio State		A	40	28
Dec. 18—Cincinnati		H	58	30
Dec. 20—Illinois		A	41	43
Dec. 28—Carnegie Tech		A	61	14
Dec. 30—St. John's		A	44	38
Jan. 8—Notre Dame		N-1	55	54
Jan. 15—Wright Field		H	61	28
Jan. 31—Ft. Knox ARC		H	76	48
Feb. 4—DePauw		H	38	35
Feb. 7—Illinois		H	51	40
Feb. 12—Cincinnati		A	38	34
Feb. 26—Ohio U.		H	51	35

SEC TOURNAMENT (Louisville)

Mar. 2—Georgia			57	29
Mar. 3—Louisiana State			55	28
Mar. 4—Tulane			62	46

NATIONAL INVITATION (New York)

Mar. 20—Utah			46	38
Mar. 22—St. John's			45	48
Mar. 26—Oklahoma A & M			45	29
SEASON TOTALS			1,095	745

N-1, Louisville.

LEADING SCORERS

Player	Pts.	Avg.
Bob Brannum, Fr., C	229	11.4
Jack Tingle, Fr., F	175	8.3
Jack Parkinson, Fr., G	145	7.0
Wilbur Schu, So., F	126	6.3
Tom Moseley, So., G	79	3.8
Walter Johnson, Fr., G	74	6.1

1944-45: Won 22, Lost 4
CAPTAIN—None

Date	Team	Site	UK	Opp.
Dec. 2—Ft. Knox		H	56	23
Dec. 4—Berea		H	56	32
Dec. 9—Cincinnati		H	66	24
Dec. 16—Indiana		N-1	61	43
Dec. 23—Ohio State		H	53	*48
Dec. 26—Wyoming		N-2	50	46
Dec. 30—Temple		A	45	44
Jan. 1—Long Island		A	62	*52
Jan. 6—Ohio U.		H	59	46
Jan. 8—Arkansas State		H	75	6
Jan. 13—Mich. State		H	66	35
Jan. 20—Tennessee		A	34	35
Jan. 22—Georgia Tech		A	64	58
Jan. 27—Notre Dame		N-1	58	*59

Jan. 29—Georgia		H	73	37
Feb. 3—Georgia Tech		H	51	32
Feb. 5—Mich. State		A	50	66
Feb. 17—Tennessee		H	40	34
Feb. 19—Ohio U.		A	61	38
Feb. 24—Cincinnati		A	65	35

SEC TOURNEY (Louisville)

Mar. 1—Florida			57	35
Mar. 2—Louisiana State			68	37
Mar. 3—Alabama			52	41
Mar. 3—Tennessee			39	35

NCAA REGIONAL (New York)

Mar. 22—Ohio State			37	45
Mar. 23—Tufts			66	56
SEASON TOTALS			1,464	1,042

*Overtime
N-1, Louisville; N-2, Buffalo, N.Y.

LEADING SCORERS

Player	Pts.	Avg.
Jack Tingle, So., F	293	11.7
Jack Parkinson, So., G	269	10.3
Wilbur Schu, Jr., F	210	8.1
Alex Groza, Fr., C	165	16.5
Kenton Campbell, Fr., C	142	6.1

1945-46: Won 28, Lost 2
CAPTAIN—Jack Parkinson

Date	Team	Site	UK	Opp.
Dec. 1—Ft. Knox		H	59	36
Dec. 7—Western Ontario		H	51	42
Dec. 8—Western Ontario		H	71	28
Dec. 15—Cincinnati		H	67	31
Dec. 18—Arkansas		H	67	42
Dec. 21—Oklahoma		H	43	33
Dec. 29—St. John's		A	73	59
Jan. 1—Temple		A	45	53
Jan. 5—Ohio U.		H	57	48
Jan. 7—Ft. Benning		H	81	25
Jan. 12—Mich. State		A	55	44
Jan. 14—Xavier		A	62	36
Jan. 19—Tennessee		A	50	32
Jan. 21—Georgia Tech		A	68	43
Jan. 26—Notre Dame		N-1	47	56
Jan. 28—Georgia Tech		H	54	46
Feb. 2—Mich State		H	59	51
Feb. 4—Vanderbilt		A	59	37
Feb. 9—Vanderbilt		N-2	64	31
Feb. 16—Tennessee		H	54	34
Feb. 19—Ohio U.		A	60	52
Feb. 23—Xavier		H	83	40

SEC TOURNAMENT (Louisville)

Feb. 28—Auburn			69	24
Mar. 1—Florida			69	32
Mar. 2—Alabama			59	30
Mar. 2—Louisiana State			59	36

POST-SEASON GAME (Louisville)

Mar. 9—Temple			54	43

NATIONAL INVITATION (New York)

Mar. 16—Arizona			77	53
Mar. 18—West Virginia			59	51
Mar. 20—Rhode Island			46	45
SEASON TOTALS			1,821	1,193

N-1, Louisville; N-2, Paducah, Ky.

LEADING SCORERS

Player	Pts.	Avg.
Jack Parkinson, Jr., G	339	11.3
Wallace Jones, Fr., C	290	9.7
Ralph Beard, Fr., G	279	9.3
Jack Tingle, Jr., F	278	9.3
Wilbur Schu, Sr., F	200	7.7

1946-47: Won 34, Lost 3
CAPTAIN—Kenny Rollins

Date	Team	Site	UK	Opp.
Nov. 28—Indiana Central		H	78	36
Nov. 30—Tulane		H	64	35
Dec. 2—Ft. Knox		H	68	31
Dec. 7—Cincinnati		A	80	49
Dec. 9—Idaho		H	65	35
Dec. 12—DePaul		N-1	65	45
Dec. 14—Texas A & M		H	83	18
Dec. 16—Miami, Ohio		H	62	49
Dec. 21—St. John's		N-2	70	50
Dec. 23—Baylor		H	75	34
Dec. 28—Wabash		H	96	24

SUGAR BOWL (New Orleans)

Dec. 30—Okla. A & M			31	37

Jan. 4—Ohio U.		H	46	36
Jan. 11—Dayton		H	70	29
Jan. 13—Vanderbilt		A	82	30
Jan. 18—Tennessee		A	54	39
Jan. 20—Georgia Tech		A	70	47
Jan. 21—Georgia		A	84	45

Jan. 25—Xavier		H	71	34
Jan. 27—Mich. State		H	86	36
Feb. 1—Notre Dame		N-1	60	30
Feb. 3—Alabama		A	48	37
Feb. 8—DePaul		A	47	53
Feb. 10—Georgia		H	81	40
Feb. 15—Tennessee		H	61	46
Feb. 17—Alabama		H	63	33
Feb. 19—Xavier		A	58	31
Feb. 21—Vanderbilt		A	84	41
Feb. 22—Georgia Tech		H	83	46

SEC TOURNAMENT (Louisville)

Feb. 27—Vanderbilt			98	29
Feb. 28—Auburn			84	18
Mar. 1—Georgia Tech			75	53
Mar. 1—Tulane			55	38

POST-SEASON GAME (Louisville)

Mar. 8—Temple			68	29

NATIONAL INVITATION (New York)

Mar. 17—Long Island			63	62
Mar. 19—N. Carolina State			60	42
Mar. 24—Utah			45	49
SEASON TOTALS			2,533	1,416

N-1, Louisville; N-2, Mad. Square Garden.

LEADING SCORERS

Player	Pts.	Avg.
Alex Groza, So., C	393	10.6
Ralph Beard, So., G	392	10.6
Kenny Rollins, Jr., G	310	8.4
Joe Holland, So., G	224	6.1
Wallace Jones, So., F-C	217	6.6

1947-48: Won 36, Lost 3
CAPTAIN—Kenny Rollins

Date	Team	Site	UK	Opp.
Nov. 29—Indiana Central		H	80	41
Dec. 1—Ft. Knox		H	80	41
Dec. 5—Tulsa		H	72	18
Dec. 6—Tulsa		H	71	22
Dec. 10—DePaul		N-1	74	50
Dec. 13—Cincinnati		A	67	31
Dec. 17—Xavier		H	79	37
Dec. 20—Temple		A	59	60
Dec. 23—St. John's		A	52	40
Jan. 2—Creighton		A	65	23
Jan. 3—Western Ontario		H	98	41
Jan. 5—Miami (Ohio)		A	67	53
Jan. 10—Mich. State		A	47	45
Jan. 12—Ohio U.		A	79	57
Jan. 17—Tennessee		A	65	54
Jan. 19—Georgia Tech		A	71	56
Jan. 20—Georgia		A	88	51
Jan. 24—Cincinnati		H	70	43
Jan. 31—DePaul		A	68	51
Feb. 2—Notre Dame		A	55	64
Feb. 5—Alabama		A	41	31
Feb. 7—Wash. (St. Louis)		N-2	69	39
Feb. 9—Vanderbilt		A	82	51
Feb. 14—Tennessee		H	69	42
Feb. 16—Alabama		H	63	33
Feb. 20—Vanderbilt		H	79	43
Feb. 21—Georgia Tech		H	78	54
Feb. 24—Temple		N-1	58	38
Feb. 28—Xavier		A	59	37

SEC TOURNAMENT (Louisville)

Mar. 4—Florida			87	31
Mar. 5—Louisiana State			63	47
Mar. 6—Tennessee			70	47
Mar. 6—Georgia Tech			54	43

NCAA TOURNAMENT (New York)

Mar. 18—Columbia			76	53
Mar. 20—Holy Cross			60	52
Mar. 23—Baylor			58	42

OLYMPIC TRIALS (New York)

Mar. 27—Louisville			91	57
Mar. 29—Baylor			77	59
Mar. 31—Bartlesville Oilers			49	53
SEASON TOTALS			2,690	1,730

EXHIBITION GAMES
(Kentucky vs. Oilers)

June 30—At Tulsa, Okla.			52	60
July 2—Kansas City, Mo.			70	**69
July 9—At Lexington, Ky.			50	56

N-1, Louisville; N-2, Memphis, Tenn.
**Two overtimes.

LEADING SCORERS

Player	Pts.	Avg.
Alex Groza, Jr., C	488	12.5
Ralph Beard, Jr., G	476	12.5
Wallace Jones, Jr., F-C	335	9.3
Jim Line, So., F	265	7.0
Kenny Rollins, Sr., G	257	6.4

Cliff Barker, Jr., F	248	6.5
Dale Barnstable, So., F	176	4.6

1948-49: Won 32, Lost 2

CAPTAIN—None.

Date	Team	Site	UK	Opp.
Nov. 29	Indiana Central	H	74	38
Dec. 8	DePaul	N-1	67	36
Dec. 10	Tulsa	H	81	27
Dec. 13	Arkansas	H	76	39
Dec. 16	Holy Cross	A	51	48
Dec. 18	St. John's	A	57	30
Dec. 22	Tulane	N-1	51	47

SUGAR BOWL (New Orleans, La.)

Dec. 29	Tulane		78	47
Dec. 30	St. Louis		40	42
Jan. 11	Bowling Green	N-2	63	61
Jan. 15	Tennessee	A	66	51
Jan. 17	Georgia Tech	A	56	45
Jan. 22	DePaul	A	56	45
Jan. 29	Notre Dame	N-1	62	38
Jan. 31	Vanderbilt	A	72	50
Feb. 2	Alabama	A	56	40
Feb. 3	Mississippi	N-3	75	45
Feb. 5	Bradley	N-4	62	52
Feb. 8	Tennessee	H	71	56
Feb. 12	Xavier	H	96	50
Feb. 14	Alabama	H	74	32
Feb. 16	Mississippi	H	85	31
Feb. 19	Georgia Tech	H	78	32
Feb. 21	Georgia	H	95	40
Feb. 24	Xavier	A	51	40
Feb. 26	Vanderbilt	H	70	37

SEC TOURNAMENT (Louisville)

Mar. 3	Florida		73	36
Mar. 4	Auburn		70	39
Mar. 5	Tennessee		83	44
Mar. 5	Tulane		68	52

NATIONAL INVITATION (New York)

Mar. 14	Chicago Loyola		56	67

NCAA REGIONAL (New York)

Mar. 21	Villanova		85	72
Mar. 22	Illinois		76	47

NCAA FINALS (Seattle)

Mar. 26	Okla. A & M		46	36
	SEASON TOTALS		2,320	1,492

N-1, Louisville; N-2 Cleveland; N-3 Memphis; N-4 Owensboro.

LEADING SCORERS

Player	Pts.	Avg.
Alex Groza, Sr., C	698	20.5
Ralph Beard, Sr. G	370	10.9
Wallace Jones, Sr., F-C	309	9.7
Cliff Barker, Sr., F-G	248	7.3
Dale Barnstable, Jr., F-G	209	6.1

1949-50: Won 25, Lost 5

CAPTAIN—Dale Barnstable.

Date	Team	Site	UK	Opp.
Dec. 3	Indiana Central	H	84	61
Dec. 10	Western Ontario	H	90	18
Dec. 15	St. John's	A	58	69
Dec. 21	DePaul	N-1	49	47
Dec. 23	Purdue		60	54

SUGAR BOWL (New Orleans)

Dec. 29	Villanova		57	*56
Dec. 30	Bradley		71	66
Jan. 2	Arkansas	A	57	53
Jan. 4	Miss. State	N-2	87	55
Jan. 9	N. Carolina	H	83	44
Jan. 14	Tennessee	A	53	66
Jan. 16	Georgia Tech	A	61	47
Jan. 17	Georgia	A	60	71
Jan. 21	DePaul	A	86	53
Jan. 23	Notre Dame	A	51	64
Jan. 26	St. Xavier	A	58	47
Jan. 28	Georgia	H	88	56
Jan. 30	Vanderbilt	A	58	54
Feb. 2	Alabama	A	66	64
Feb. 4	Mississippi	N-3	61	55
Feb. 11	Tennessee	H	79	52
Feb. 13	Alabama	H	77	57
Feb. 15	Mississippi	H	90	50
Feb. 18	Georgia Tech	H	97	62
Feb. 23	Xavier	H	58	53
Feb. 25	Vanderbilt	H	70	66

SEC TOURNAMENT (Louisville)

Mar. 3	Miss. State		56	46
Mar. 3	Georgia		79	63
Ma. 4	Tennessee		95	58

NATIONAL INVITATION (New York)

Mar. 14	City College of N.Y.		50	89
	SEASON TOTALS		2,089	1,696

N-1, Louisville, N-2, Owensboro; N-3, Memphis.
*Overtime.

LEADING SCORERS

Player	Pts.	Avg.
Bill Spivey, So., C	578	19.3
Jim Line, Sr., F	394	13.1
Walt Hirsch, Jr., F	297	9.9
Bobby Watson, So., G	227	7.5
Dale Barnstable, Sr., F	179	5.9

1950-51: Won 32, Lost 2

CAPTAIN—Walt Hirsch

Date	Team	Site	UK	Opp.
Dec. 1	W. Texas State	H	73	43
Dec. 9	Purdue	H	70	52
Dec. 12	Xavier	A	67	56
Dec. 14	Florida	H	85	37
Dec. 16	Kansas	H	68	39
Dec. 23	St. John's	A	43	37

SUGAR BOWL (New Orleans)

Dec. 29	St. Louis		42	*43
Dec. 30	Syracuse		69	59
Jan. 5	Auburn	H	79	35
Jan. 8	DePaul	H	63	55
Jan. 13	Alabama	H	65	48
Jan. 15	Notre Dame	H	69	44
Jan. 20	Tennessee	A	70	45
Jan. 22	Georgia Tech	A	82	61
Jan. 27	Vanderbilt	A	74	49
Jan. 29	Tulane	A	104	68
Jan. 31	Louisiana State	A	81	59
Feb. 2	Miss. State	A	80	60
Feb. 3	Mississippi	N-1	86	39
Feb. 9	Georgia Tech	H	75	42
Feb. 13	Xavier	H	78	51
Feb. 17	Tennessee	H	86	61
Feb. 19	DePaul	A	60	57
Feb. 23	Georgia	H	88	41
Feb. 24	Vanderbilt	H	89	57

SEC TOURNAMENT (Louisville)

Mar. 1	Miss. State		92	70
Mar. 2	Auburn		84	54
Mar. 3	Georgia Tech		82	56
Mar. 3	Vanderbilt		57	61

POST-SEASON GAME

Mar. 13	Chicago Loyola	H	97	61

NCAA TOURNAMENT
(First Round, Raleigh, N.C.)

Mar. 20	Louisville		79	68

(Eastern Regional, New York)

Mar. 22	St. John's		59	43
Mar. 24	Illinois		76	74

(NCAA Finals, Minneapolis)

Mar. 27	Kansas State		68	58
	SEASON TOTALS		2,540	1,783

N-1, Owensboro.
*Overtime.

SCORING LEADERS

Player	Pts.	Avg.
Bill Spivey, Jr., C	635	19.2
Shelby Linville, Jr., F	355	10.4
Bobby Watson, Jr., G	353	10.4
Frank Ramsey, So., G	345	10.1
Walt Hirsch, Sr., F	274	9.1
Cliff Hagan, So., F	183	9.2

1951-52: Won 29, Lost 3

CAPTAIN—Bobby Watson

Date	Team	Site	UK	Opp.
Dec. 8	Wash. & Lee	H	96	46
Dec. 10	Xavier	A	97	72
Dec. 13	Minnesota	A	57	61
Dec. 17	St. John's	H	81	40
Dec. 20	DePaul	H	98	60
Dec. 26	UCLA	H	84	53

SUGAR BOWL (New Orleans)

Dec. 28	Brigham Young		84	64
Dec. 29	St. Louis		60	61
Jan. 2	Mississippi-x	N-1	116	58
Jan. 5	Louisiana State	H	57	47
Jan. 7	Xavier	H	83	50
Jan. 12	Florida	A	99	52
Jan. 16	Georgia	N-2	99	55
Jan. 19	Tennessee	A	65	56
Jan. 21	Georgia Tech	A	96	51
Jan. 26	Alabama	A	71	67
Jan. 28	Vanderbilt	A	88	51
Jan. 30	Auburn	A	88	48
Feb. 2	Notre Dame	N-3	71	66
Feb. 4	Tulane	H	103	54
Feb. 6	Mississippi	H	81	61
Feb. 9	Georgia Tech	H	93	42
Feb. 11	Miss. State	H	110	66
Feb. 16	Tennessee	H	95	40
Feb. 21	Vanderbilt	H	75	45
Feb. 23	DePaul	A	63	61

SEC TOURNAMENT (Louisville)

Feb. 28	Georgia Tech		80	59
Feb. 29	Tulane		85	61
Mar. 1	Tennessee		81	66
Mar. 1	Louisiana State		44	43

NCAA REGIONAL (Raleigh, N.C.)

Mar. 21	Penn State		82	54
Mar. 22	St. John's		57	64
	SEASON TOTALS		2,639	1,774

N-1, Owensboro; N-2, Louisville; N-3, Chicago.
x-Not an SEC game.

LEADING SCORERS

Player	Pts.	Avg.
Cliff Hagan, Jr., C	692	21.6
Frank Ramsey, Jr., G	509	15.9
Bobby Watson, Sr., G	421	13.1
Lou Tsioropoulos, Jr., F	254	7.9
Lucian Whitaker, Sr., F-G	242	7.8
Billy Evans, So., F	162	5.2

1952-53: No Schedule

Under suspension by the NCAA and SEC.

1953-54: Won 25, Lost 0

COCAPTAINS—Cliff Hagan, Frank Ramsey

Date	Team	Site	UK	Opp.
Dec. 5	Temple	H	86	59
Dec. 12	Xavier	A	81	66
Dec. 14	Wake Forest	H	101	69
Dec. 18	St. Louis	A	71	59

UK INVITATIONAL TOURNEY

Dec. 21	Duke	H	85	69
Dec. 22	LaSalle	H	73	60
Dec. 28	Minnesota	H	74	59
Jan. 4	Xavier	H	77	71
Jan. 9	Georgia Tech	H	105	53
Jan. 11	DePaul	H	81	63
Jan. 16	Tulane	H	94	43
Jan. 23	Tennessee	A	97	71
Jan. 30	Vanderbilt	A	85	63
Feb. 2	Georgia Tech	N-1	99	48
Feb. 4	Georgia	H	106	55
Feb. 6	Georgia	N-2	100	68
Feb. 8	Florida	A	97	55
Feb. 13	Mississippi	H	88	62
Feb. 15	Miss. State	H	81	49
Feb. 18	Tennessee	H	90	63
Feb. 20	DePaul	H	76	61
Feb. 22	Vanderbilt	H	100	64
Feb. 27	Auburn	N-3	109	79
Mar. 1	Alabama	A	68	43
Mar. 9	Louisiana	N-4	63	56
	SEASON TOTALS		2,187	1,508

N-1, Louisville; N-2, Owensboro; N-3, Montgomery, Ala.; N-4, Nashville, playoff for NCAA berth. UK won but declined the bid.

LEADING SCORERS

Player	Pts.	Avg.
Cliff Hagan, Sr., C	600	24.0
Frank Ramsey, Sr., G	490	19.6
Lou Tsioropoulos, Sr., F	363	14.5
Billy Evans, Jr., F-G	221	8.4
Gayle Rose, Jr., G	154	6.7
Phil Grawemeyer, So., F	147	5.9
Linville Puckett, So., G	123	4.9

1954-55: Won 23, Lost 3

CAPTAIN—Billy Evans

Date	Team	Site	UK	Opp.
Dec. 4	Louisiana State-x	H	74	58
Dec. 11	Xavier	A	73	69
Dec. 18	Temple	H	79	61

UK INVITATIONAL

Date	Team	Site	UK	Opp.
Dec. 21—Utah		H	70	65
Dec. 22—LaSalle		H	63	54
Dec. 30—St. Louis		H	82	65
Jan. 1—Temple		A	101	69
Jan. 8—Georgia Tech		H	58	59
Jan. 10—DePaul		H	92	59
Jan. 15—Tulane		A	58	44
Jan. 17—Louisiana State		A	64	62
Jan. 22—Tennessee		A	84	66
Jan. 29—Vanderbilt		A	75	71
Jan. 31—Georgia Tech		A	59	65
Feb. 3—Florida		H	87	63
Feb. 5—Mississippi		N-1	84	66
Feb. 7—Miss. State		A	61	56
Feb. 9—Georgia		H	86	40
Feb. 14—Xavier		H	66	55
Feb. 19—DePaul		A	76	72
Feb. 21—Vanderbilt		H	77	59
Feb. 26—Auburn		H	93	59
Feb. 28—Alabama		H	66	52
Mar. 5—Tennessee		H	104	61

NCAA REGIONAL (Evanston, Ill.)

Mar. 11—Marquette			71	79
Mar. 12—Penn State			84	59
SEASON TOTALS			1,987	1,588

N-1, Memphis.
x-Not an SEC game.

LEADING SCORERS

Player	Pts.	Avg.
Bob Burrow, Jr., C	495	19.0
Billy Evans, Sr., G	333	13.9
Jerry Bird, Jr., F	278	10.7
Phil Grawemeyer, Jr., F	260	13.0
Gayle Rose, Sr., G	177	7.4
John Brewer, So., F	102	5.7

1955-56: Won 20, Lost 6

CAPTAIN—Phil Grawemeyer

Date	Team	Site	UK	Opp.
Dec. 3—Louisiana State-x		A	62	52
Dec. 10—Temple		H	61	73
Dec. 12—DePaul		H	71	69
Dec. 15—Maryland		A	62	61
Dec. 17—Idaho		H	91	49

UK INVITATIONAL

Dec. 20—Minnesota			72	65
Dec. 21—Dayton			74	89
Dec. 28—St. Louis		A	101	80
Jan. 7—Georgia Tech		H	104	51
Jan. 12—Tulane		H	85	63
Jan. 14—Louisiana State		H	107	65
Jan. 21—Tennessee		A	95	68
Jan. 28—Vanderbilt		A	73	81
Jan. 30—Georgia Tech		A	84	62
Feb. 1—Duke		H	81	76
Feb. 4—Auburn		N-1	82	81
Feb. 6—Florida		A	81	70
Feb. 11—Mississippi		H	88	49
Feb. 13—Miss. State		H	86	65
Feb. 18—DePaul		A	79	81
Feb. 20—Vanderbilt		H	76	55
Feb. 25—Alabama		N-1	77	101
Feb. 27—Georgia		N-2	143	66
Mar. 3—Tennessee		H	101	77

NCAA REGIONAL (Iowa City, Iowa)

Mar. 16—Wayne			84	64
Mar. 17—Iowa			77	89
SEASON TOTALS			2,197	1,802

N-1, Montgomery, Ala.; N-2, Louisville.
x—Not an SEC game.

LEADING SCORERS

Player	Pts.	Avg.
Bob Burrow, Sr., C	528	21.1
Jerry Bird, Sr., F	421	16.2
Vernon Hatton, So., G	346	13.3
Gerry Calvert, Jr., G	291	11.2
Phil Grawemeyer, Sr., F	219	8.4

1956-57: Won 23, Lost 5

COCAPTAINS—Gerry Calvert, Ed Beck

Date	Team	Site	UK	Opp.
Dec. 1—Wash. & Lee		H	94	66
Dec. 3—Miami (Fla.)		H	114	75
Dec. 8—Temple		A	73	58
Dec. 10—St. Louis		H	70	71
Dec. 15—Maryland		H	76	55
Dec. 18—Duke		A	84	85

UK INVITATIONAL

Dec. 21—Southern Methodist		H	73	67
Dec. 22—Illinois		H	91	70

SUGAR BOWL (New Orleans)

Dec. 28—Virginia Tech			56	55
Dec. 29—Houston			111	76
Jan. 5—Georgia Tech		H	95	72
Jan. 7—Chicago Loyola		H	81	62
Jan. 12—Louisiana State		A	51	46
Jan. 14—Tulane		A	60	68
Jan. 19—Tennessee		H	97	72
Jan. 26—Vanderbilt		A	91	83
Jan. 28—Georgia Tech		A	76	65
Jan. 30—Georgia		H	84	53
Feb. 2—Florida		H	88	61
Feb. 8—Mississippi		N-1	75	69
Feb. 11—Miss. State		A	81	89
Feb. 15—Chicago Loyola		H	115	65
Feb. 18—Vanderbilt		H	80	65
Feb. 23—Alabama		H	79	60
Feb. 25—Auburn		H	103	85
Mar. 2—Tennessee		H	93	75

NCAA REGIONAL (Lexington)

Mar. 15—Pittsburgh		H	98	92
Mar. 16—Mich. State		H	68	80
SEASON TOTALS			2,357	1,953

SCORING LEADERS

Player	Pts.	Avg.
Johnny Cox, So., F	544	19.4
Gerry Calvert, Sr., G	427	15.2
Vernon Hatton, Jr., G	311	14.8
John Crigler, Jr., F	289	10.3
Ed Beck, Jr., C	259	9.5
Adrian Smith, Jr., G	158	7.1

1957-58: Won 23, Lost 6

CAPTAIN—Ed Beck

Date	Team	Site	UK	Opp.
Dec. 2—Duke		H	78	74
Dec. 4—Ohio State		A	61	54
Dec. 7—Temple		H	85	***83
Dec. 9—Maryland		A	62	71
Dec. 14—St. Louis		A	73	60
Dec. 16—Southern Methodist		A	64	65

UK INVITATIONAL

Dec. 20—West Virginia		H	70	77
Dec. 21—Minnesota		H	78	58
Dec. 23—Utah State		H	92	64
Dec. 30—Chicago Loyola		H	75	42
Jan. 4—Georgia Tech		H	76	60
Jan. 6—Vanderbilt		A	86	81
Jan. 11—Louisiana State		H	97	52
Jan. 13—Tulane		H	86	50
Jan. 18—Tennessee		H	77	68
Jan. 27—Georgia Tech		A	52	71
Jan. 29—Georgia		N-1	74	55
Jan. 31—Florida		A	78	56
Feb. 8—Mississippi		H	96	65
Feb. 10—Miss. State		H	72	62
Feb. 15—Chicago Loyola		A	56	57
Feb. 17—Vanderbilt		H	65	61
Feb. 22—Alabama		N-2	45	*43
Feb. 24—Auburn		N-3	63	64
Mar. 1—Tennessee		A	77	66

NCAA REGIONAL (Lexington)

Mar. 14—Miami (Ohio)		H	94	70
Mar. 15—Notre Dame		H	89	56

NCAA FINALS (Louisville)

Mar. 21—Temple			61	60
Mar. 22—Seattle			84	72
SEASON TOTALS			2,166	1,817

N-1, Atlanta; N-2, Montgomery; N-3, Birmingham.
*One overtime; ***Three overtimes.

LEADING SCORERS

Player	Pts.	Avg.
Vernon Hatton, Sr., G	496	17.1
Johnny Cox, Jr., F	432	14.9
John Crigler, Sr., F	382	13.6
Adrian Smith, Sr., G	360	12.4
Ed Beck, Sr., C	163	5.6

1958-59: Won 24, Lost 3

CAPTAIN—Johnny Cox

Date	Team	Site	UK	Opp.
Dec. 1—Florida State		H	91	68
Dec. 6—Temple		A	76	71
Dec. 8—Duke		A	78	64
Dec. 11—Southern Methodist		H	72	60
Dec. 13—St. Louis		H	76	57
Dec. 15—Maryland		H	58	*56

UK INVITATIONAL

Dec. 19—Ohio State		H	95	76
Dec. 20—West Virginia		H	97	91
Dec. 29—Navy		H	82	69
Dec. 30—Illinois		N-1	76	75
Jan. 3—Georgia Tech		H	72	62
Jan. 6—Vanderbilt		A	66	75
Jan. 10—Louisiana State		A	76	61
Jan. 12—Tulane		A	85	68
Jan. 17—Tennessee		H	79	58
Jan. 26—Georgia Tech		A	94	70
Jan. 29—Georgia		H	108	55
Jan. 31—Florida		H	94	51
Feb. 7—Mississippi		N-2	97	72
Feb. 9—Miss. State		A	58	66
Feb. 14—Notre Dame		N-3	71	52
Feb. 18—Vanderbilt		H	83	71
Feb. 21—Auburn		H	75	56
Feb. 23—Alabama		H	39	32
Feb. 28—Tennessee		A	69	56

NCAA REGIONAL (Evanston, Ill.)

Mar. 13—Louisville			61	76
Mar. 14—Marquette			98	69
SEASON TOTALS			2,126	1,737

N-1, Louisville; N-2, Jackson, Miss.; N-3, Chicago.
*Overtime.

LEADING SCORERS

Player	Pts.	Avg.
Johnny Cox, Sr., F	485	17.9
Bill Lickert, So., F-G	338	13.5
Bennie Coffman, Jr., G	291	10.7
Don Mills, Jr., C	275	10.5
Dick Parsons, So., G	216	8.0
Sid Cohen, Jr., G	203	8.1

1959-60: Won 18, Lost 7

CAPTAINS—Bill Lickert, Don Mills

Date	Team	Site	UK	Opp.
Dec. 1—Colorado State		H	106	73
Dec. 4—UCLA		A	68	66
Dec. 5—Southern Cal		A	73	87
Dec. 12—St. Louis		A	61	73
Dec. 14—Kansas		A	77	*72

UK INVITATIONAL TOURNAMENT

Dec. 18—North Carolina		H	76	70
Dec. 19—West Virginia		H	70	79
Dec. 20—Temple		N-1	97	92
Dec. 28—Ohio State		H	96	93
Jan. 2—Georgia Tech		H	54	62
Jan. 5—Vanderbilt		A	76	59
Jan. 9—Louisiana State		H	77	45
Jan. 11—Tulane		H	68	42
Jan. 16—Tennessee		A	78	68
Jan. 25—Georgia Tech		A	44	65
Jan. 27—Georgia		N-2	84	60
Jan. 29—Florida		A	75	62
Feb. 6—Mississippi		H	61	43
Feb. 8—Mississippi State		H	90	59
Feb. 13—Notre Dame		H	68	65
Feb. 16—Vanderbilt		H	68	60
Feb. 20—Auburn		A	60	61
Feb. 22—Alabama		N-3	75	55
Feb. 27—Tennessee		H	63	65
Mar. 5—Pittsburgh		H	73	66
SEASON TOTALS			1,838	1,642

*One overtime period.
N-1, Louisville; N-2, Columbus, Ga.; N-3, Montgomery, Ala.

LEADING SCORERS

Player	Pts.	Avg.
Don Mills, Jr., C-F	319	12.7
Bill Lickert, Jr., F-G	288	14.4
Sid Cohen, Sr., G	268	10.7
Bennie Coffman, Sr., G	235	10.2
Ned Jennings, Jr., C	193	8.8
Dick Parsons, Jr., G	160	6.9
Carroll Burchett, So., F	155	7.0

1960-61: Won 19, Lost 9

CAPTAIN—Dick Parsons

Date	Team	Site	UK	Opp.
Dec. 1—Virginia Military		H	72	56
Dec. 3—Florida State		H	58	63
Dec. 7—Notre Dame		N-1	68	62
Dec. 13—North Carolina		N-2	70	65
Dec. 17—Temple		A	58	66

UK INVITATIONAL

Date	Team	Site	UK	Opp.
Dec. 21—Illinois		H	83	78
Dec. 22—St. Louis		H	72	*74
Dec. 31—Missouri		H	81	69
Jan. 2—Miami (Ohio)		H	70	58
Jan. 7—Georgia Tech		H	89	79
Jan. 9—Vanderbilt		A	62	64
Jan. 13—Louisiana State		A	59	73
Jan. 14—Tulane		A	70	72
Jan. 21—Tennessee		H	83	54
Jan. 30—Georgia Tech		A	60	62
Feb. 4—Florida		H	89	68
Feb. 7—Georgia		H	74	67
Feb. 11—Mississippi		N-3	74	60
Feb. 13—Mississippi State		A	68	62
Feb. 17—UCLA		H	77	76
Feb. 21—Vanderbilt		H	60	59
Feb. 25—Alabama		H	80	53
Feb. 27—Auburn		H	77	51
Mar. 4—Tennessee		A	68	61

SEC PLAYOFF (Knoxville, Tenn.)

Date	Team	Site	UK	Opp.
Mar. 9—Vanderbilt			88	67
Mar. 11—Marquette		N-4	72	88

NCAA REGIONAL (Louisville)

Date	Team	Site	UK	Opp.
Mar. 17—Morehead			71	64
Mar. 18—Ohio State			74	87
SEASON TOTALS			2,027	1,858

N-1, Louisville; N-2, Greensboro, N.C.; N-3, Jackson, Miss.; N-4, Chicago.

LEADING SCORERS

Player	Pts.	Avg.
Bill Lickert, Sr., F-G	450	16.0
Roger Newman, Sr., F-G	397	14.1
Larry Pursiful, Jr., G	375	13.4
Ned Jennings, Sr., C	323	11.5
Carroll Burchett, Jr., F-C	144	5.1
Dick Parsons, Sr., G	135	5.6

1961-62: Won 23, Lost 3

CAPTAIN—Larry Pursiful

Date	Team	Site	UK	Opp.
Dec. 2—Miami (Ohio)		H	93	61
Dec. 4—Sou. California		H	77	79
Dec. 11—St. Louis		H	86	77
Dec. 16—Baylor		H	94	60
Dec. 18—Temple		H	78	55

UK INVITATIONAL

Date	Team	Site	UK	Opp.
Dec. 22—Tennessee		H	96	69
Dec. 23—Kansas State		H	80	67
Dec. 27—Yale		H	79	58
Dec. 30—Notre Dame		N-1	100	53
Jan. 2—Virginia		H	93	73
Jan. 6—Georgia Tech		H	89	70
Jan. 8—Vanderbilt		A	77	68
Jan. 12—Louisiana State		A	84	63
Jan. 15—Tennessee		A	95	82
Jan. 29—Georgia Tech		A	71	62
Jan. 31—Georgia		N-2	86	59
Feb. 2—Florida		H	81	69
Feb. 10—Mississippi		H	83	60
Feb. 12—Mississippi State		H	44	49
Feb. 19—Vanderbilt		H	87	80
Feb. 24—Alabama		A	73	65
Feb. 26—Auburn		A	63	60
Mar. 5—Tulane		H	97	72
Mar. 10—Tennessee		H	90	59

NCAA REGIONAL (Iowa City, Iowa)

Date	Team	Site	UK	Opp.
Mar. 16—Butler			81	60
Mar. 17—Ohio State			64	74
SEASON TOTALS			2,141	1,704

N-1, Louisville; N-2, Atlanta.

SCORING LEADERS

Player	Pts.	Avg.
Charles Nash, So., C-F	608	23.4
Larry Pursiful, Sr., G	497	19.1
Carroll Burchett, Sr., F-C	279	11.2
Scotty Baesler, Jr., G	283	10.9
Roy Roberts, Jr., F	181	7.0

1962-63: Won 16, Lost 9

CAPTAIN—Scotty Baesler

Date	Team	Site	UK	Opp.
Dec. 1—Virginia Tech		H	77	80
Dec. 8—Temple		A	56	52
Dec. 12—Florida State		H	83	54
Dec. 15—Northwestern		H	71	60
Dec. 17—North Carolina		H	66	68

UK INVITATIONAL

Date	Team	Site	UK	Opp.
Dec. 21—Iowa		H	94	69
Dec. 22—West Virginia		H	79	75
Dec. 27—Dartmouth		H	95	49
Dec. 29—Notre Dame		N-1	78	70
Dec. 31—St. Louis		A	63	87
Jan. 5—Georgia Tech		H	85	**86
Jan. 7—Vanderbilt		H	106	82
Jan. 11—Louisiana State		A	63	56
Jan. 12—Tulane		A	81	72
Jan. 19—Tennessee		H	69	*78
Jan. 26—Xavier		H	90	76
Jan. 28—Georgia Tech		A	62	66
Jan. 31—Georgia		H	74	67
Feb. 2—Florida		H	94	71
Feb. 9—Mississippi		N-2	75	69
Feb. 11—Mississippi State		A	52	56
Feb. 18—Vanderbilt		H	67	69
Feb. 23—Auburn		H	78	59
Feb. 25—Alabama		H	80	63
Mar. 2—Tennessee		A	55	63
SEASON TOTALS			1,893	1,697

*One overtime; **two overtimes.
N-1, Louisville; N-2, Jackson, Miss.

SCORING LEADERS

Player	Pts.	Avg.
Charles Nash, Jr., F-C	514	20.6
Scotty Baesler, Sr., G	243	9.7
Ted Deeken, Jr., F	235	9.8
Roy Roberts, Sr., F	226	9.0
Charles Ishmael, Jr., G	212	11.1

1963-64: Won 21, Lost 6

CAPTAINS—Charles Nash, Ted Deeken

Date	Team	Site	UK	Opp.
Nov. 30—Virginia		H	75	64
Dec. 2—Texas Tech		H	107	91
Dec. 7—Northwestern		A	95	63
Dec. 9—North Carolina		H	100	80
Dec. 14—Baylor		H	101	65

UK INVITATIONAL

Date	Team	Site	UK	Opp.
Dec. 20—Wisconsin		H	108	85
Dec. 21—Wake Forest		H	98	75
Dec. 28—Notre Dame		N-1	101	81

SUGAR BOWL (At New Orleans)

Date	Team	Site	UK	Opp.
Dec. 30—Loyola (La.)			86	64
Dec. 31—Duke			81	79
Jan. 4—Georgia Tech		A	67	76
Jan. 6—Vanderbilt		A	83	85
Jan. 10—Louisiana State		H	103	84
Jan. 11—Tulane		H	105	63
Jan. 18—Tennessee		H	66	57
Jan. 25—Georgia Tech		H	79	62
Feb. 1—Florida		A	77	72
Feb. 3—Georgia		A	103	83
Feb. 8—Mississippi		H	102	59
Feb. 10—Mississippi State		H	65	59
Feb. 17—Vanderbilt		H	104	73
Feb. 22—Auburn		N-2	99	79
Feb. 24—Alabama		H	59	65
Feb. 29—Tennessee		A	42	38
Mar. 2—St. Louis		H	60	67

NCAA REGIONAL (Minneapolis, Minn.)

Date	Team	Site	UK	Opp.
Mar. 13—Ohio University			69	85
Mar. 14—Chicago Loyola			91	100
SEASON TOTALS			2,326	1,954

N-1, Louisville; N-2, Montgomery, Ala.

LEADING SCORERS

Player	Pts.	Avg.
Cotton Nash, Sr., F-C	648	24.0
Ted Deeken, Sr., F	493	18.5
Larry Conley, So., F	331	12.2
Terry Mobley, Jr., G	225	9.4
Randy Embry, Jr., G	174	7.2

1964-65: Won 15, Lost 10

CAPTAIN—Randy Embry

Date	Team	Site	UK	Opp.
Dec. 4—Iowa		H	85	77
Dec. 7—North Carolina		N-1	67	82
Dec. 9—Iowa State		H	100	74
Dec. 12—Syracuse		H	110	77

UK INVITATIONAL

Date	Team	Site	UK	Opp.
Dec. 18—West Virginia		H	102	78
Dec. 19—Illinois		H	86	91
Dec. 22—St. Louis		A	75	80
Dec. 29—Notre Dame		N-2	97	111
Jan. 2—Dartmouth		H	107	67
Jan. 5—Vanderbilt		H	79	97
Jan. 9—Louisiana State		A	79	66
Jan. 11—Tulane		A	102	72
Jan. 16—Tennessee		H	58	77
Jan. 18—Auburn		H	73	67
Jan. 23—Florida		A	68	84
Jan. 25—Georgia		A	102	82
Jan. 30—Florida		H	78	61
Feb. 1—Georgia		H	96	64
Feb. 6—Mississippi		H	102	65
Feb. 8—Miss. State		H	74	56
Feb. 16—Vanderbilt		A	90	91
Feb. 20—Auburn		A	69	88
Feb. 22—Alabama		A	71	75
Feb. 27—Tennessee		H	61	60
Mar. 1—Alabama		H	78	72
SEASON TOTALS			2,109	1,914

N-1, Charlotte, N.C.; N-2, Louisville.

LEADING SCORERS

Player	Pts.	Avg.
Louie Dampier, So., G	426	17.0
Pat Riley, So., F	375	15.0
John Adams, Sr., C	296	11.8
Larry Conley, Jr. F	290	11.6
Tom Kron, Jr., G-F	284	12.3
Terry Mobley, Sr., G	226	9.0

1965-66: Won 27, Lost 2

CAPTAIN—None

Date	Team	Site	UK	Opp.
Dec. 1—Hardin-Simmons		H	83	55
Dec. 4—Virginia		A	99	73
Dec. 8—Illinois		A	86	68
Dec. 11—Northwestern		H	86	75

UK INVITATIONAL

Date	Team	Site	UK	Opp.
Dec. 17—Air Force		H	78	58
Dec. 18—Indiana		H	91	56
Dec. 22—Texas Tech		A	89	73
Dec. 29—Notre Dame		N-1	103	69
Jan. 3—St. Louis		H	80	70
Jan. 8—Florida		A	78	64
Jan. 10—Georgia		A	69	**65
Jan. 15—Vanderbilt		H	96	83
Jan. 24—Louisiana State		H	111	85
Jan. 29—Auburn		H	115	78
Jan. 31—Alabama		H	82	62
Feb. 2—Vanderbilt		A	105	90
Feb. 5—Georgia		H	74	50
Feb. 7—Florida		H	85	75
Feb. 12—Auburn		A	77	64
Feb. 14—Alabama		A	90	67
Feb. 19—Miss. State		H	73	69
Feb. 21—Mississippi		A	108	65
Feb. 26—Tennessee		H	78	64
Mar. 5—Tennessee		A	62	69
Mar. 7—Tulane		H	103	74

NCAA REGIONAL (Iowa City)

Date	Team	Site	UK	Opp.
Mar. 11—Dayton			86	79
Mar. 12—Michigan			84	77

NCAA FINALS (College Park, Md.)

Date	Team	Site	UK	Opp.
Mar. 18—Duke			83	79
Mar. 19—Texas Western			65	72
SEASON TOTALS			2,519	2,028

N-1, Louisville.
*Overtime.

LEADING SCORERS

Player	Pts.	Avg.
Pat Riley, Jr., F	637	21.9
Louie Dampier, Jr., G	612	21.1
Thad Jaracz, So., C	383	13.2
Larry Conley, Sr., F	313	11.5
Tom Kron, Sr., G	297	10.2

1966-67: Won 13, Lost 13

CAPTAIN—None

Date	Team	Site	UK	Opp.
Dec. 3—Virginia		H	104	84
Dec. 5—Illinois		H	97	*98
Dec. 10—Northwestern		A	118	116
Dec. 13—North Carolina		H	55	64
Dec. 17—Florida		H	75	78

UK INVITATIONAL

Date	Team	Site	UK	Opp.
Dec. 22—Oregon State		H	96	66
Dec. 23—Kansas State		H	83	79
Dec. 28—Cornell		H	77	92
Dec. 31—Notre Dame		N-1	96	85
Jan. 5—Vanderbilt		H	89	*91
Jan. 14—Florida		A	72	89
Jan. 16—Georgia		A	40	49
Jan. 21—Auburn		H	60	58
Jan. 23—Tennessee		H	50	**52
Jan. 28—Louisiana State		H	102	72
Jan. 30—Mississippi		H	96	53
Feb. 4—Louisiana State		A	105	84
Feb. 6—Mississippi		A	79	70
Feb. 11—Miss. State		H	72	*77
Feb. 13—Tennessee		A	57	76
Feb. 18—Miss. State		A	103	74
Feb. 20—Georgia		H	101	76
Feb. 25—Alabama		A	71	81
Feb. 27—Auburn		A	49	60
Mar. 4—Vanderbilt		A	94	110
Mar. 6—Alabama		H	110	78
SEASON TOTALS			2,151	2,012

N-1, Louisville.
*Overtime; **Two overtimes.

LEADING SCORERS

Player	Pts.	Avg.
Louie Dampier, Sr., G	537	20.6
Pat Riley, Sr., F	452	17.4
Thad Jaracz, Jr., C	293	11.3
Cliff Berger, Jr., C	226	11.3
Phil Argento, So., G	110	5.2

1967-68: Won 22, Lost 5

CAPTAIN—Thad Jaracz

Date	Team	Site	UK	Opp.
Dec. 2—Michigan		H	96	79
Dec. 4—Florida		H	99	76
Dec. 6—Xavier		H	111	76
Dec. 9—Pennsylvania		H	64	49
Dec. 12—North Carolina		N-1	77	84

UK INVITATIONAL

Date	Team	Site	UK	Opp.
Dec. 22—Dayton			88	85
Dec. 23—South Carolina			76	66
Dec. 30—Notre Dame		N-2	81	73
Jan. 6—Vanderbilt		A	94	78
Jan. 8—Alabama		A	84	76
Jan. 13—Florida		A	78	96
Jan. 15—Georgia		H	104	73
Jan. 20—Auburn		A	73	74
Jan. 22—Tennessee		A	59	87
Jan. 27—Louisiana State		A	121	95
Jan. 29—Mississippi		A	85	76
Feb. 3—Louisiana State		H	109	96
Feb. 5—Mississippi		H	78	62
Feb. 10—Miss. State		A	92	84
Feb. 12—Tennessee		H	60	59
Feb. 17—Miss. State		H	107	81
Feb. 19—Georgia		A	106	87
Feb. 24—Alabama		H	96	83
Feb. 26—Auburn		H	89	57
Mar. 2—Vanderbilt		H	85	80

NCAA REGIONAL (Lexington)

Date	Team	Site	UK	Opp.
Mar. 15—Marquette			107	89
Mar. 16—Ohio State			81	82
SEASON TOTALS			2,400	2,103

N-1, Greensboro, N.C.; N-2, Louisville.

LEADING SCORERS

Player	Pts.	Avg.
Mike Casey, So., G	541	20.1
Dan Issel, So., C	444	16.4
Mike Pratt, So., F	380	14.1
Thad Jaracz, Sr., F	306	11.3
Phil Argento, Jr., G	185	13.2
Steve Clevenger, Sr., G	156	6.0

1968-69: Won 23, Lost 5

CAPTAIN—Phil Argento

Date	Team	Site	UK	Opp.
Nov. 30—Xavier		H	115	77
Dec. 2—Miami		A	86	77
Dec. 7—North Carolina		H	77	87
Dec. 14—Pennsylvania		A	102	78

UK INVITATIONAL

Date	Team	Site	UK	Opp.
Dec. 20—Michigan		H	112	104
Dec. 21—Army		H	80	65
Dec. 28—Notre Dame		N-1	110	90
Dec. 31—Wisconsin		N-2	65	69
Jan. 4—Mississippi		A	69	59
Jan. 6—Miss. State		A	91	72
Jan. 11—Florida		H	88	67
Jan. 13—Georgia		A	88	68
Jan. 18—Tennessee		A	69	66
Jan. 25—Louisiana State		A	108	96
Jan. 27—Alabama		A	83	70
Feb. 1—Vanderbilt		H	103	89
Feb. 3—Auburn		H	105	93
Feb. 8—Mississippi		H	104	68
Feb. 10—Miss. State		H	91	69
Feb. 15—Florida		A	81	82
Feb. 17—Georgia		A	85	77
Feb. 22—Louisiana State		H	103	89
Feb. 26—Alabama		H	108	79
Mar. 1—Vanderbilt		A	99	101
Mar. 3—Auburn		A	90	86
Mar. 8—Tennessee		H	84	69

NCAA REGIONAL (Madison, Wis.)

Date	Team	Site	UK	Opp.
Mar. 13—Marquette			74	81
Mar. 15—Miami			72	71
SEASON TOTALS			2,542	2,199

SCORING LEADERS

Player	Pts.	Avg.
Dan Issel, Jr., C	746	26.6
Mike Casey, Jr., G	534	19.1
Mike Pratt, Jr., F	439	16.9
Phil Argento, Sr., G	281	10.0
Larry Steele, So., F	242	8.6

1969-70: Won 26, Lost 2

CAPTAIN—Dan Issel, Mike Pratt

Date	Team	Site	UK	Opp.
Dec. 1—West Virginia		H	106	87
Dec. 6—Kansas		H	115	85
Dec. 8—North Carolina		A	94	87
Dec. 13—Indiana		H	109	92

UK INVITATIONAL

Date	Team	Site	UK	Opp.
Dec. 19—Navy		H	73	59
Dec. 20—Duke		H	98	76
Dec. 27—Notre Dame		N-1	102	100
Dec. 29—Miami (Ohio)		H	80	58
Jan. 3—Mississippi		H	95	73
Jan. 5—Miss. State		H	111	76
Jan. 10—Florida		A	88	69
Jan. 12—Georgia		A	72	71
Jan. 17—Tennessee		H	68	52
Jan. 24—Louisiana State		H	109	96
Jan. 26—Alabama		H	86	71
Jan. 31—Vanderbilt		A	81	89
Feb. 2—Auburn		H	84	83
Feb. 7—Mississippi		A	120	85
Feb. 9—Miss. State		A	86	57
Feb. 14—Florida		H	110	66
Feb. 16—Georgia		H	116	86
Feb. 21—Louisiana State		A	121	105
Feb. 23—Alabama		A	98	89
Feb. 28—Vanderbilt		H	90	86
Mar. 2—Auburn		H	102	81
Mar. 7—Tennessee		A	86	69

NCAA REGIONAL (Columbus, Ohio)

Date	Team	Site	UK	Opp.
Mar. 12—Notre Dame			109	99
Mar. 14—Jacksonville			100	106
SEASON TOTALS			2,709	2,253

N-1, Louisville.

LEADING SCORERS

Player	Pts.	Avg.
Dan Issel, Sr., C	948	33.9
Mike Pratt, Sr., F	540	19.3
Tom Parker, So., F	260	10.4
Terry Mills, Jr., G	237	9.1
Larry Steele, Jr., F	225	9.8
Jim Dinwiddie, Jr., G.	125	4.5

1970-71: Won 22, Lost 6

COCAPTAINS—Mike Casey, Larry Steele

Date	Team	Site	UK	Opp.
Dec. 1—Northwestern		A	115	100
Dec. 5—Michigan		H	104	93
Dec. 7—West Virginia		A	106	100
Dec. 12—Indiana		A	95	93

UK INVITATIONAL

Date	Team	Site	UK	Opp.
Dec. 18—DePaul		H	106	85
Dec. 19—Purdue		H	83	89
Dec. 22—Oregon State		H	84	78
Dec. 29—Notre Dame		N-1	92	99
Jan. 2—Mississippi		A	103	95
Jan. 4—Miss. State		A	79	71
Jan. 9—Florida		H	101	75
Jan. 11—Georgia		H	79	66
Jan. 16—Tennessee		A	71	75
Jan. 23—Louisiana State		A	82	79
Jan. 25—Alabama		A	86	73
Jan. 30—Vanderbilt		H	102	92
Feb. 1—Auburn		H	114	76
Feb. 6—Mississippi		H	121	86
Feb. 8—Miss. State		H	102	83
Feb. 13—Florida		A	65	74
Feb. 15—Georgia		A	107	95
Feb. 20—Louisiana State		H	110	73
Feb. 22—Alabama		H	101	74
Feb. 27—Vanderbilt		A	119	90
Mar. 1—Auburn		A	102	83
Mar. 6—Tennessee		H	84	78

NCAA REGIONAL (Athens, Ga.)

Date	Team	Site	UK	Opp.
Mar. 18—Western Ky.			83	107
Mar. 20—Marquette			74	91
SEASON TOTALS			2,670	2,373

N-1, Louisville.

SCORING LEADERS

Player	Pts.	Avg.
Tom Parker, Jr., F	492	17.6
Tom Payne, So., C	473	16.9
Mike Casey, Sr., G	460	17.0
Larry Steele, Sr., F	314	13.1
Kent Hollenbeck, Jr., G	308	14.0

1971-72: Won 21, Lost 7

CAPTAIN—None

Date	Team	Site	UK	Opp.
Dec. 1—Northwestern		H	94	85
Dec. 4—Kansas		A	79	69
Dec. 6—Kansas State		A	71	64
Dec. 11—Indiana		N-1	89	**90
Dec. 13—Michigan State		H	85	91

UK INVITATIONAL

Date	Team	Site	UK	Opp.
Dec. 17—Missouri		H	83	79
Dec. 18—Princeton		H	96	82
Dec. 28—Notre Dame		N-1	83	67
Jan. 8—Mississippi		H	93	82
Jan. 10—Miss. State		H	104	76
Jan. 15—Florida		A	70	72
Jan. 17—Georgia		A	73	85
Jan. 22—Tennessee		H	72	70
Jan. 24—Vanderbilt		H	106	80
Jan. 29—Louisiana State		H	89	71
Jan. 31—Alabama		H	77	74
Feb. 5—Vanderbilt		A	85	*80
Feb. 7—Auburn		H	78	72
Feb. 12—Mississippi		A	90	82
Feb. 14—Miss. State		A	63	55
Feb. 19—Florida		H	95	68
Feb. 21—Georgia		H	87	63
Feb. 26—Louisiana State		A	71	88
Feb. 28—Alabama		A	70	73
Mar. 6—Auburn		H	102	67
Mar. 9—Tennessee		A	67	66

NCAA REGIONAL (Dayton, Ohio)

Date	Team	Site	UK	Opp.
Mar. 16—Marquette			85	69
Mar. 18—Florida State			54	73
SEASON TOTALS			2,311	2,093

N-1, Louisville.

LEADING SCORERS

Player	Pts.	Avg.
Jim Andrews, Jr., C	602	21.5
Tom Parker, Sr., F	486	18.0
Stan Key, Sr., G	349	12.4
Ronnie Lyons, So., G	344	13.2
Larry Stamper, Jr., F	289	10.3